GRADES 1-2

AMERICAN EDUCATION PUBLISHING™

An imprint of Carson-Dellosa Publishing
Greensboro, NC

American Education Publishing™
An imprint of Carson-Dellosa Publishing LLC
P.O. Box 35665
Greensboro, NC 27425 USA

ISBN 978-1-60996-784-0

01-363117811

TABLE OF CONTENTS

TABLE OF CONTENTS

TIME TO THE QUARTER-HOUR

TIME TO THE MINUTE

TIME REVIEW

TABLE OF CONTENTS

TABLE OF CONTENTS

COINS AND BILLS

MONEY REVIEW

ANSWER KEY

TIME

Face Clocks: Introduction

What is the best way to tell what time it is? A clock! There are all kinds of clocks.

Circle the ones you have seen.

Face Clocks: Identifying Parts

A clock can tell you what time it is. A clock has different parts.

Read and trace each part of the clock.

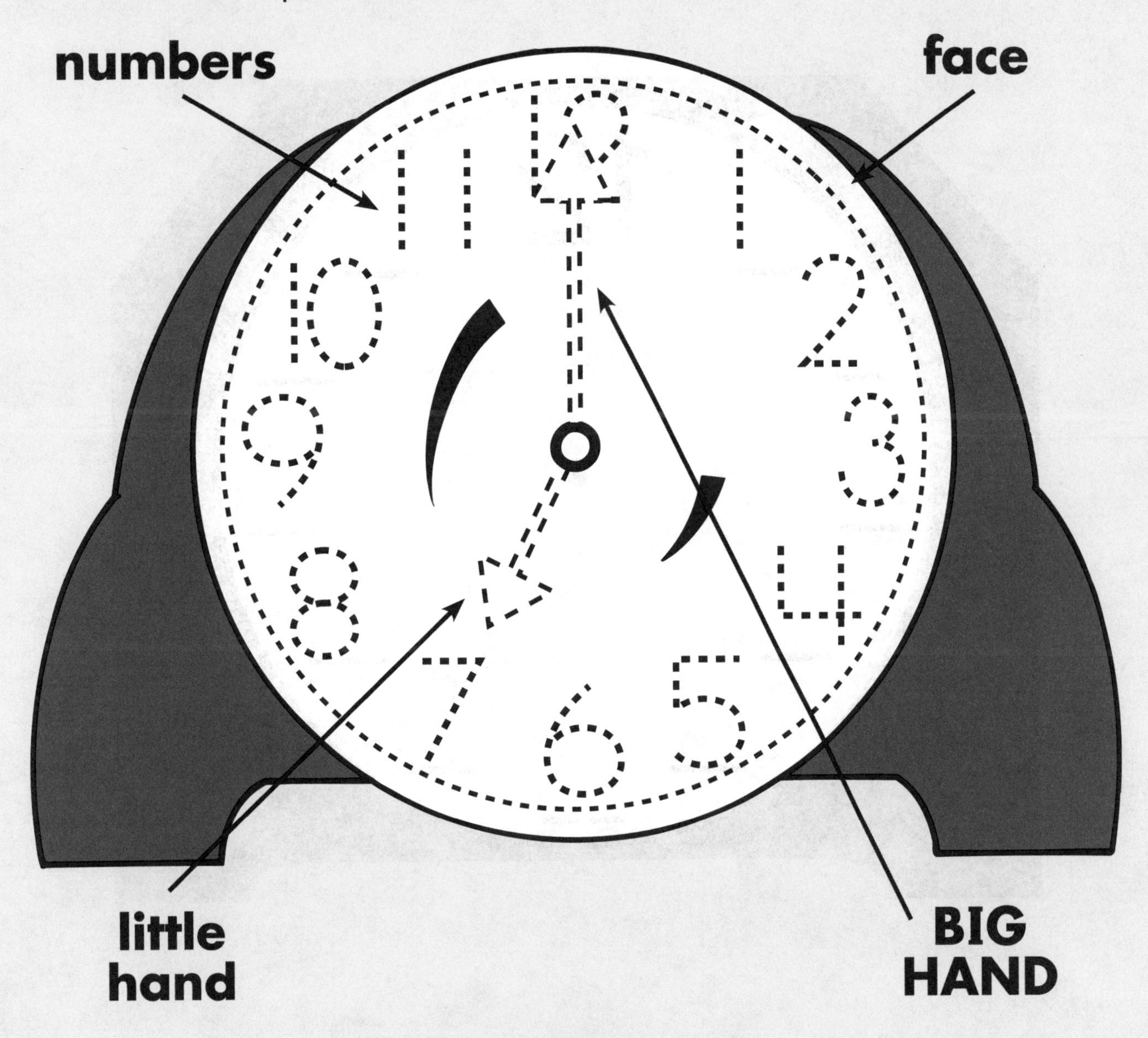

The **BIG HAND** is on **12**.
The **little hand** tells the hour.

Writing the Time

Write the numbers on the clock face. Draw the BIG HAND to 12. Draw the little hand to 5.

What time is it? ________________ o'clock

Writing the Time

An hour is 60 minutes long. It takes an hour for the BIG HAND to go around the clock. When the BIG HAND is on 12, and the little hand points to a number, that is the hour.

Color the BIG HAND **red**. Color the little hand **blue**.

The BIG HAND is on ________________. The little hand is on ________________.

It is ________8________ o'clock.

Writing the Time

Color the little hour hand **red**. Fill in the blanks.

The BIG HAND is on ______________.

The little hand is on ______________.

It is ______________ o'clock.

The BIG HAND is on ______________.

The little hand is on ______________.

It is ______________ o'clock.

The BIG HAND is on ______________.

The little hand is on ______________.

It is ______________ o'clock.

The BIG HAND is on ______________.

The little hand is on ______________.

It is ______________ o'clock.

Drawing the Hour Hand

Draw the little hour hand on each clock.

8 o'clock

1 o'clock

7 o'clock

Drawing the Hour Hand

Draw the little hour hand on each clock.

2 o'clock

10 o'clock

9 o'clock

Circling the Hour Hand

Circle the little hour hand on each clock. What time is it? Write the time below.

_______________ o'clock

_______________ o'clock

_______________ o'clock

_______________ o'clock

_______________ o'clock

_______________ o'clock

Practice

Draw the little hour hand on each clock.

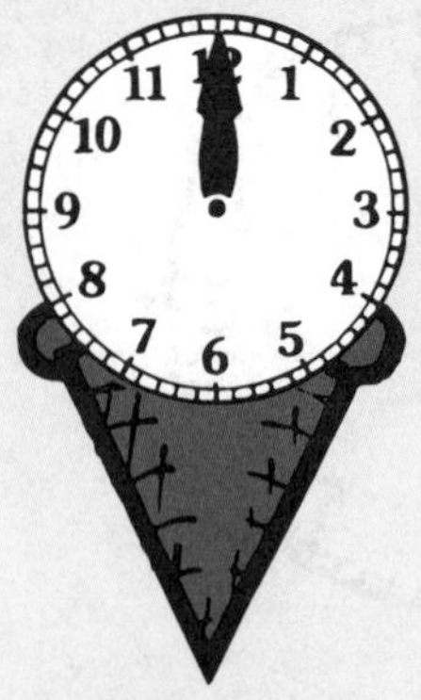

8 o'clock

4 o'clock

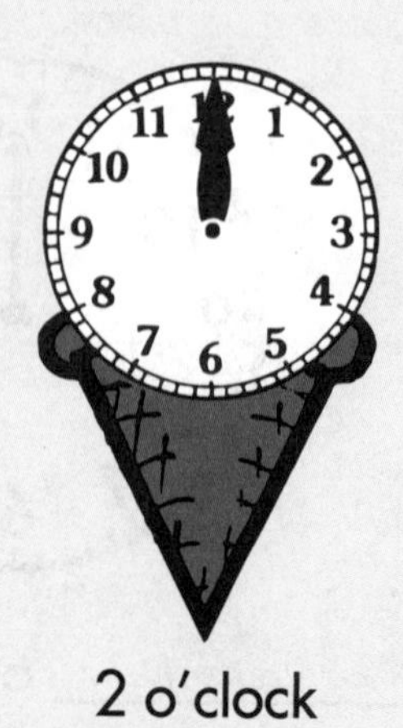

2 o'clock

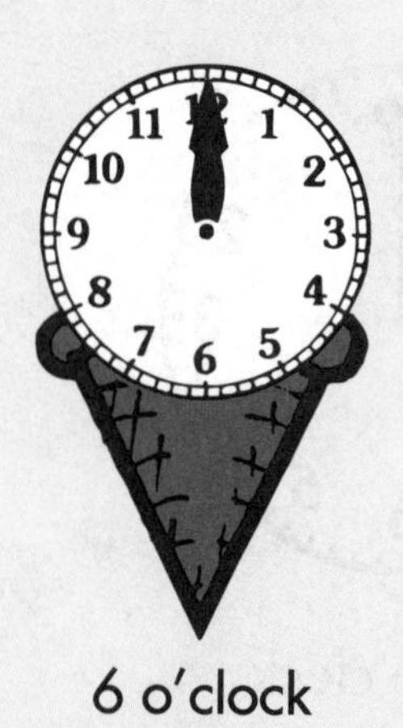

6 o'clock

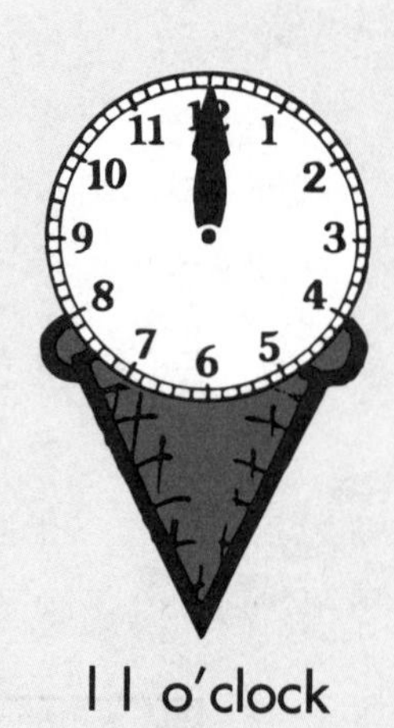

11 o'clock

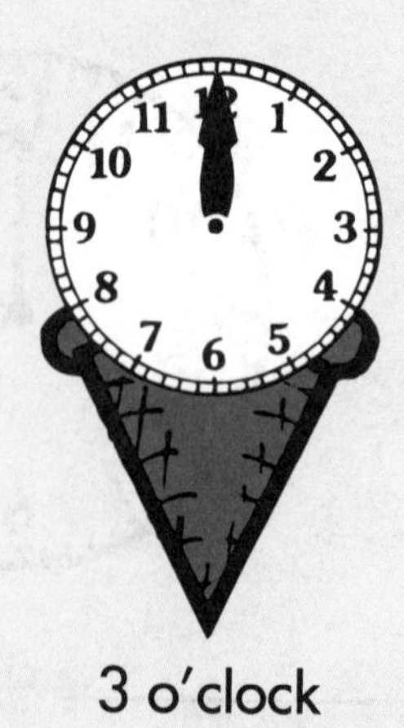

3 o'clock

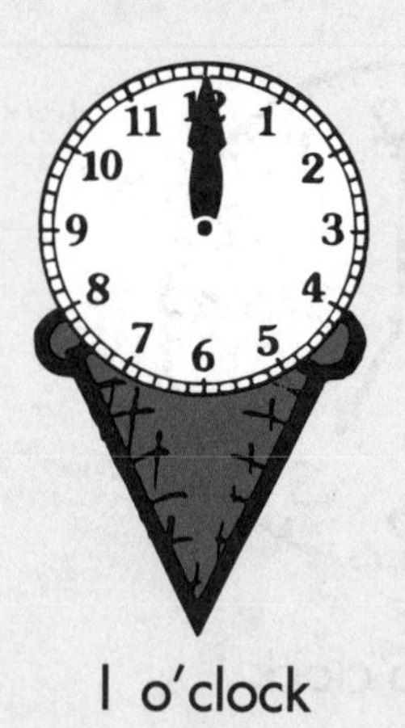

1 o'clock

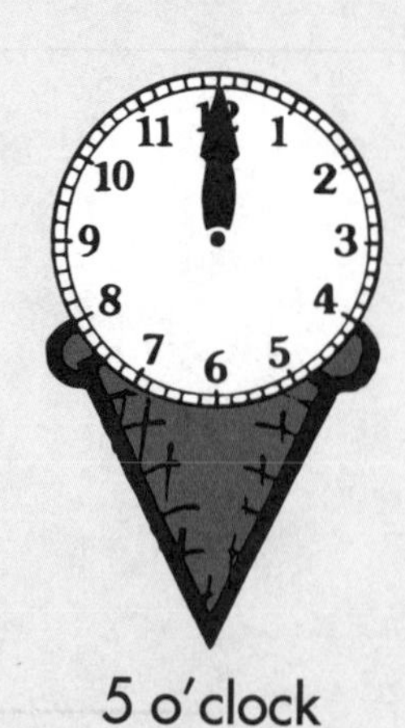

5 o'clock

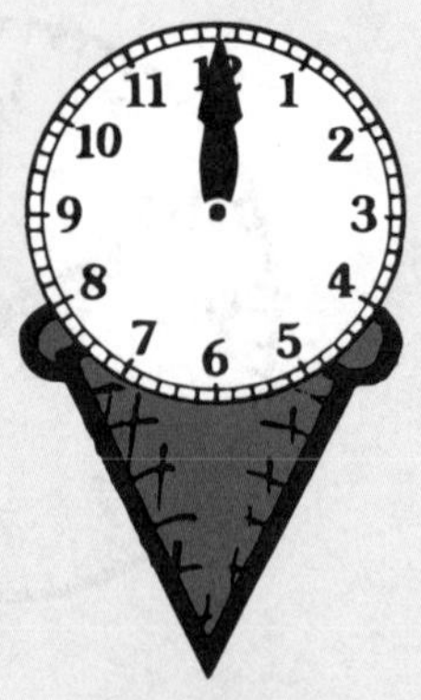

7 o'clock

Practice

What is the time?

Writing the Time: One Hour Later

Write the original time and 1 hour later.

one hour later

one hour later

Time Poems

Read each poem. Draw a line to the clock that matches.

1. It is 7 o'clock.
Time to rise and shine.
First it will rain,
Then turn out fine.

2. It is 10 o'clock.
We are at the pool.
We're happy today
Because there is no school!

3. It is 4 o'clock.
It is time to play!
We will see friends
Outside today.

Digital Clocks: Introduction

A digital clock tells time with numbers. First, it tells the hour, then the minutes.

Draw the little hour hand on this face clock below to read 10 o'clock.

Both clocks show that it is 10 o'clock. Make a **green** circle around the kinds of clocks you have at home.

Matching Digital and Face Clocks

Trace the time on the digital clocks.

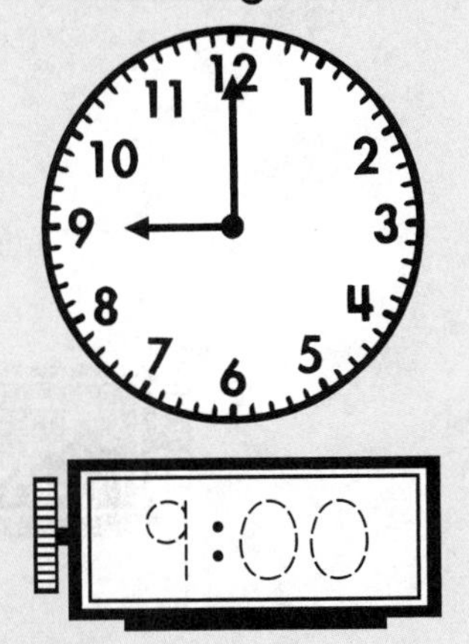

Match the clocks.

Matching Digital and Face Clocks

Long ago, there were only wind-up clocks. Today, we also have electric and battery clocks. We even have solar clocks!

Match these digital and face clocks.

Digital Clocks

Write the time on the digital clocks.

Drawing the Hour Hand: Matching Digital and Face Clocks

Look at the digital clock. Say the time. Draw the little hour hand on each face clock.

Time Two Ways

Show each time two ways. Draw the hands on each clock face. Then, write the time on each digital clock.

1. Bessie Bear gets up at **6 o'clock**.

2. Bernie Bear eats breakfast at **7 o'clock**.

3. What time do you get up for school?
Draw it below!

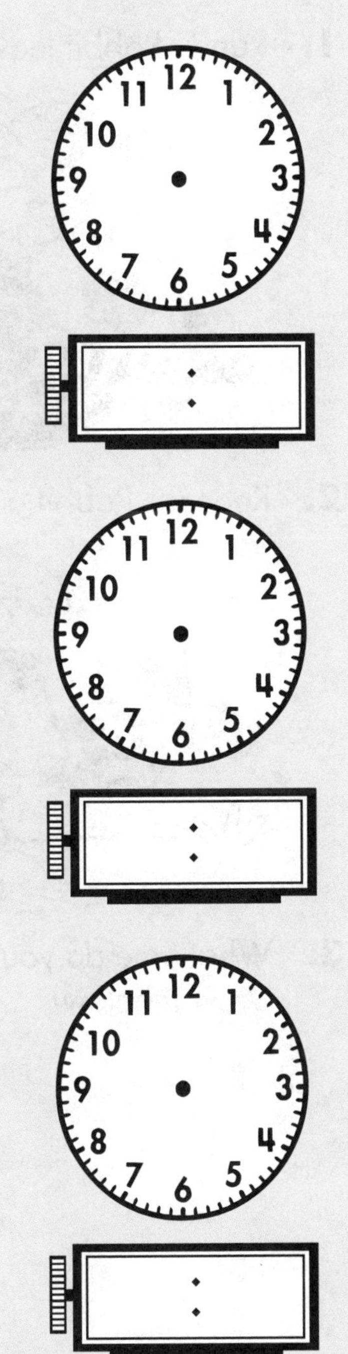

Time Two Ways

Show each time two ways. Draw the hands on each clock face. Then, write the time on each digital clock.

1. Randy Rabbit leaves for school at **8 o'clock**.

2. Rebecca Rabbit goes out to recess at **10 o'clock**.

3. What time do you go out for recess? Draw it below!

Time Two Ways

Show each time two ways. Draw the hands on each clock face. Then, write the time on each digital clock.

1. Fernando Frog eats lunch at **12 o'clock**.

2. Fanny Frog goes to the library at **1 o'clock**.

3. What time do you eat lunch?
Draw it below!

Time Two Ways

Show each time two ways. Draw the hands on each clock face. Then, write the time.

1. At **9 o'clock**, Frog goes for a swim.

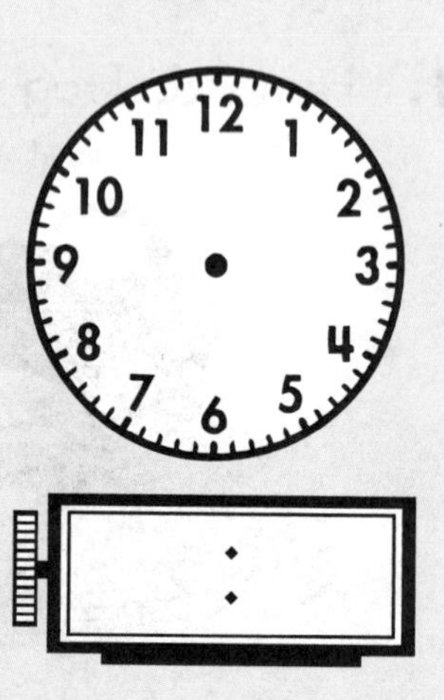

2. At **11 o'clock**, Frog sits on a lily pad.

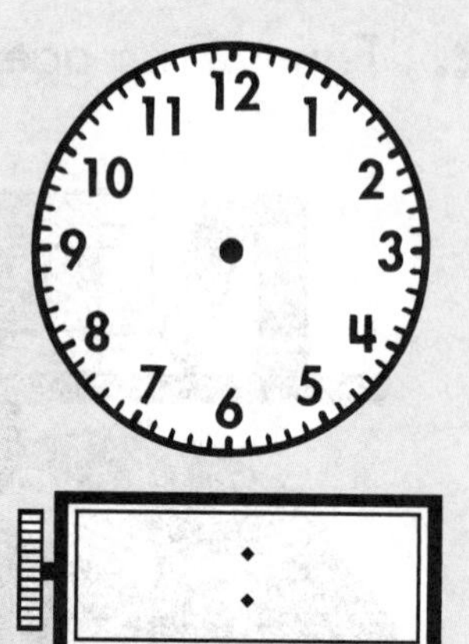

3. At **12 o'clock**, Frog eats a sandwich.

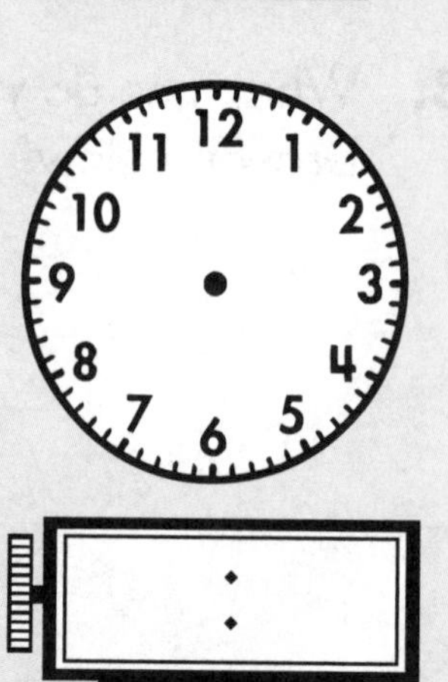

Time Stories

Read each story. Draw the hands on each clock face.

1. At **11:00**, Mouse starts to cook. Yum! Cheese soup is good.

2. At **12 o'clock**, Mouse sets the table. Oh no! He drops a spoon.

3. At **7:00**, Mouse reads a book. What a funny story!

4. Time for bed. It is **9 o'clock**, and Mouse is sleepy.

Time Stories

Read each story. Draw the hands on each clock face.

1. Rabbit is hungry. It is **6 o'clock**—time for supper and some carrot stew.

2. At **8:00**, Rabbit washes the dishes. Scrub, scrub, the pot is sticky.

3. Rabbit works in his garden. It is **4 o'clock**, and he is picking lettuce.

4. At **5:00**, Rabbit makes a lettuce salad. What a tasty meal!

Time to the Half-Hour: Introduction

This clock face shows the time gone by since 8 o'clock.
Thirty minutes, or half an hour, has gone by.
There are three ways to say time to the half-hour.
We say eight thirty, thirty past eight, or half past eight.

Half-hour later

9:30

30 minutes past 

o'clock

Half-hour later

__________ __________

__________ minutes past __________ o'clock

Writing Time on the Half-Hour

Trace the big minute hand **green**. Trace the little hour hand **yellow**. Write the time on the line.

Matching Digital and Face Clocks

These digital numbers got lost. Write them in the correct clocks on this page and page 34.

6:30	12:30	3:30	8:30	9:30	5:30

Matching Digital and Face Clocks

Drawing the Hour Hand

Say the time. Draw the little hour hand on each clock.

Telling Time: Hour and Half-Hour

Draw a line from the clock to the correct time.

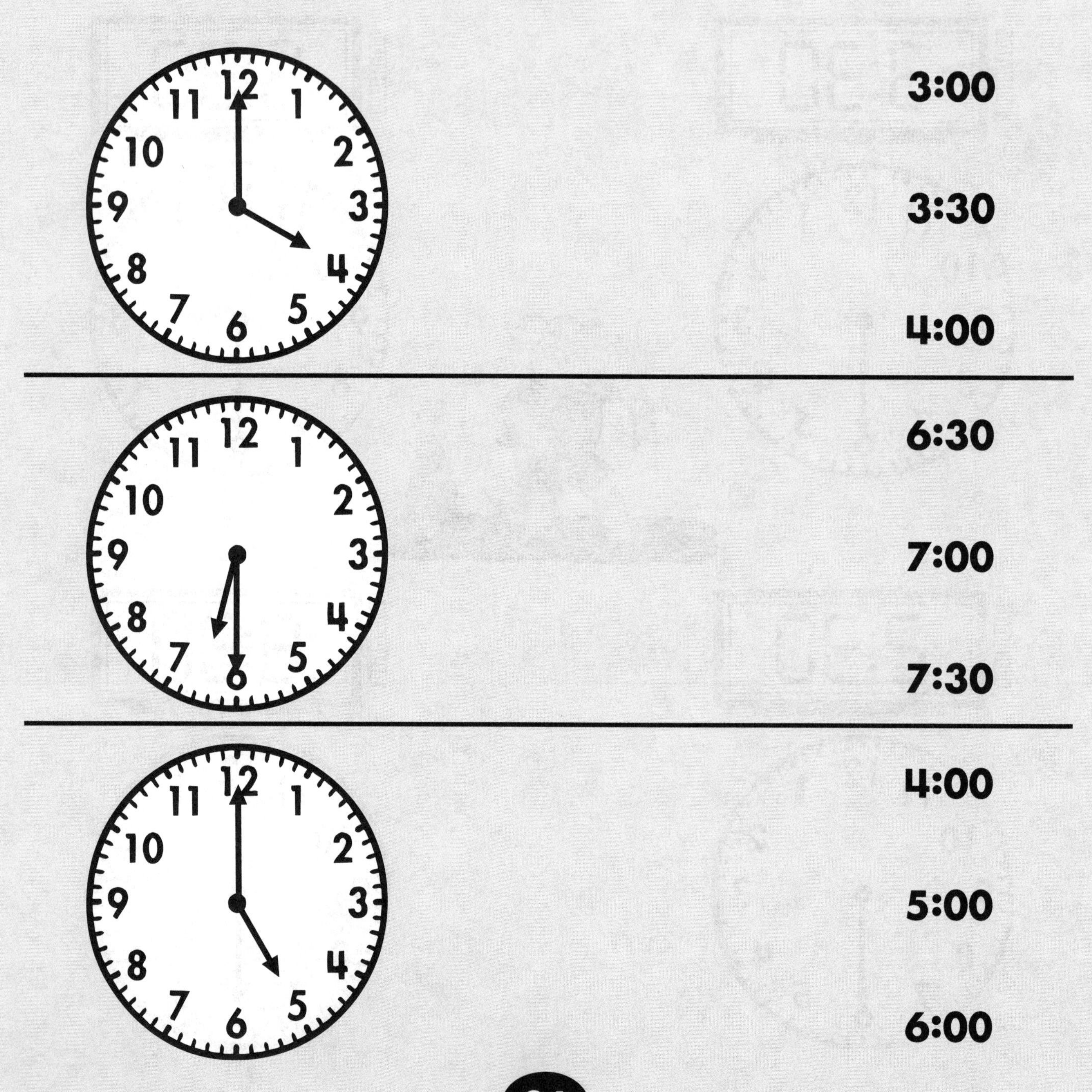

Writing the Time: Practice

Draw the hands on the sock clocks.

Writing the Time: Practice

What time is it?

3:00

:

:

:

:

:

:

:

:

:

:

:

Matching Digital and Face Clocks

Match each clock to the correct time.

Time Stories

Read each story. Draw the hands on each clock face.

1. It is **5:30**, and the sun is coming up. Bird is ready for the day.

2. At **6:30**, Bird is looking for breakfast. Watch out, worms!

3. Bird is resting after breakfast. It is **9:30** and almost time for flying practice.

4. At **12:30**, Bird naps before lunch. Flying is hard work!

Time Lapse: Hours

Can you tell how much time has passed?

_____ : _____

_____ : _____

If it started snowing at **3:00** and snowed until **6:00**, it snowed __________ hours.

What time did the spider start spinning the web? _____ : _____

What time did she finish? _____ : _____

_____ : _____

_____ : _____

The spider took __________ hours to spin the web.

Time Lapse: Hours

1. Steve went to play baseball at **3:30**.
   Mom told him to be home in **2 hours**.

   He should be home at ______:______.

Show the time on this watch.

2. Tiffany went to Latonia's house to ride bikes at **10:00**.
   Dad asked her to be home in **3 hours**.

   She should be home at ______:______.

Show the time on this watch.

Time Lapse: Hours

1. Kristen took her sister to the movies at **7:30**.
   Mom said she would meet them in **2 hours**.

   She will meet them at ______:______.

Show the time on this watch.

2. Latrissa went to the library for story hour. She got there at **1:00**.
   She stayed **1 hour**.

   Story hour should be over at ______:______.

Show the time on this watch.

Drawing the Hour Hand: A Half-Hour Later

Draw the hands on each clock face.

1. At **8:00**, it starts to rain.

What time is it one half-hour later?

2. At **11:00**, the sun comes out.

What time is it one half-hour later?

3. At **3:00**, we skip home from school.

What time is it one half-hour later?

Time Stories

Read each story. Draw the hands on each clock face.

1. Tom makes a huge sandwich at **1:00**. He finishes the whole sandwich **one half-hour** later. What time does Tom finish the sandwich?

2. Tom gets home from school at **3:00**. He goes out to play **30 minutes** later. What time does Tom go out to play?

3. Tom goes to bed at **8:30**. He falls asleep **one half-hour** later. What time does Tom fall asleep?

Time Stories

Read each story. Draw the hands on each clock face.

1. Maria makes lunch at **7:00**. She gets on the bus **30 minutes** later. What time does she get on the bus?

2. Maria helps make dinner at **5:30**. Everyone eats it **one half-hour** later. What time does everyone eat?

3. Maria's family plays a game at **8:30**. They stop playing **30 minutes** later. What time do they stop playing?

Time Two Ways

Draw the hands on each clock face. Write the time on the digital clock.

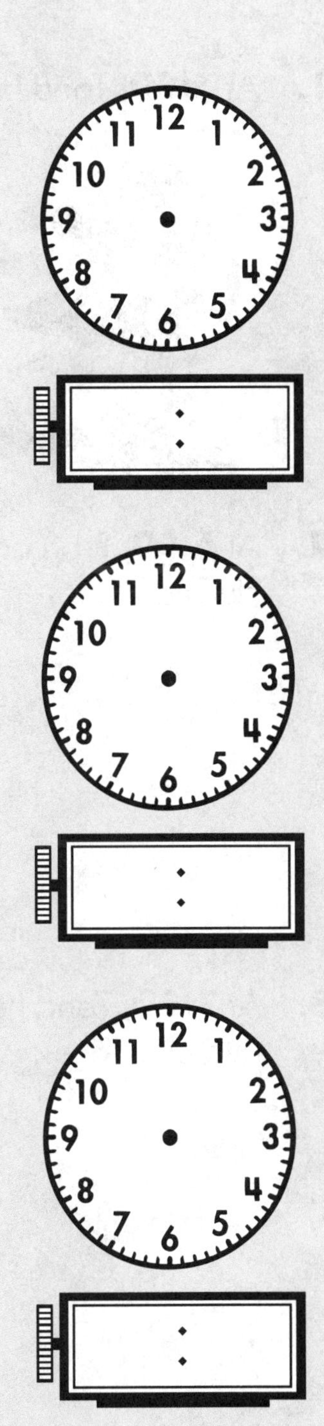

1. At **1:30**, Squirrel hides seven nuts.

2. At **2:00**, Squirrel runs down the tree to find more nuts.

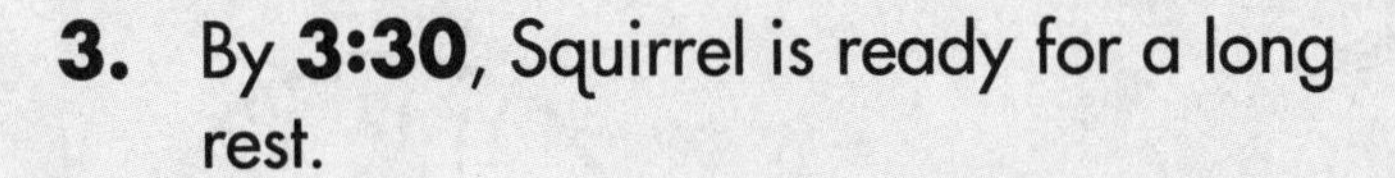

3. By **3:30**, Squirrel is ready for a long rest.

Time Two Ways

Draw the hands on each clock face. Write the time on the digital clock.

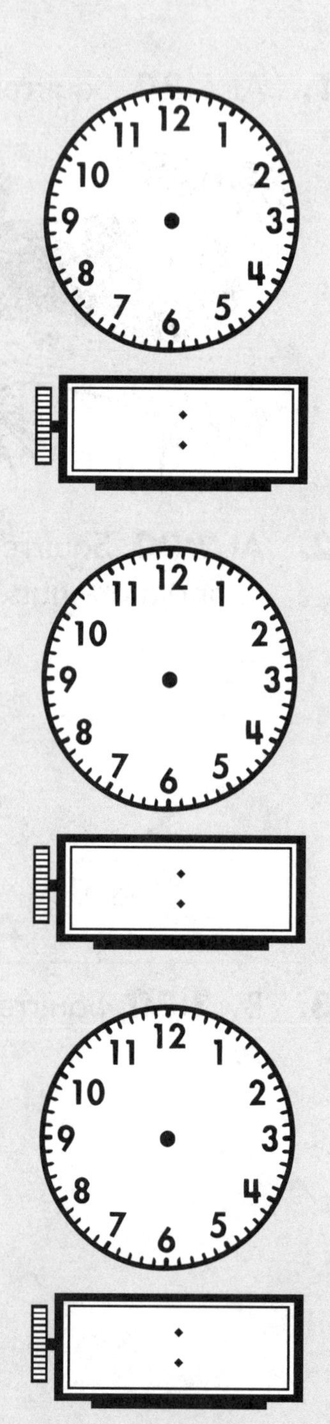

1. At **5:30**, Toad hops over to visit Frog.

2. At **6:00**, Frog and Toad are sipping Fine Fly Tea.

3. At **7:30**, Toad heads home, full of tea and bug cakes.

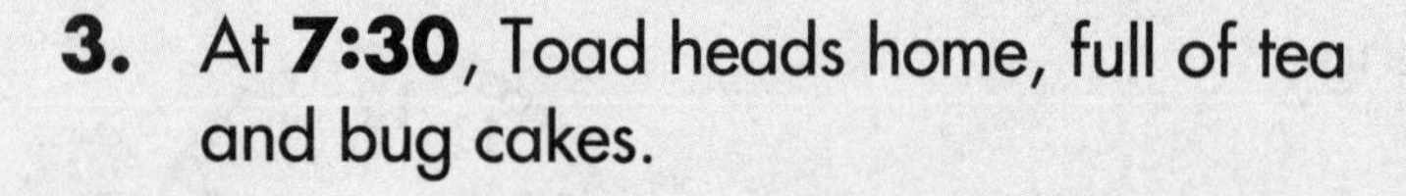

Time Two Ways

Draw the hands on each clock face. Write the time on the digital clock.

1. Ricardo Raccoon starts his lunch at **12:00**. He finishes his lunch **30 minutes after 12:00**.

2. Rachel Raccoon sits down at the computer at **7:00**. She gets up from the computer a **half-hour after 7:00**.

Time Stories

Read the story. Write the time two ways. Choose a time for everyone to eat lunch!

Bear is going on a picnic today with his brother and sister. They leave for the park at **9:00**. They get to the park at **10:00**. Bear helps carry the food to a picnic table. Then, he gets out his kite. Bear flies his kite at **10:30**. Later, at ___________, everyone has a picnic lunch!

Put the story in order by writing what time Bear did each thing.

Time Stories

Read the story. Write the time two ways. Choose a time for everyone to go home!

Pig wakes up at **7:00**. Pig's grandmother is taking her to the zoo today! They get to the zoo at **10:30**. They walk and walk. They stop to eat at **12:30**. They walk some more. Pig and her grandmother don't get home until ____________. They had a wonderful day!

Put the story in order by writing what time Pig did each thing.

1. ________________

2. ________________

3. ________________

4. ________________

Time Stories

Read the story. Write the time two ways. Choose a time for everyone to wake up!

It's a hot summer day. Frog and Turtle begin to walk to the lake at **11:00**. They jump into the cold water at **12:30**. They swim and dive. Then, they enjoy lunch at **1:30**. They fall asleep after lunch. Later, at ____________, Frog and Turtle wake up. They hurry home!

Put the story in order by writing what time Frog and Turtle did each thing.

1. ____________________

2. ____________________

3. ____________________

4. ____________________

Time Puzzles

Read each clue and guess what time it might be. Draw the hands on each clock. Write the time.

It's dark outside. Everyone is asleep.

Ring, ring! Time to get up.

Here comes the school bus.
Run, so you won't be late!

I'm hungry! Soon it will be time for lunch.

Time Puzzles

Read each clue and guess what time it might be. Draw the hands on each clock. Write the time.

School is out! We're going home.

Here comes the mail! I hope I get a letter.

It's getting dark. Time to go inside.

It's light tonight. Look, a big full moon!

Time Puzzles

Read each clue and guess what time it might be. Draw the hands on each clock. Write the time.

Sometimes, I have homework to do.

Sometimes, I have jobs to do.

The best time is when I can do just what I want to do.

On Saturday and Sunday, I play with friends.

Time to the Quarter-Hour: Introduction

Each hour has 60 minutes.
An hour has 4 quarter-hours.
A quarter-hour is 15 minutes.

This clock face shows a quarter of an hour.

From the 12 to the 3 is 15 minutes.

From the **12** to the **3** is **15 minutes**.

15 minutes past 8 o'clock is 8 : 15

Telling Time

Each hour has 4 quarter-hours. A quarter-hour is 15 minutes. Write the times.

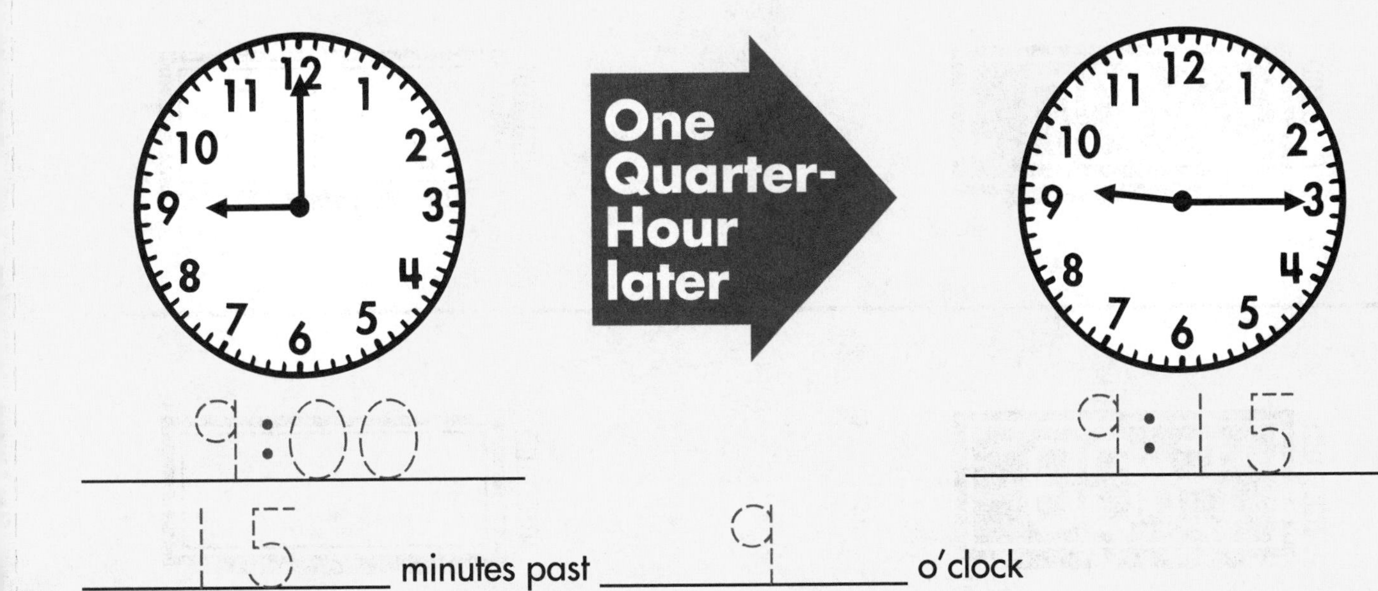

One Quarter-Hour later

______________________ ______________________

__________ minutes past __________ o'clock

Digital Clocks

Your digital clock has quarter-hours, too. It also shows 15 minutes. Write the times one quarter-hour later.

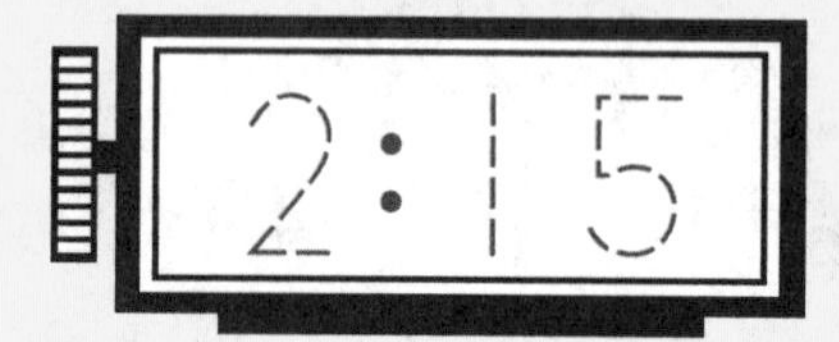

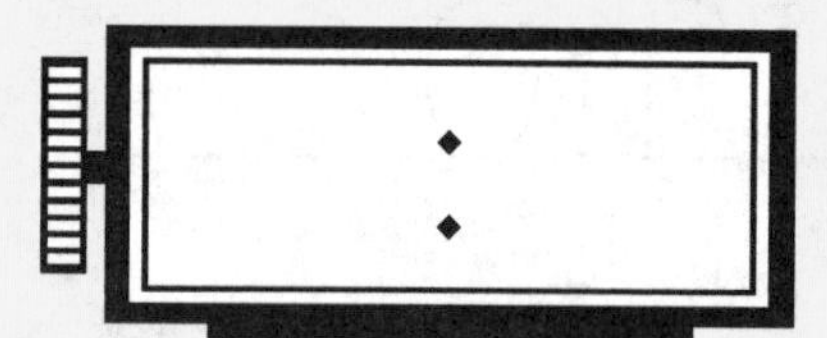

Telling Time

Count by fives to see how many minutes have passed.

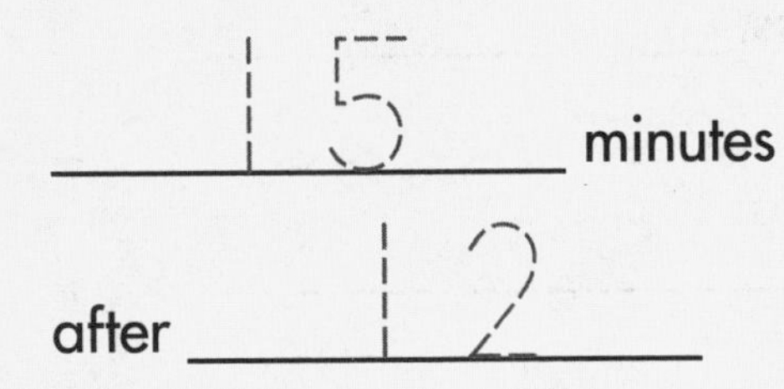

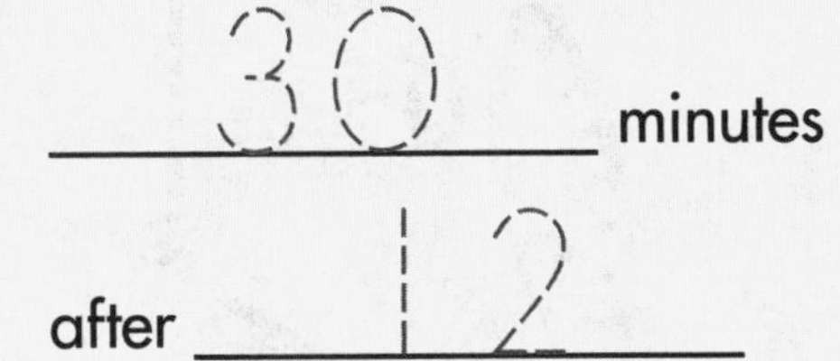

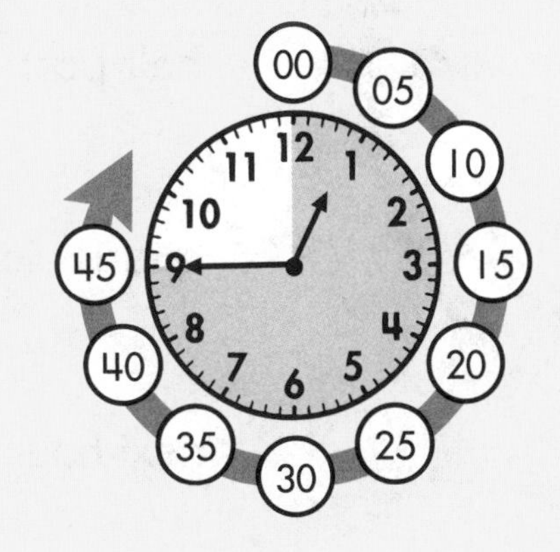

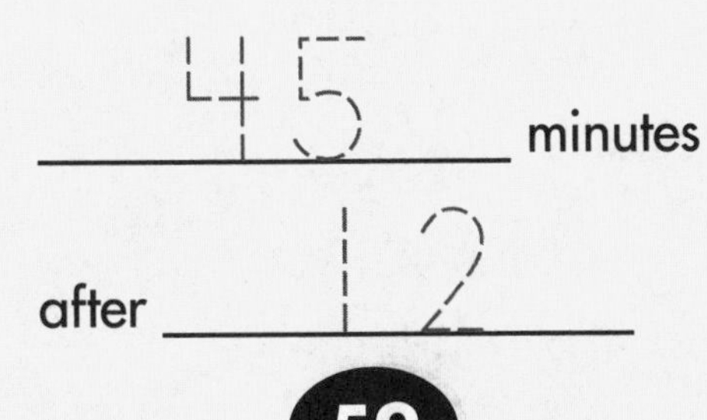

Telling Time

Quarter after means 15 minutes after the hour.

Half past means 30 minutes after the hour.

Quarter to means 15 minutes until the next hour.

Write the quarter-hours from this time.

8 o'clock

quarter past ______

half past ______

quarter to ______

next hour: ______ o'clock

Telling Time

Circle the time.

10:45

12:45

9:45

3:45

7:30

6:45

10:00

2:00

6:15

6:45

10:30

10:45

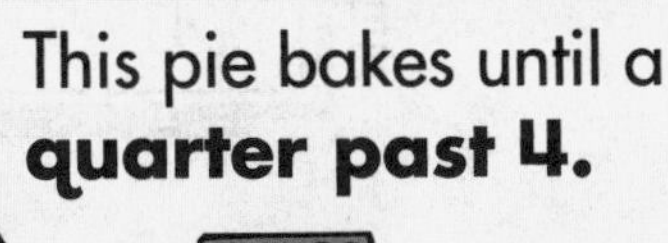

This pie bakes until a **quarter past 4.**

4:45

4:15

Telling Time

Write the time on the digital clocks.

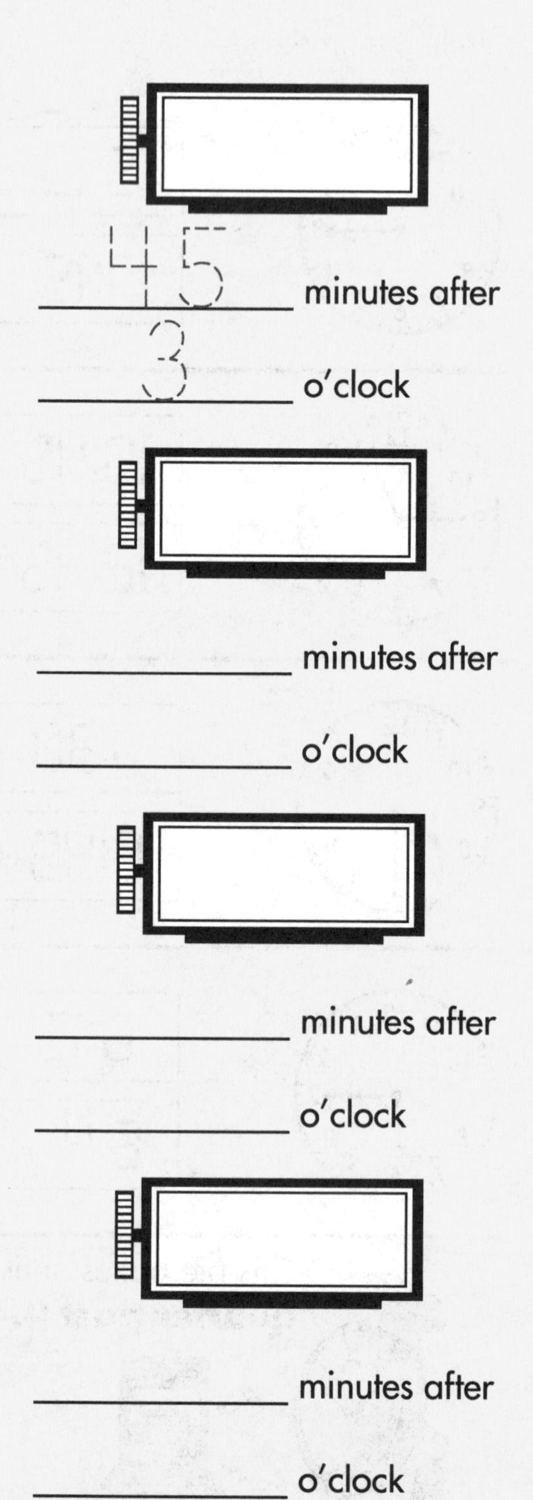

45 minutes after

3 o'clock

______ minutes after

______ o'clock

______ minutes after

______ o'clock

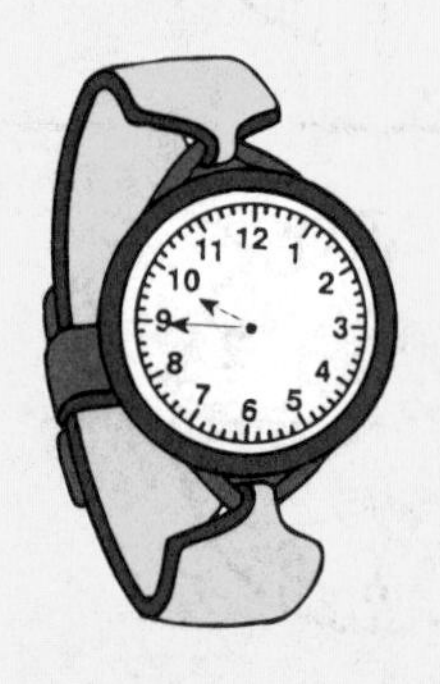

______ minutes after

______ o'clock

Time Two Ways

Draw the hands on each clock face. Write the time.

1. Marta begins writing a letter at **3:30**. She stops **30 minutes later**.

Begins

Stops

:

:

2. Arnold begins drying dishes at **8:00**. He stops **15 minutes later**.

Begins

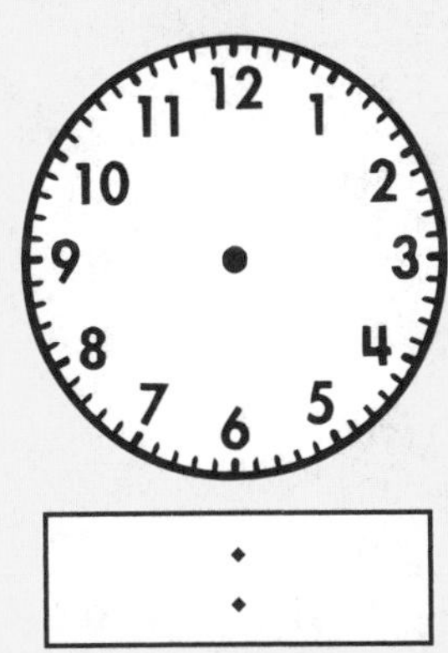

Stops

:

:

3. Write your own time story.

____

____

____

Begins

:

Stops

:

Time Two Ways

Draw the hands on each clock face. Write the time.

1. Darius begins throwing balls for the dog at **5:00**. He stops **15 minutes later**.

Begins

:

Stops

12 1 2 3 4 5 6 7 8 9 10 11

:

2. Olga begins playing frisbee at **4:15**. She stops **15 minutes later**.

Begins

:

Stops

:

3. Write your own time story.

____

____

____

Begins

:

Stops

:

Time Two Ways

Draw the hands on each clock face. Write the time.

1. Alberto begins working in the yard at **10:30**. He stops **45 minutes later**.

Begins

Stops

2. Darlene begins playing catch at **2:30**. She stops **15 minutes later**.

Begins

Stops

3. Write your own time story.

____

____

____

Begins

Stops

Time Two Ways

Draw the hands on each clock face. Write the time.

1. Lucia begins practicing for the play at **3:00**. She stops **45 minutes later**.

Begins

Stops

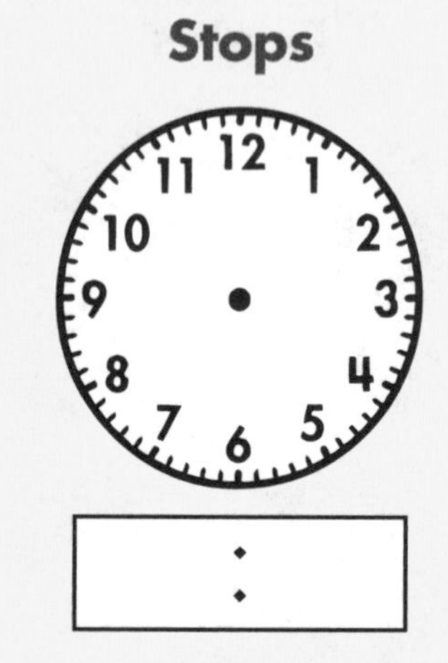

:

:

2. Ann begins sorting her baseball cards at **7:30**. She stops **15 minutes later**.

Begins

Stops

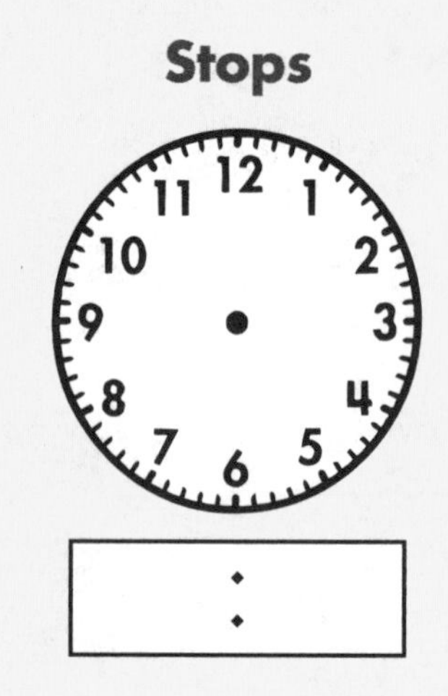

:

:

3. Solve this puzzle.

When did Ray begin biking? Ray biked for **30 minutes**. He stopped biking at **5:30**.

Began

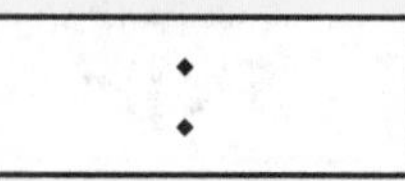

Stopped

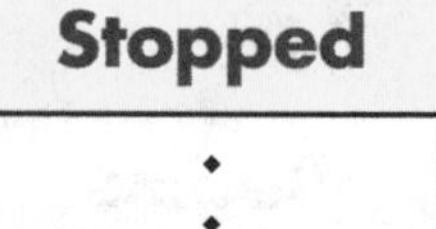

Time to the Minute Intervals: Introduction

Each number on the clock face stands for 5 minutes.

Count by fives beginning at 12.

Write the numbers here: **00** 05 10 15 20 25

It is 25 minutes after 8 o'clock.

It is written **8:25**.

Count by fives.

00 _____ _____ _____ _____ _____ _____ _____

It is _____ minutes after _____ o'clock.

_____ : _____

Time to the Minute Intervals: Introduction

Write the time both ways.

00 ______ ______

______ minutes after ______ o'clock

______ : ______

00 ______ ______ ______ ______

______ minutes after ______ o'clock

______ : ______

00 ______ ______ ______ ______ ______ ______
______ ______

______ minutes after ______ o'clock

______ : ______

00 ______ ______ ______ ______ ______ ______
______ ______ ______ ______ ______

______ minutes after ______ o'clock

______ : ______

Drawing the Minute Hand

Read the time. Draw the minute hand with a pencil. Color over it with a **red** crayon.

2:05

__5__ minutes after __2__ o'clock

Drawing the Minute Hand

Draw the hands on these fish clocks.

Drawing the Minute Hand

Draw the clock hands to show the time you watch these cartoons.

What is your favorite cartoon? ____________________

What time does it come on? ____________________

Digital Clocks

Can you read a digital clock?

First read the hour. Then, read the minutes.

This clock is read **four twenty** or **twenty minutes past 4 o'clock**.

Match the digital and face clocks.

Digital Clocks

Circle the words to match the times.

five twenty  five fifty

six twenty-five  six thirty-five

seven ten  seven twenty

one fifty-five  eleven fifty-five

Writing the Time

What time is it?

Drawing Clock Hands

Draw the hands. Write the time.

Three thirty

Five forty-five

Eleven twenty

Eight ten

Two fifty-five

Nine forty

Time Two Ways

Draw the hands on each clock face. Write the time.

1. 30 minutes after 6:00

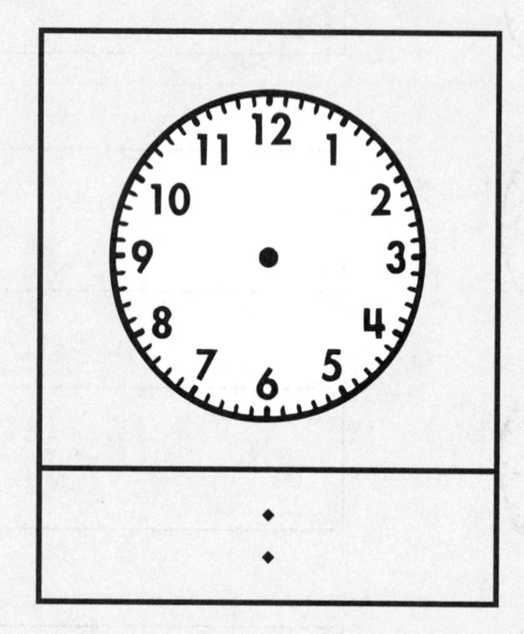

2. 20 minutes before 6:00

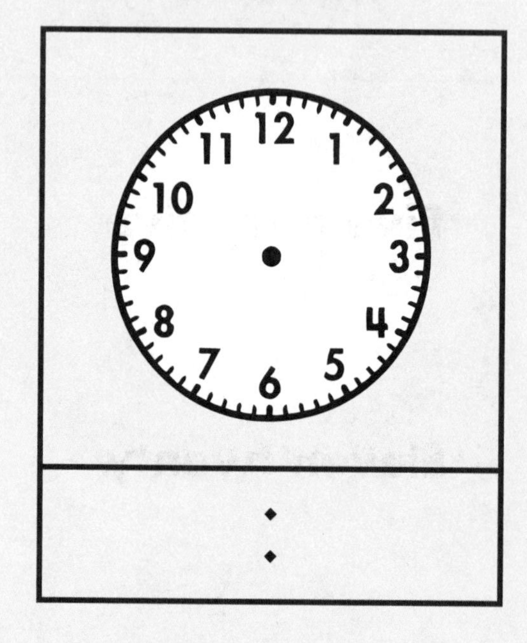

3. Exactly 6 o'clock

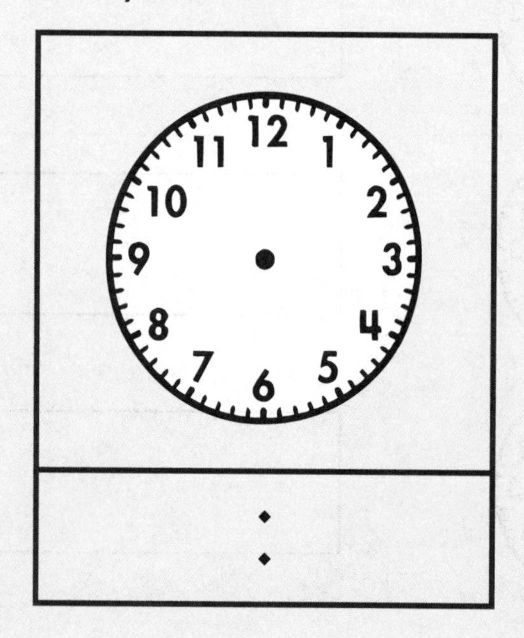

4. 20 minutes after 6:00

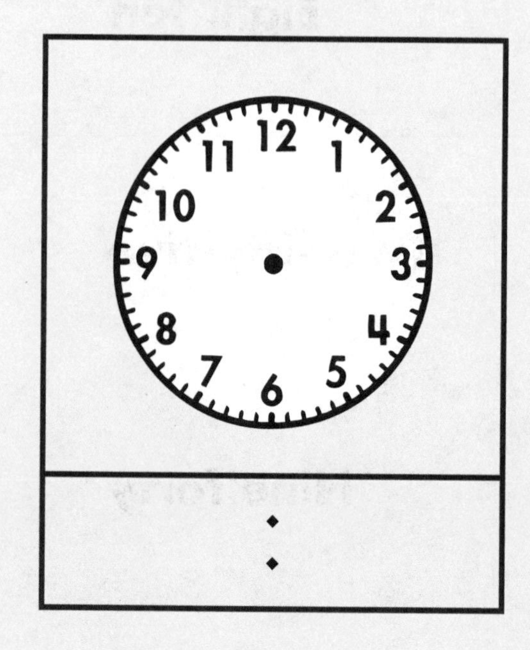

Time Two Ways

Draw the hands on each clock face. Write the time.

1. Exactly noon

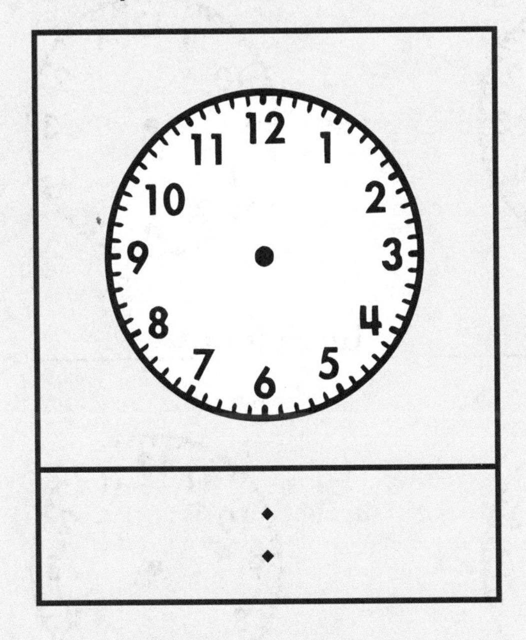

2. Quarter past 12:00

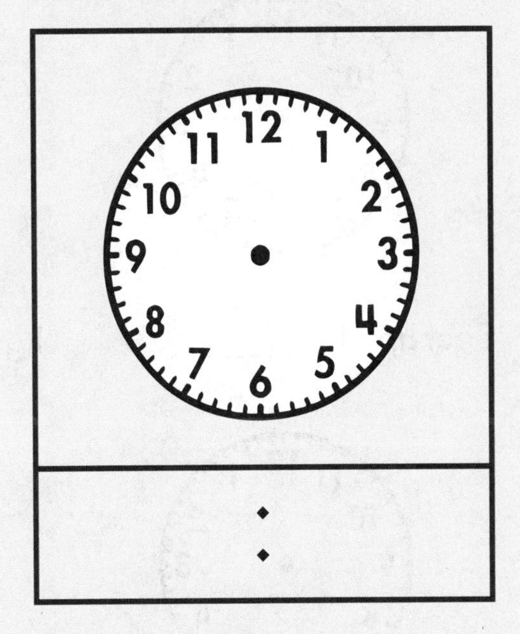

3. 15 minutes before 12:00

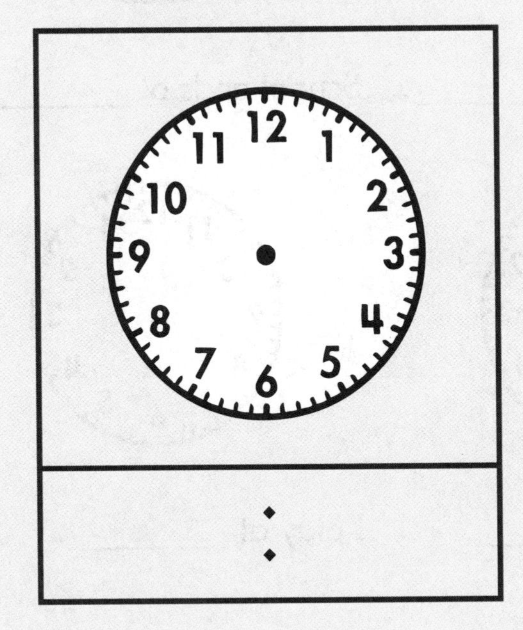

4. Half past 12:00

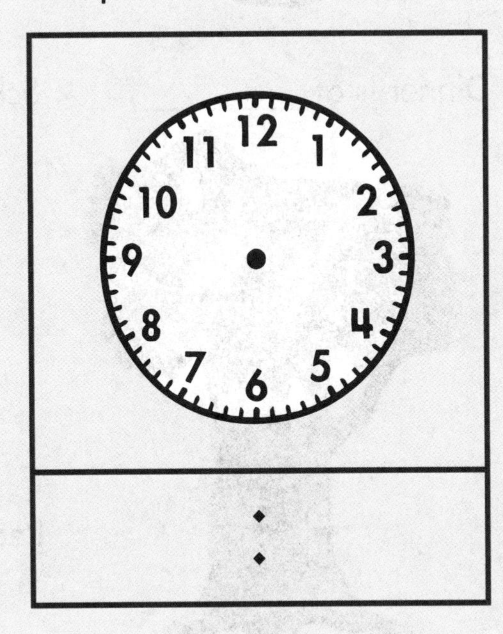

Writing Familiar Times: Family "Time Tree"

Write the time. Draw the hands on each clock.

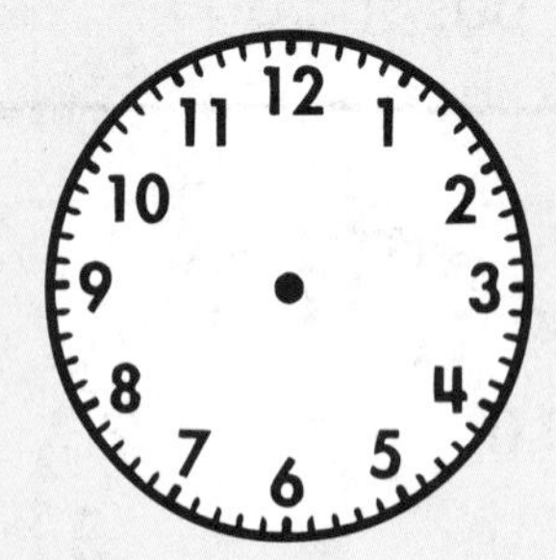

I get up at _________.

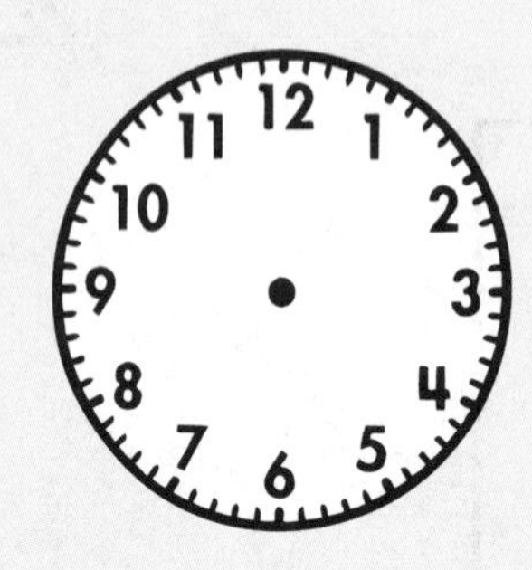

I go to bed at _________.

Lunch is at _________.

Dinner is at _________.

School starts at _________.

School ends at _________.

Recess is at _________.

I play at _________.

Time Lapse: Minutes

How much time did each activity take?

1. Jimmy played darts from 1:20 to 1:40.

He played for ___20___ minutes.

2. Marietta rode a pony for 15 minutes. She began at 1:00.

She finished at ________ : ________.

3. She had so much fun, she rode another 15 minutes.

She finished at ________ : ________.

Time Lapse: Minutes

How much time did each activity take?

1. Tim worked at the snow cone booth. The first clock shows the time he started. He worked 1 hour and 30 minutes.

Show the time he finished on the second clock.

2. Andrea won the juggling contest. She kept the balls in the air for 5 minutes. She began juggling at 1:25.

She finished at ________ : ________.

Circle the clock that shows the correct time.

Drawing Clock Hands

Read each story. Draw the hands on each clock face.

1. Rabbit hops into his garden at **6:00**. He finishes working in the garden **one and one-half hours later**.

Hops in garden

Finishes work

2. Rabbit gets out lettuce and carrots at **8:30**. He finishes eating **45 minutes later**.

Gets out lettuce and carrots

Finishes eating

3. Rabbit lies down for a nap at **4:00**. He wakes up **55 minutes later**.

Lies down

Wakes up

Drawing Clock Hands

Read each story. Draw the hands on each clock face.

1. Pig takes a mud bath at **9:00**. She showers off **15 minutes later**.

Takes mud bath

Showers off

2. On Monday, Pig begins cleaning at **noon**. Her house is clean and neat **90 minutes later**.

Begins cleaning

House is clean

3. On Tuesday, Pig goes to the market at **12:45**. She comes home with a basket full of goodies **30 minutes later**.

Goes to market

Comes home

Time Stories

Read the story. Write the times on each digital clock.

Val and Phil go out to the backyard at **6:00**. They put up their tent. This takes them **1 hour and 30 minutes**. They get in the tent and talk for **1 hour**. Then, they fall asleep. They sleep for **2 hours**, until a dog barks and wakes them up.

1. Go to backyard

2. Finish putting up tent

3. Fall asleep

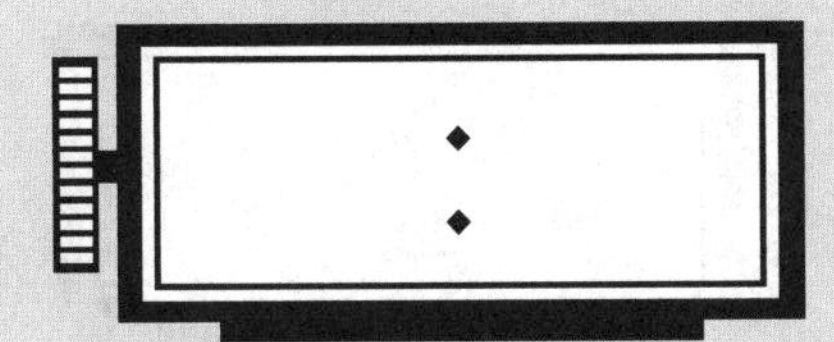

4. Dog barks

5. How long are Val and Phil in the yard before the dog wakes them up?

______________ hours ______________ minutes

Time Stories

Read the story. Write the times on each digital clock.

Joe and José put on roller skates at **8:30**. They skate for **2 hours**, then stop to rest. They rest for **one half-hour**, then start skating again. They reach the park **1 hour and 45 minutes later**.

1. Put on roller skates

2. Stop to rest

3. Start skating again

4. Get to park

5. How long does Joe and José's trip to the park take?

____________ hours ____________ minutes

Time Stories

Read each time story. Write the times on each digital clock.

1. Andrea took her dog for a walk. They left home at **5:30**. They walked for **20 minutes**. What time did they get home?

Leave home **Get home**

2. Rhiannon and her mother were making cookies. They put the cookies in the oven at **7:15**. After **10 minutes** they took the cookies out of the oven. Yum! What time did they take them out?

Cookies in oven **Cookies out of oven**

3. Solve the time puzzle.

When did Anita begin playing ping-pong? Anita played ping-pong with her brother for **30 minutes**. They stopped playing at **4:30**.

Begin playing **Stop playing**

Time Stories

Read each time story. Write the times on each digital clock.

1. Benito went for a ride on the roller coaster. He got on the roller coaster at **2:30**. He rode for **15 minutes**. What time did he get off?

2. Valerie and her sister went hiking. They started hiking at **9:00**. They hiked for **one hour and 30 minutes**. What time did they stop hiking?

3. Solve the time puzzle.

When did Ben and his mother get on the subway? Ben and his mother rode the subway for **20 minutes**. They got off the subway at **4:30**.

Time Puzzles

Write any time that fits the time clues.

1. Between 11:00 and 12:00.

2. Between 30 minutes after 2:00 and 3:00.

3. After quarter-past 7:00 and before 8:00.

4. Make up your own time clues. Ask a friend to solve your time puzzle!

____

____

____

Time Puzzles

Write any time that fits the time clues.

1. Between 4:15 and 5:15.

6:45

Time to brush my teeth!

2. After 6:00 and before quarter to 7:00.

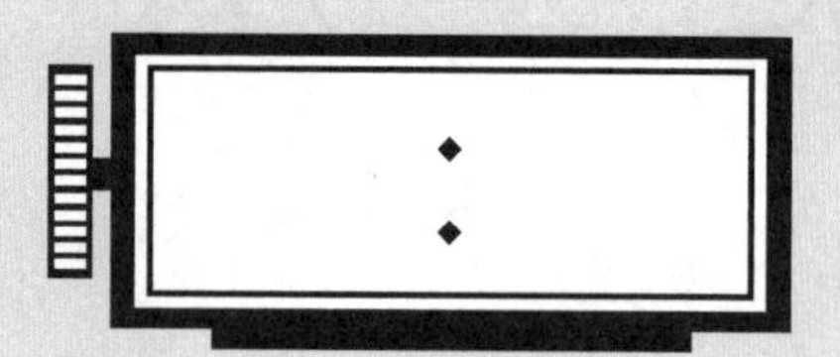

3. Between noon and 1:00.

4. Make up your own time clues. Ask a friend to solve your time puzzle!

____

____

____

Time Stories

Read the story. Write the time on each clock.

Erin and her brother Harry were shopping for dinner. First, they went into the bakery at **5:00** to buy fresh bread. This took **5 minutes**. Next, they walked to the market for vegetables and cereal. This took them **20 minutes**. Then, they walked next door for a treat at Fanny's Famous Fudge. This took them **15 minutes**. Then, they met their brother Andrew outside.

1. Go into bakery

2. Leave bakery

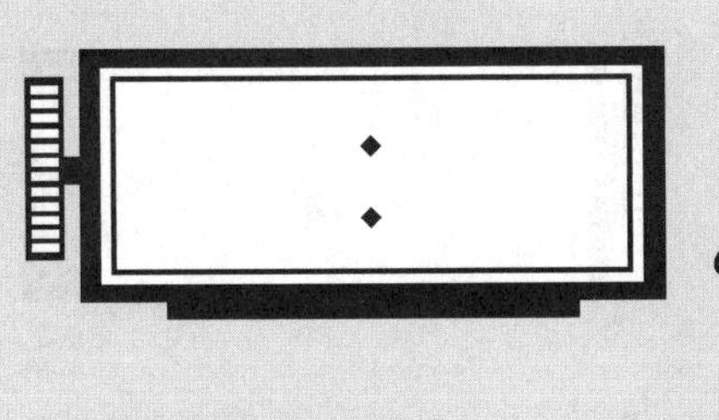

3. Leave market

4. See Andrew

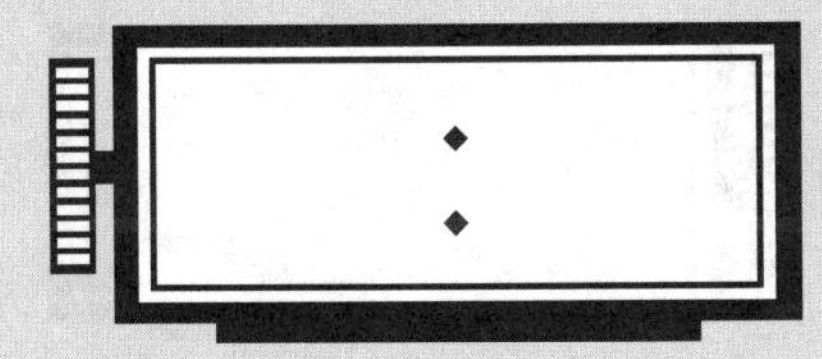

5. How long had Erin and Harry been shopping when they saw Andrew?

____

6. Make up your own story about shopping. What do you do, and how long does each thing take? Make up a starting time. Use your clock to find the ending time.

Time Stories

Read the story. Write the time on each clock.

Hanna and Shawn got to the fair at **3:00**. They threw balls at the clown's pocket for **10 minutes**. No luck! Then, they rode the Big Dipper for **30 minutes**. They got wet! After this, they ate pizza for **15 minutes**. Then, they saw their friend Mary.

1. **Go to fair**

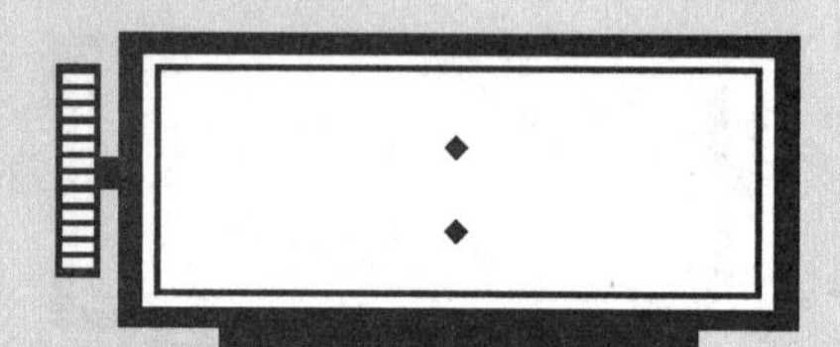

2. **Stop throwing balls**

3. **Stop riding Big Dipper**

4. **See Mary**

5. How long had Hanna and Shawn been at the fair when they saw Mary?

____

6. Make up your own story about being at a fair. What do you do, and how long does each thing take? Make up a starting time. Use your clock to find the ending time.

Telling Time: Using Charts

Gull Air	10:45	12:10	1:45
Far West Airlines	9:25	10:10	11:40
Swift Flights	12:30	1:15	2:20

Use the chart. Write the time that each pair took a flight.

1. Teresa and her aunt flew on the plane that left closest to **10:30**.

   Airline: ____________________

   Left at: ____________________

2. Kelly and her mother flew on the plane that left closest to **11:00**.

   Airline: ____________________

   Left at: ____________________

3. Leticia and her father flew on the plane that left closest to **12:15**.

   Airline: ____________________

   Left at: ____________________

4. Make up your own time puzzle about the Main Airport.

Telling Time: Using Charts

Otters	2:00	3:30	5:00
Dolphins	11:30	3:15	5:20
Sharks	2:30	4:00	5:45

Use the chart. Write the time that each pair went to a feeding.

1. Francisco and José went to the feeding that was closest to **3:00**.

Animal: ____________________

Feeding at: ____________________

2. Alex and Shannon went to the feeding that was closest to **6:00**.

Animal: ____________________

Feeding at: ____________________

3. Kim and Amanda went to the feeding that was closest to **5:30**.

Animal: ____________________

Feeding at: ____________________

4. Make up your own time puzzle about the Bayside Aquarium.

MONEY

Pennies: Introduction

This is a penny.

It is worth 1 cent. It has 2 sides.

This is the cent symbol. Trace it.

Color the pennies **brown**.

Pennies: Introduction

Find each penny. Color it **brown**.

How many pennies did you find? ___________

Counting Pennies

Count the pennies.

___3___ pennies = ___3___¢

________ pennies = ________¢

________ penny = ________¢

Counting Pennies

Count the pennies on the flowers. Write the cents in the center.

Counting Pennies

Draw a line from the pennies to the correct numbers.

Example:

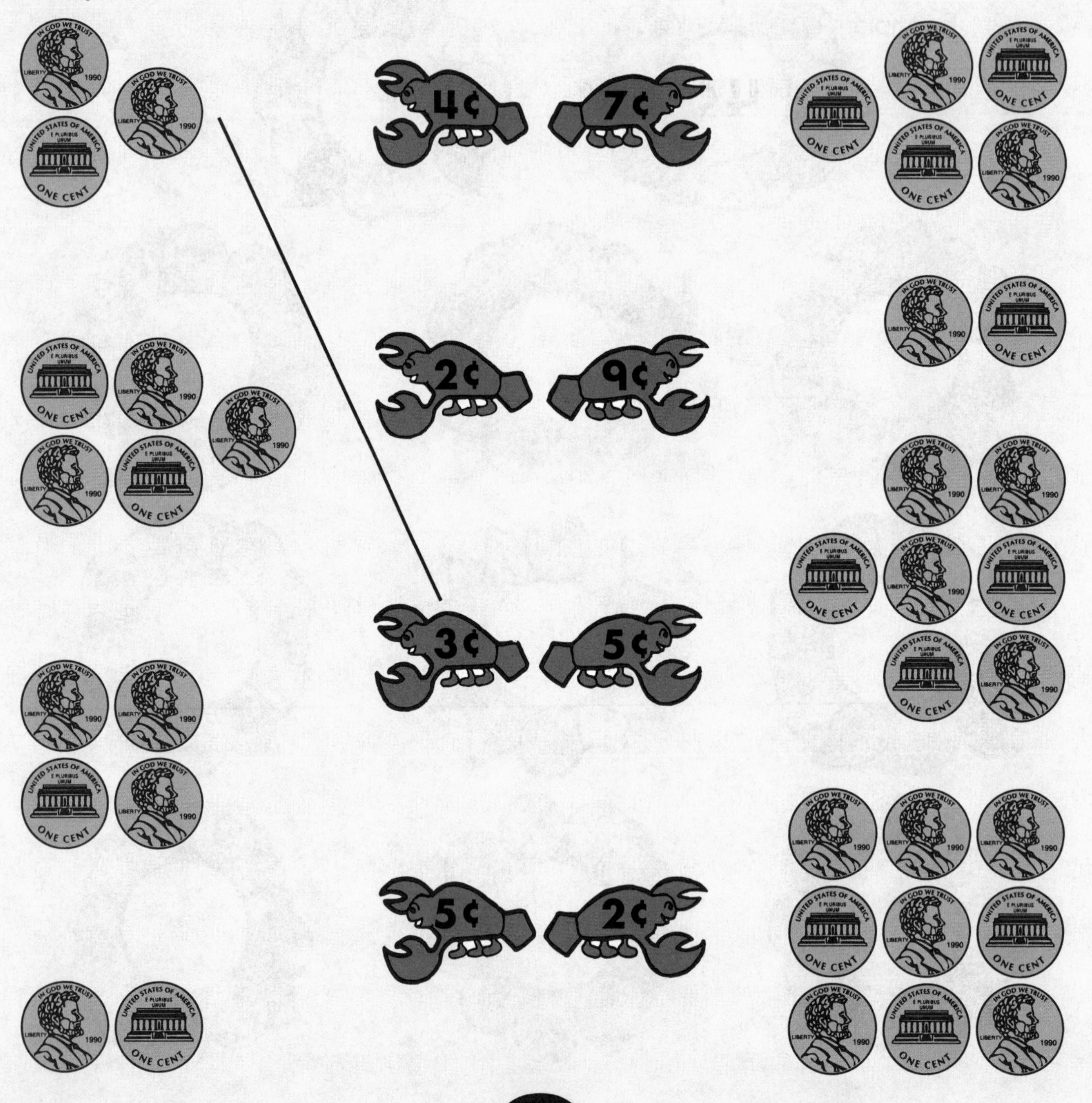

Counting Pennies

Write the number of pennies on each bag. Color each penny.

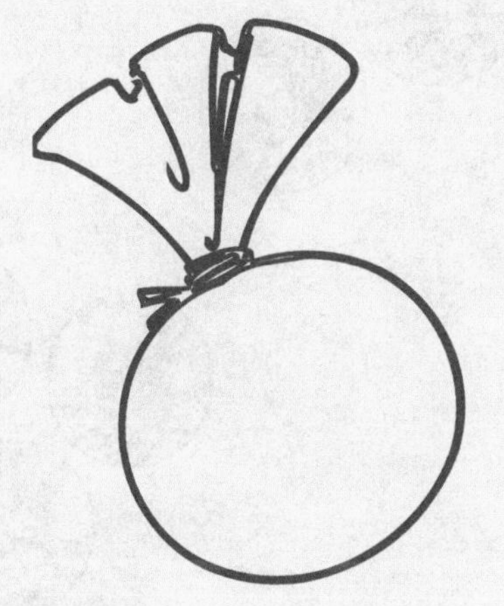

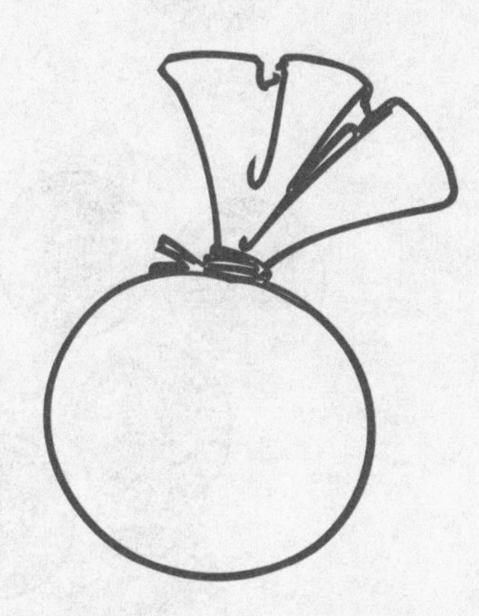

Counting Pennies

Count the pennies in each group. Match it to the correct bag.

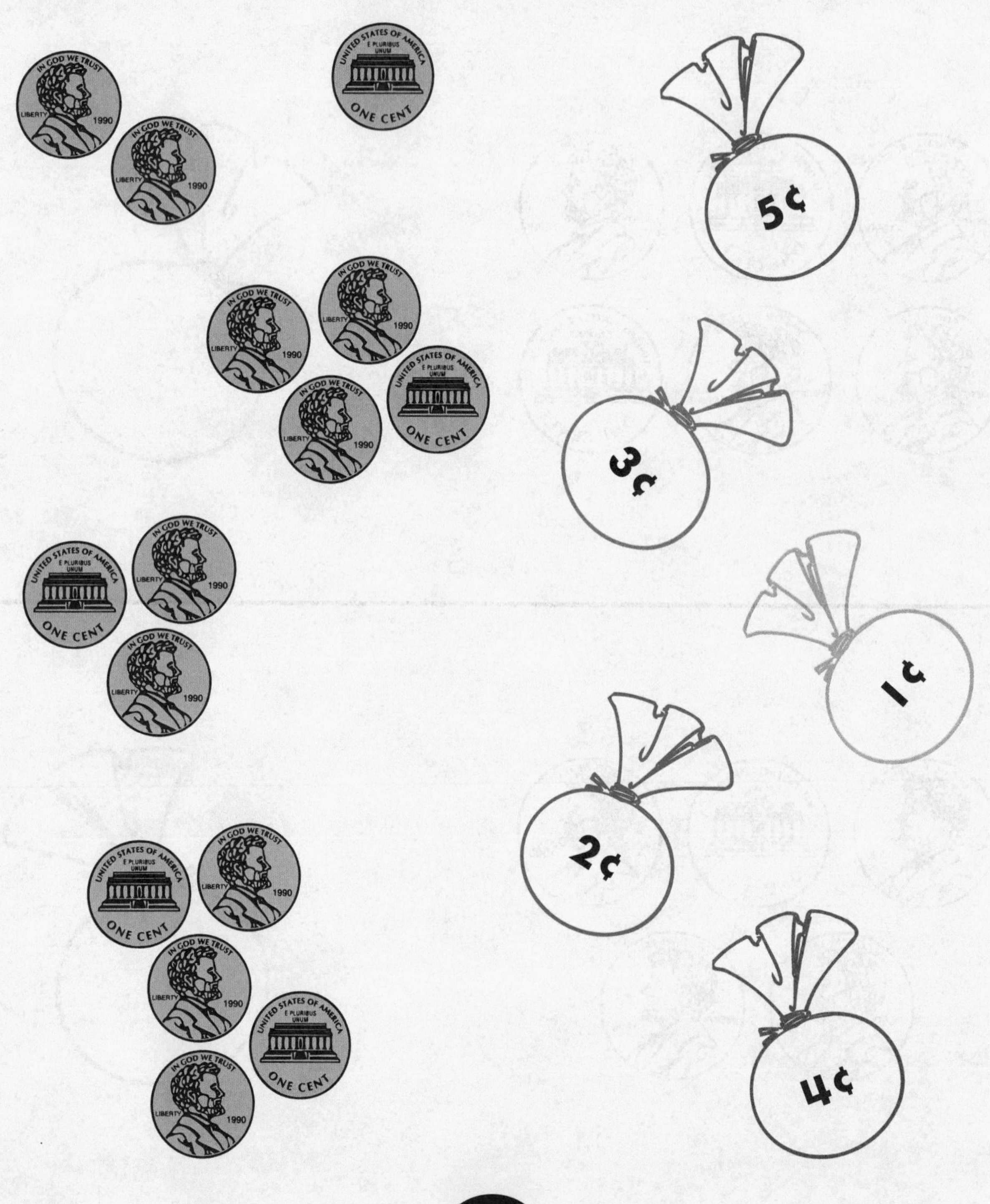

Counting Pennies

Count the pennies. Write the number of pennies on the line. Color each ride.

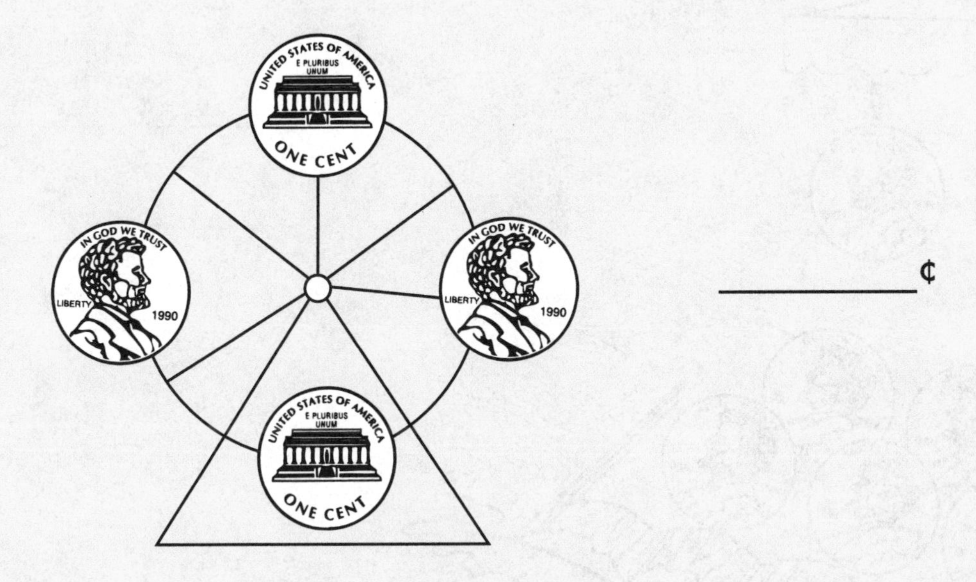

_______________ ¢

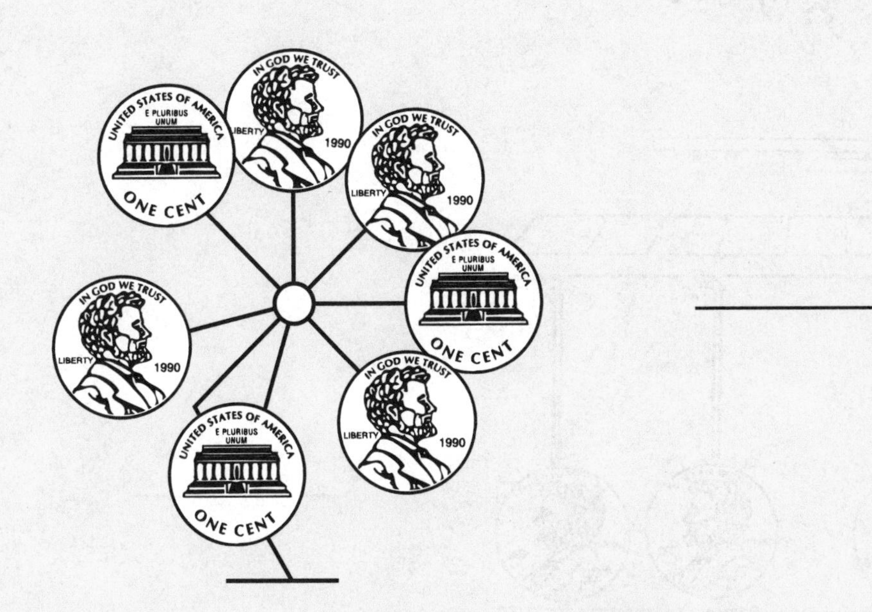

_______________ ¢

Counting Pennies

Count the pennies. Write the number of pennies on the line. Color each ride.

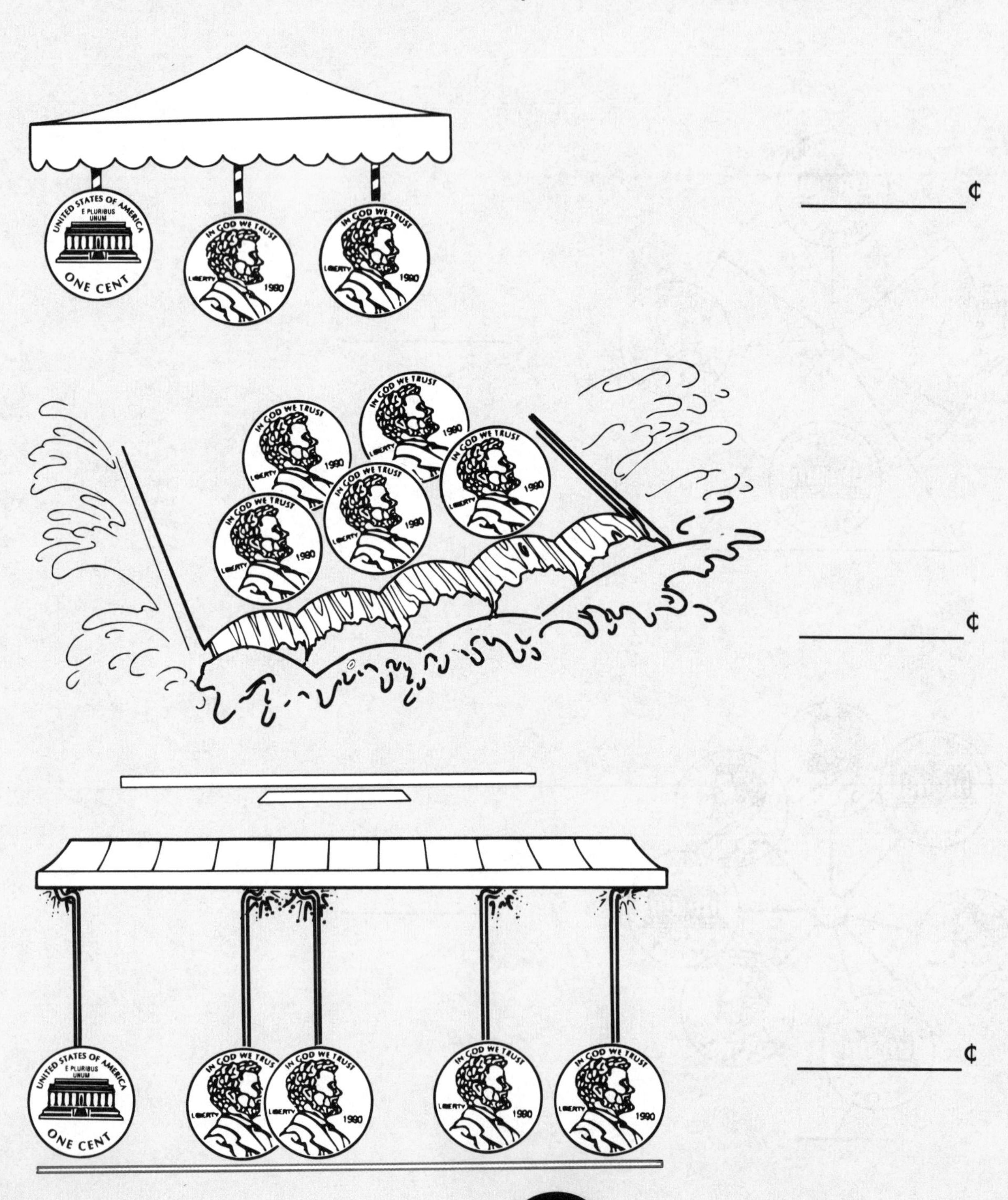

Counting Pennies

Count the money. How much?

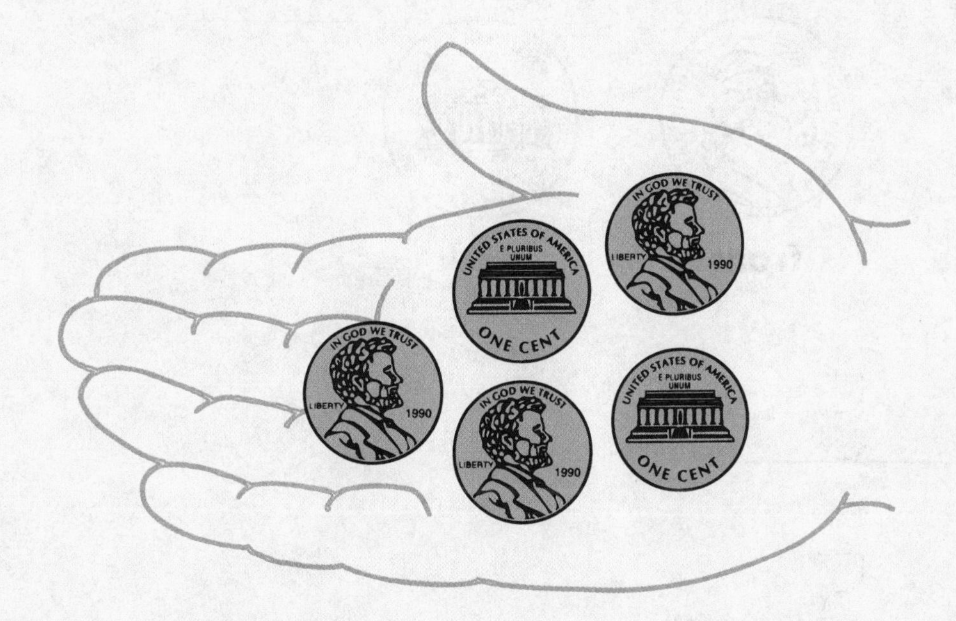

__________ ¢

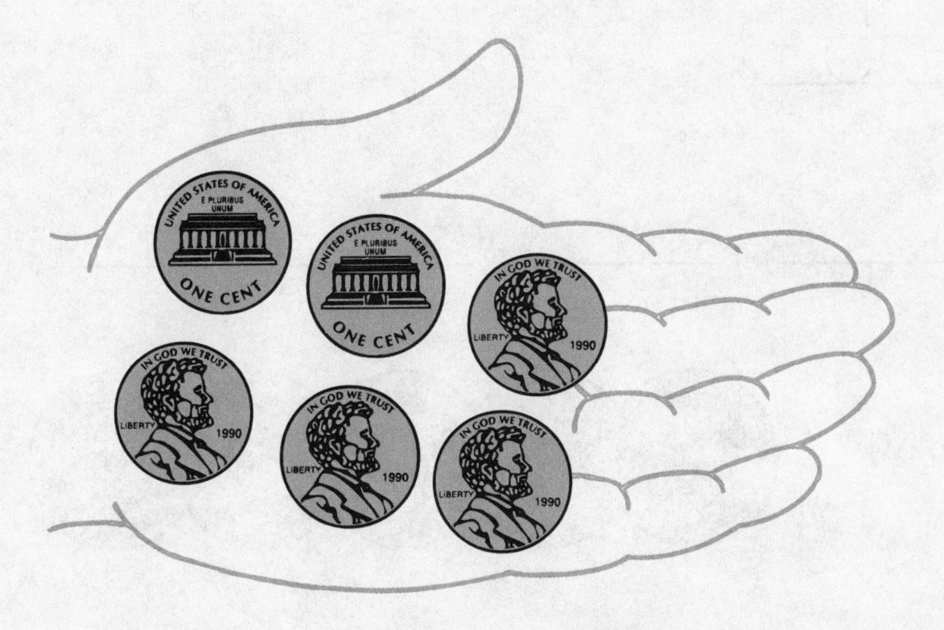

__________ ¢

Nickels: Introduction

This is a nickel. Color the nickels **silver**.

front

back

1 nickel = 5 pennies

1 nickel = 5 cents

1 nickel = 5 ¢

5¢ = ______¢ + ______¢ + ______¢ + ______¢ + ______¢

=

Counting with Nickels and Pennies

A nickel is worth 5¢. Count the money.

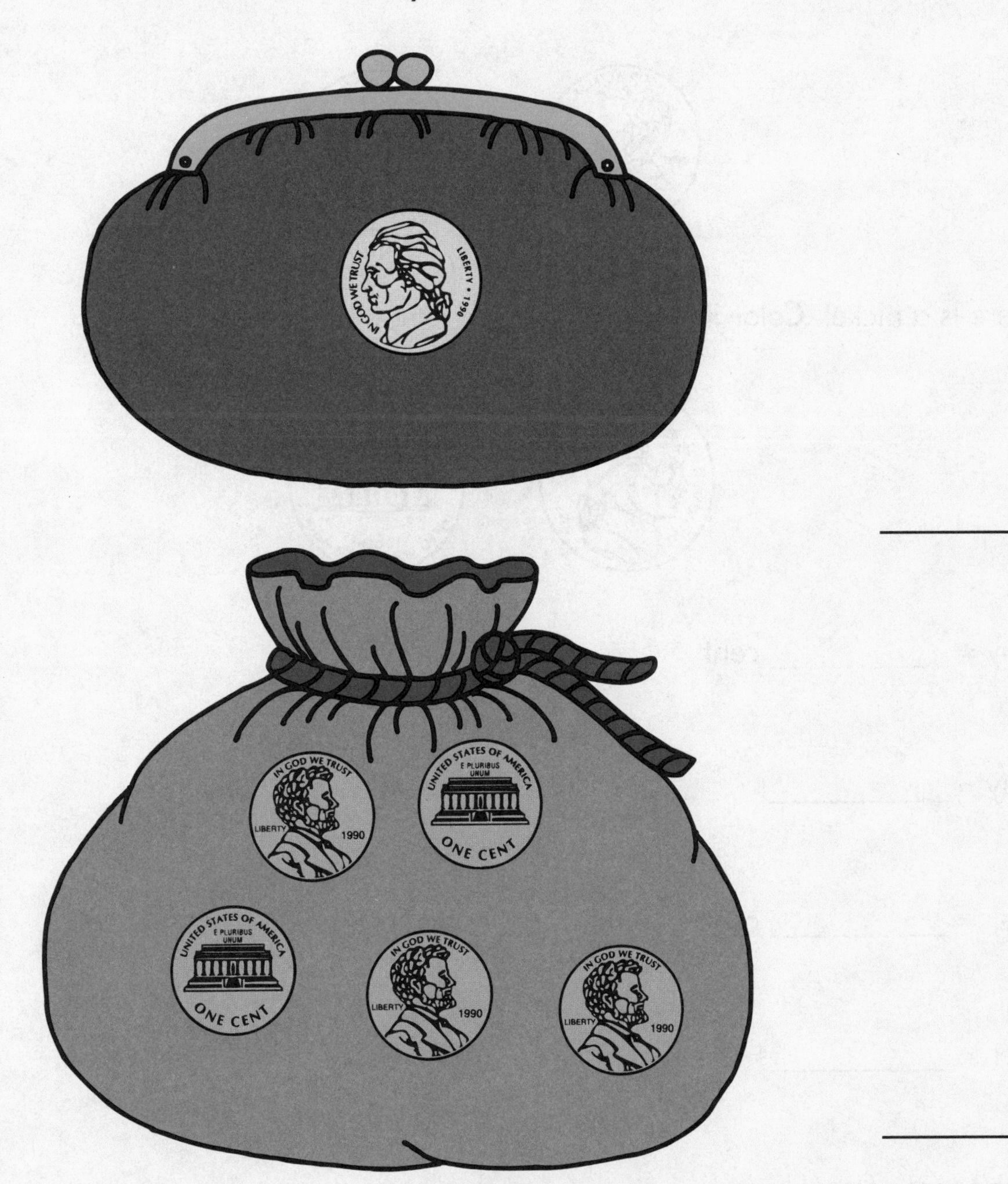

_______¢

_______¢

Counting with Nickels and Pennies

Here is a penny. Color it **brown**.

And here is a nickel. Color it **silver**.

1 penny = __________ cent

1 penny = __________¢

1 nickel = __________ cents

1 nickel = __________¢

Make the cent symbol here: __________

Counting with Nickels and Pennies

Count the money. Start with the nickel. Then, count the pennies. Write the amount.

______¢

______¢

______¢

______¢

______¢

______¢

Counting with Nickels and Pennies

Who has more money? Count the money. Write the amount.

_________¢

_________¢

Who has more money? Circle the answer.

Counting with Nickels and Pennies

Each nickel is worth 5 cents. Show how much these nickels are worth.

= ________¢

= ________¢

= ________¢ = ________¢

= ________¢

= ________¢

= ________¢ = ________¢

= ________¢

= ________¢

= ________¢

= ________¢ = ________¢

Nickels: Counting By Fives

Count by fives. See how far you can count.

5, 10, 15, 20, 25,

30, 35, 40, 45, 50,

55, 60, 65, 70, 75,

80, 85, 90, 95, 100

This is how to count nickels! Practice counting by fives!

Nickels: Counting By Fives

Count the nickels. Write the money in the meter.

Example:

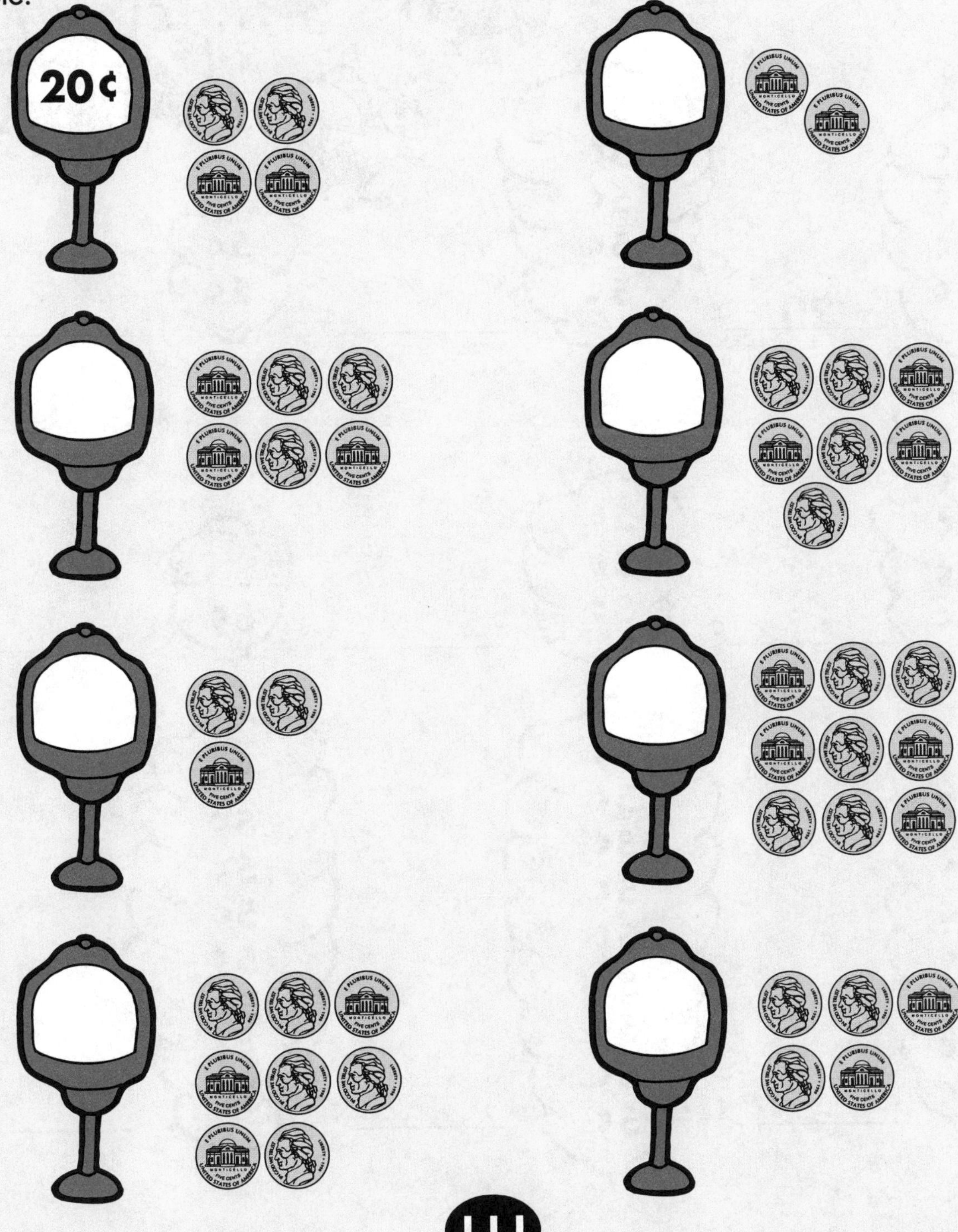

Nickels: Counting By Fives

How much money is in each hive?

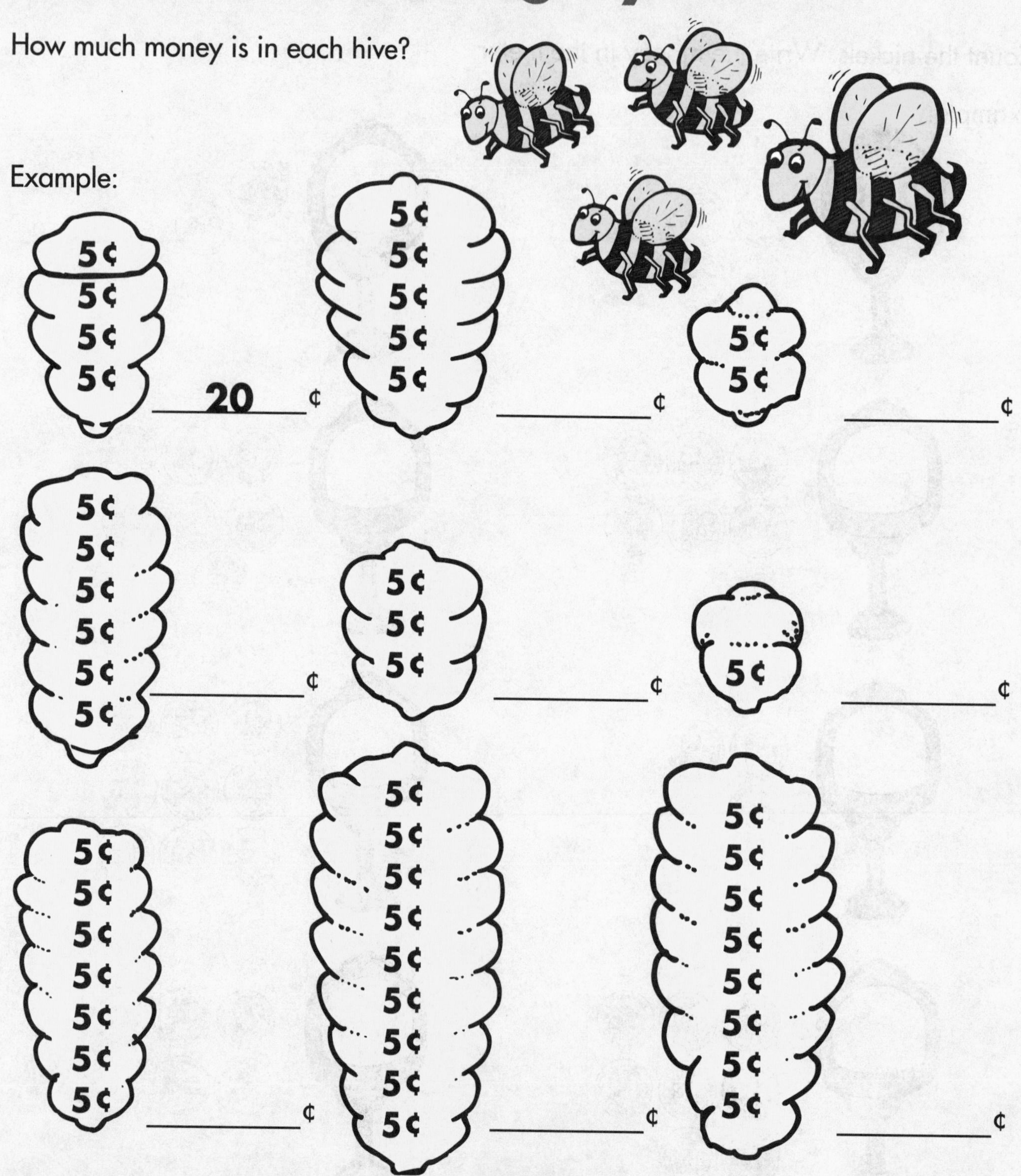

Counting with Nickels and Pennies

Count the coins. Write the amount under each bunny's carrot.

Example:

Counting with Nickels and Pennies

Look at the price on each toy. Color it if there are enough nickels.

Adding with Nickels and Pennies

Write an addition sentence for each problem.

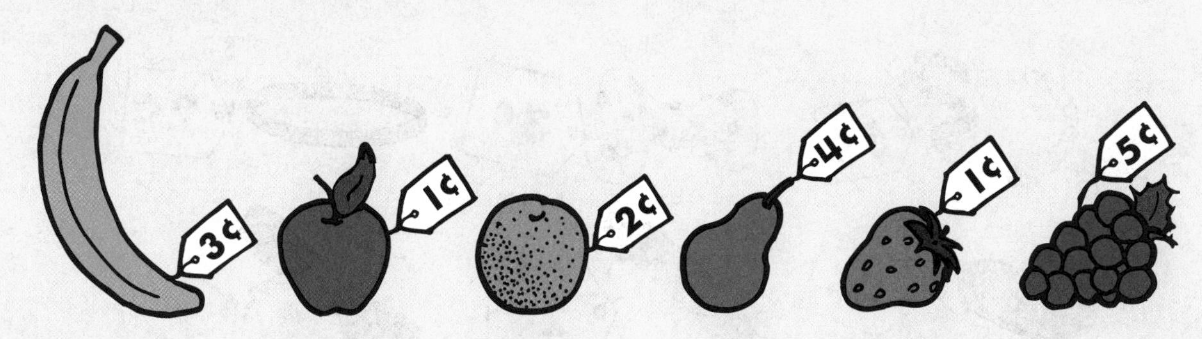

Example:

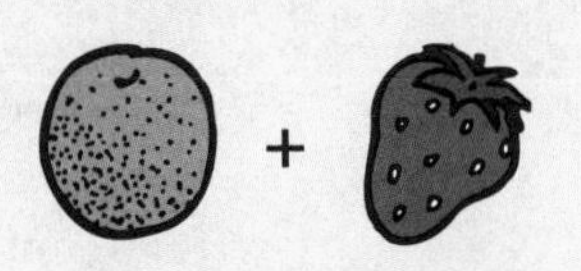

2¢ + 1¢ = 3¢

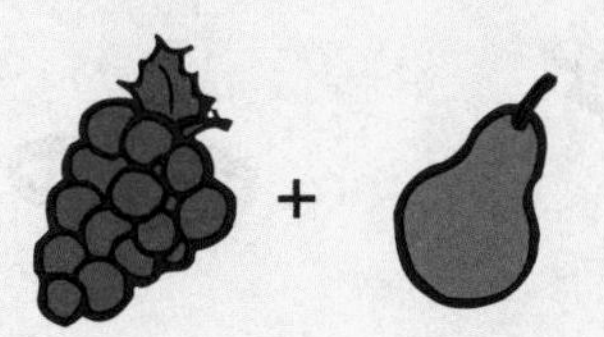

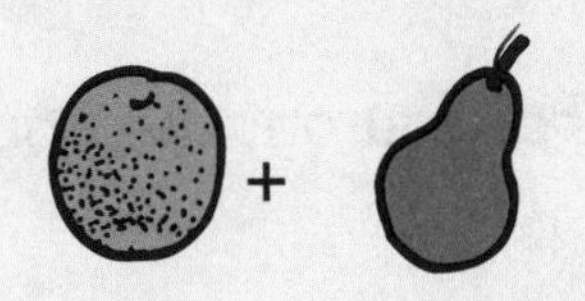

Adding with Nickels and Pennies

Kristen is having a birthday party. Let's see what she bought for her three friends.

For Cassie, she bought the and the .

She paid __________¢.

For Terri, she bought the  and the .

She paid __________¢.

For Lauren, she bought the  and the .

She paid __________¢.

Adding with Nickels and Pennies

Use page 116 to help you answer the questions below.

Every birthday party needs balloons. Draw one for each girl, including Kristen.

They cost 5¢ each. Count by fives. She paid __________¢.

She also bought bubble wands. Draw one for each girl.

They cost 2¢ each. Count by twos. She paid __________¢.

Finally! The presents! Color the presents.

Dimes: Introduction

A dime is small, but quite strong. It can buy more than a penny or nickel.

UNITED STATES OF AMERICA
ONE DIME

front **back**

Each side of a dime is different. It has ridges on its edge. Color the dime **silver**.

=

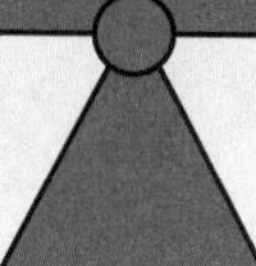

1 dime = 10 pennies

1 dime = 10 cents

1 dime = 10 ¢

Counting with Dimes and Pennies

Dimes and pennies are easy to count.

+

= ______¢

______ ______ ______

Always begin with the dime. Then, add the pennies.

+

= ______¢

______ ______ ______ ______

+

= ______¢

______ ______

+

______ ______ ______ ______

= ______¢

______ ______ ______

Dimes: Counting By Tens

Count by tens.

10¢

20¢

30¢

40¢

50¢

60¢

70¢

80¢

90¢

100¢

Dimes: Counting By Tens

Count by tens. Write the number. Circle the group with more.

__________¢ or __________¢

__________¢ or __________¢

__________¢ or __________¢

Counting with Dimes and Pennies

Count the dimes by tens. Then, count the pennies. How much?

Example:

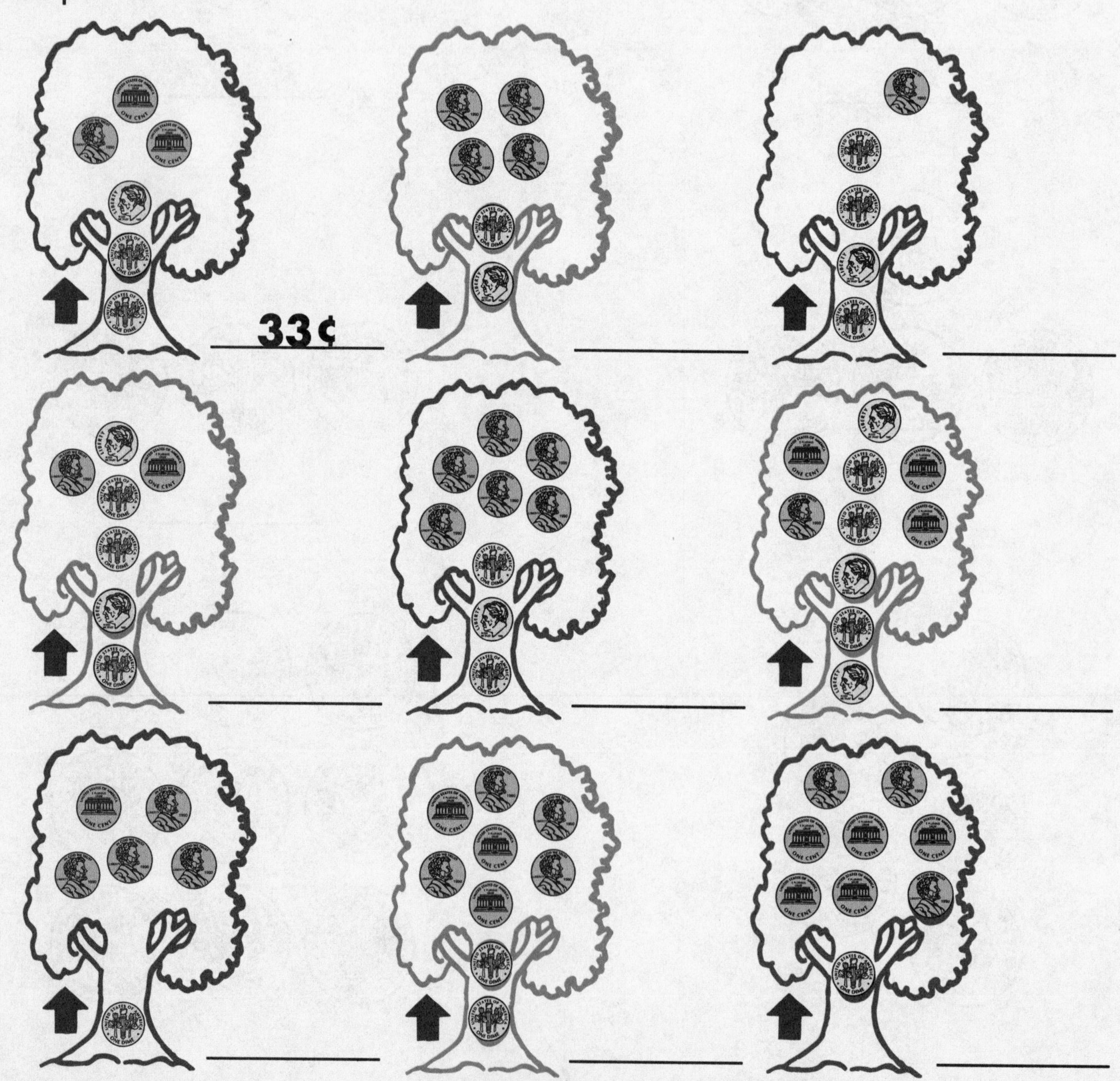

Counting with Dimes and Nickels

Do you like to do tricks? Here is a trick for counting dimes and nickels.

Look carefully at these dimes and nickels. Circle two nickels, then two more, until all the nickels are circled. Then, count by tens to see how much money is here.

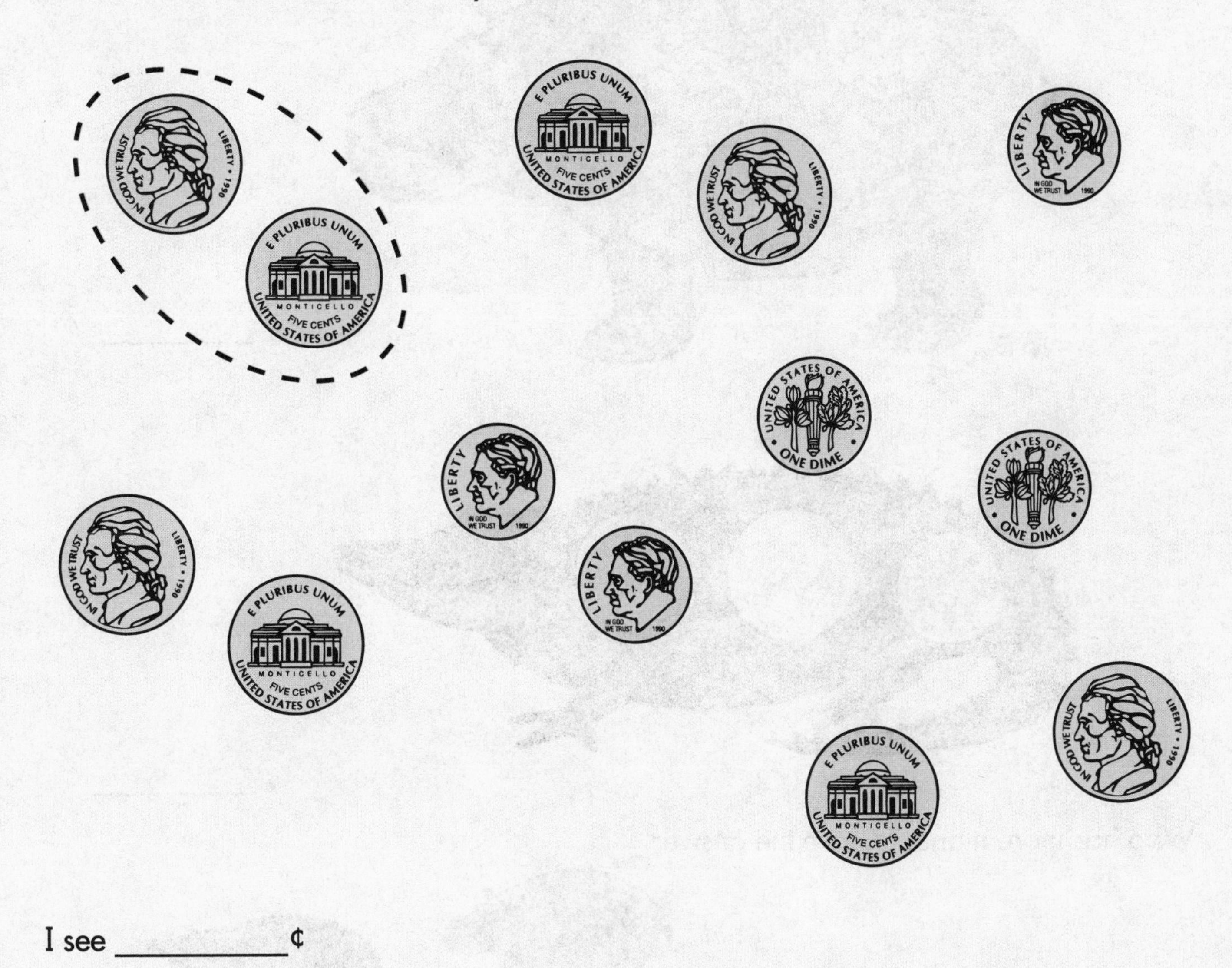

I see ____________¢

Counting with Dimes, Nickels, and Pennies

Count the money. Start with the dime. Write the amount.

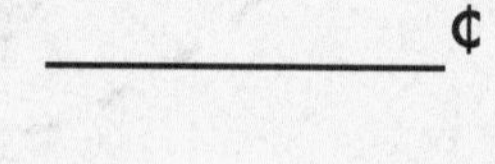
______¢

______¢

Who has more money? Circle the answer.

Counting with Dimes, Nickels, and Pennies

Count the money. Start with the dime. Write the amount.

_______________¢

_______________¢

Counting with Dimes, Nickels, and Pennies

Write how many cents.

1.

__________ ¢

2.

__________ ¢

3.

__________ ¢

If you add 1 more penny to number 1, you will have __________ ¢

If you add 1 more penny to number 2, you will have __________ ¢

If you add 1 more penny to number 3, you will have __________ ¢

Counting with Dimes, Nickels, and Pennies

There is a bake sale at school today.

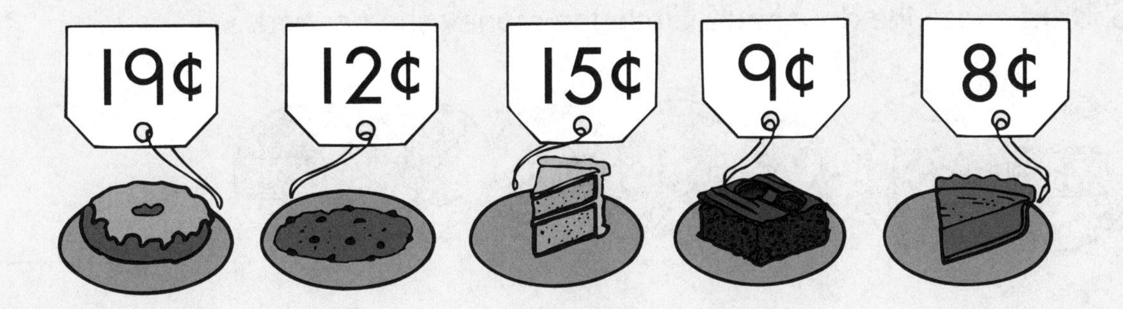

Decide which one you want. In the space below, draw enough money to pay for it.

Counting with Dimes, Nickels, and Pennies

Use page 127 to help you answer the questions below.

1. Sharita chose the doughnut. Circle the money she needed.

__________¢

2. Robert loves brownies. Circle the money he needed.

__________¢

3. Tom had 3 of these.

He had __________¢.
He spent it all on something good. Draw it here.

Counting with Dimes, Nickels, and Pennies

Circle the coins to equal the right amount.

Example:

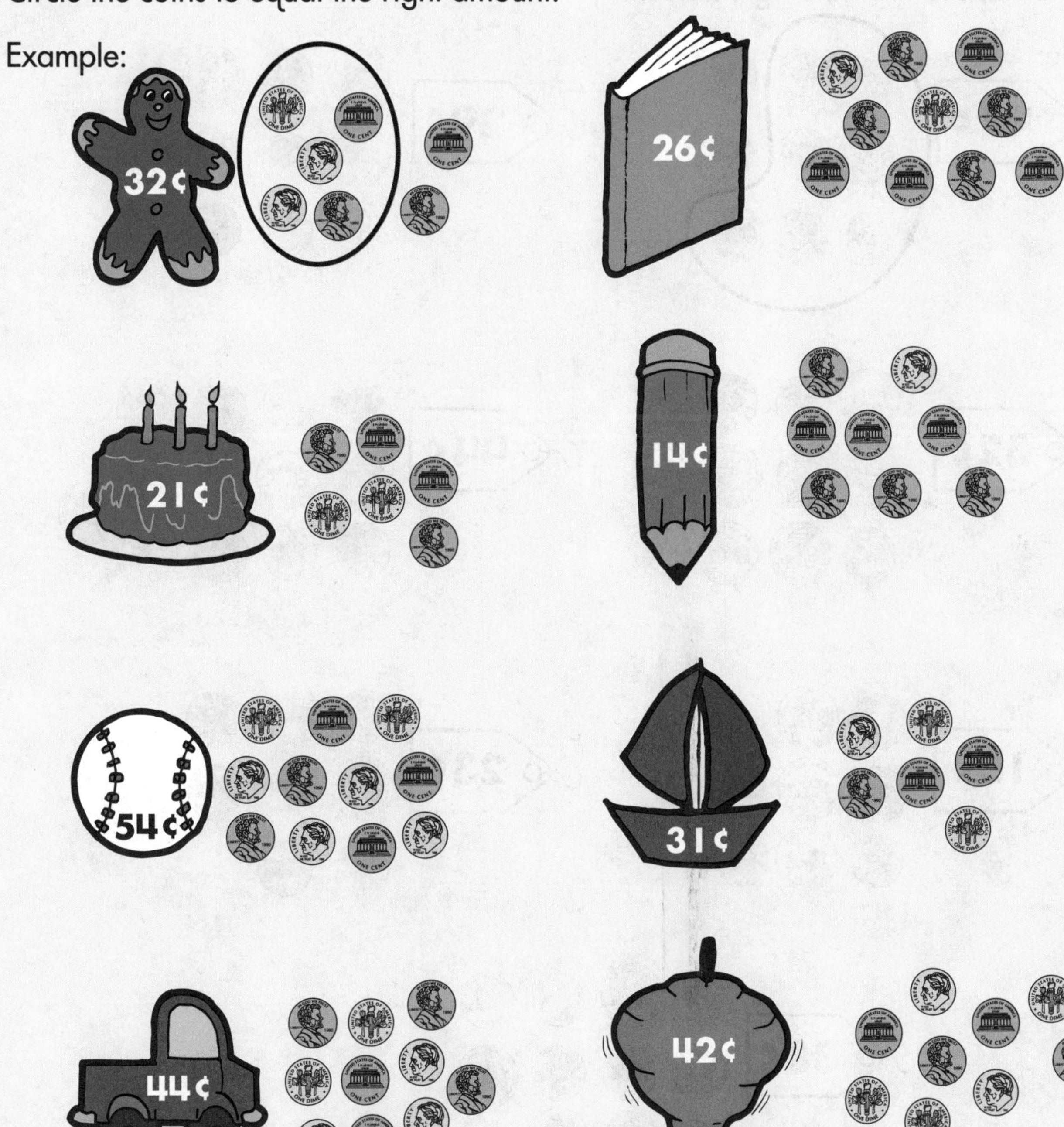

Counting with Dimes, Nickels, and Pennies

Circle the coins to show the right amount.

Example:

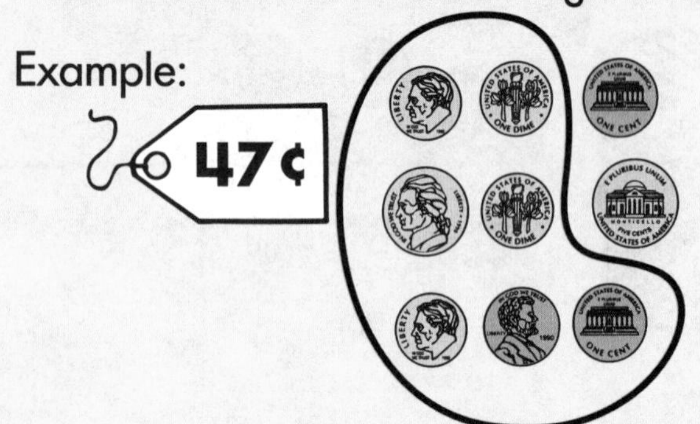

Subtracting with Dimes, Nickels, and Pennies

Earning money is fun! So is spending it! See what the children buy with their money.

Draw an **X** on the coins needed. Write how much money is left.

José wants:

He has:

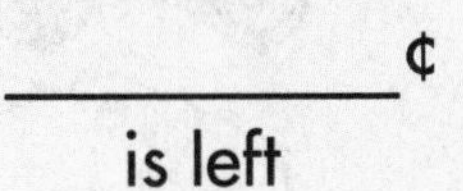

______¢
is left

Catherine wants:

She has:

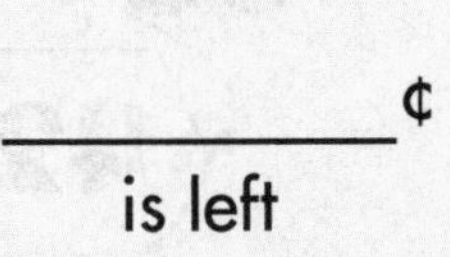

______¢
is left

Subtracting with Dimes, Nickels, and Pennies

Andrew wants:

He has:

_______¢ is left

Sherry wants:

She has:

_______¢ is left

Robert wants:

He has:

Can Robert buy the truck? __________

Quarters: Introduction

This is a quarter. The United States' first president, George Washington, is on the front.

front

back

___1___ quarter = ___25___ pennies

___1___ quarter = ___25___ cents

___1___ quarter = ___25___¢

Count these nickels by fives. Is this another way to make 25¢? Circle the answer.

yes **no**

Quarters: Introduction

Follow each path to see how many quarters Mike and Maria found. The bananas cost 25¢ each. How many can they buy?

Mike found quarters to buy __________ bananas.

Maria found quarters to buy __________ bananas.

Quarters: Combinations of 25 Cents

These are ways to make 25¢. Color each coin.

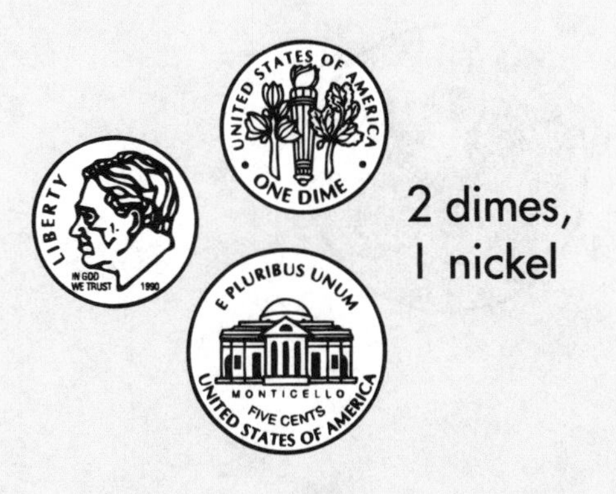

2 dimes,
1 nickel

5 nickels

25 pennies

Quarters: More or Less Than 50 Cents

The tooth fairy left 2 quarters for your shiny baby tooth.

How much money do you have?

Each quarter is worth 25¢.

Two quarters = 50¢

Color each toy you can buy.

Quarters: More or Less Than 50 Cents

Some children had fun spending the allowance they earned. The boys bought some cars.

Terry paid 5¢ for each blue car. Color Terry's cars **blue**.

How much did Terry pay for the blue cars? __________¢

Lucas liked the red cars. They were the same price. Color his cars **red**.

How much did Lucas pay for the red cars? __________¢

Which boy paid more? ____________________

Quarters: More or Less Than 50 Cents

Patty bought some pears at the store. She paid 25¢ for each pear. Color the pears.

Draw the quarters she spent.

How much money did she spend? __________¢

Jennifer bought these bananas. She paid 10¢ for each one. Color the bananas.

10¢
each

Draw the dimes she spent.

How much money did she spend? __________¢

Which girl spent less? ______________________________

Counting with Quarters, Dimes, Nickels, and Pennies

Count the money. Start with the quarters. Then, count the dimes, nickels, and pennies.

1.

25¢

35¢

40¢

41¢
Total

2.

25¢

35¢

36¢

37¢

38¢

39¢

40¢
Total

Counting with Quarters, Dimes, Nickels, and Pennies

Count the money. Write the amount.

1. ______¢ ______¢ ______¢ ______¢ Total

2. ______¢ ______¢ ______¢ ______¢ Total

3. Put more than 50¢ in the bank. Show the coins.

______¢ Total

Counting with Quarters, Dimes, Nickels, and Pennies

Count the money. Start with the quarters. Then, count the dimes, nickels, and pennies.

1.

_______ ¢ _______ ¢ _______ ¢ _______ ¢ _______ ¢

Total

2.

_______ ¢ _______ ¢ _______ ¢ _______ ¢ _______ ¢

_______ ¢ _______ ¢ _______ ¢

Total

Counting with Quarters, Dimes, Nickels, and Pennies

Count the money. Start with the quarter. Write the amount.

__________¢

__________¢

Counting with Quarters, Dimes, Nickels, and Pennies

Count the money. Start with the quarter. Write the amount.

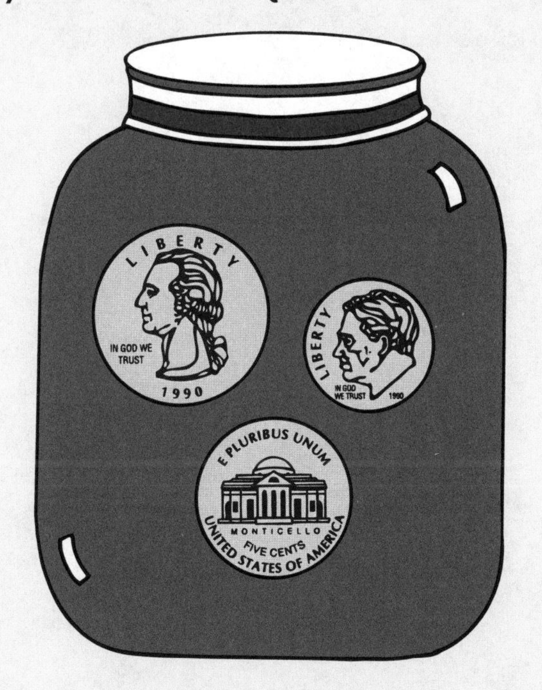

__________¢

__________¢

Counting with Quarters, Dimes, Nickels, and Pennies

Match the money with the amount.

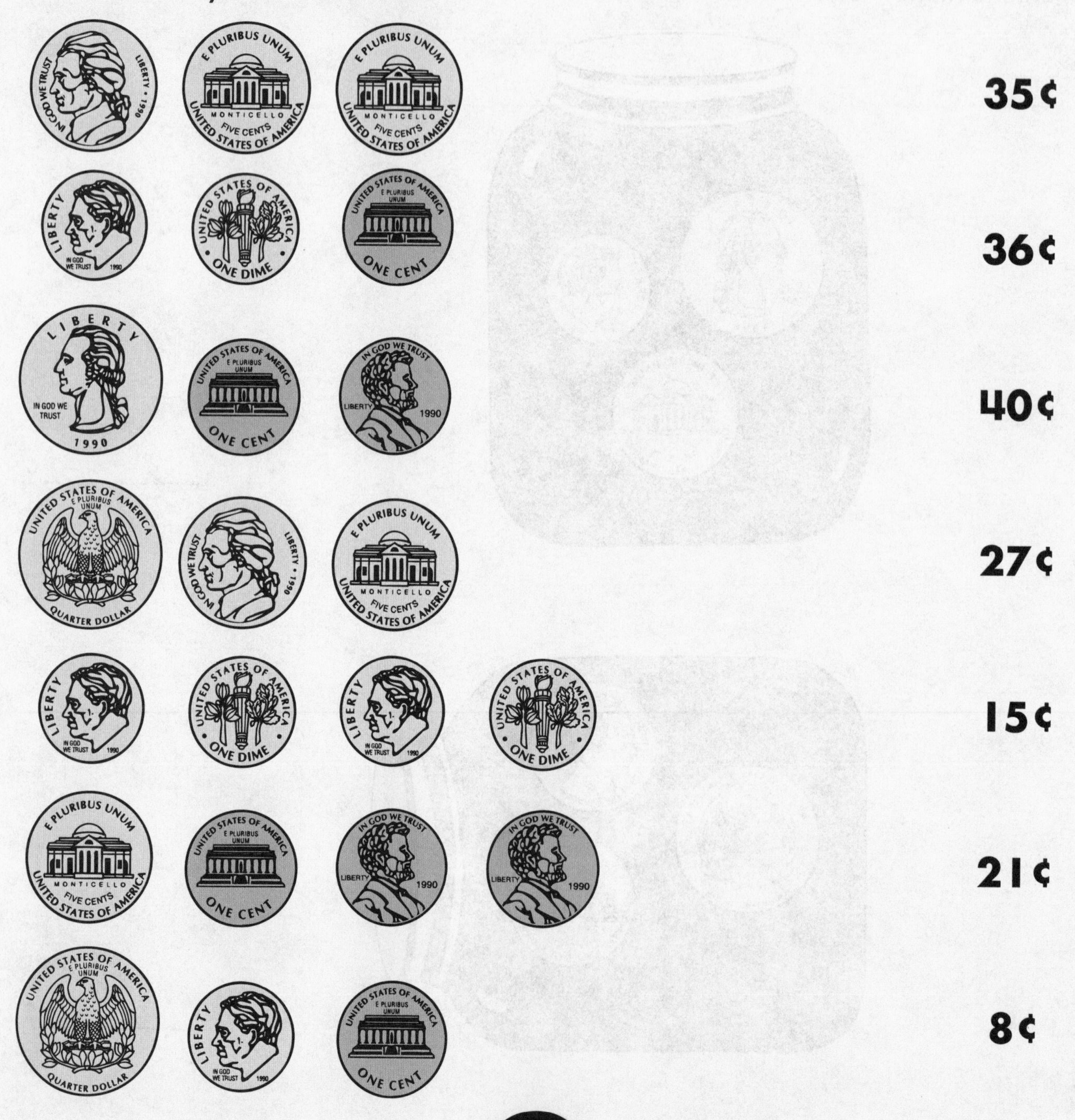

35¢

36¢

40¢

27¢

15¢

21¢

8¢

Counting with Quarters, Dimes, Nickels, and Pennies

Count the coins. Start with the quarters. Write the amount in each football.

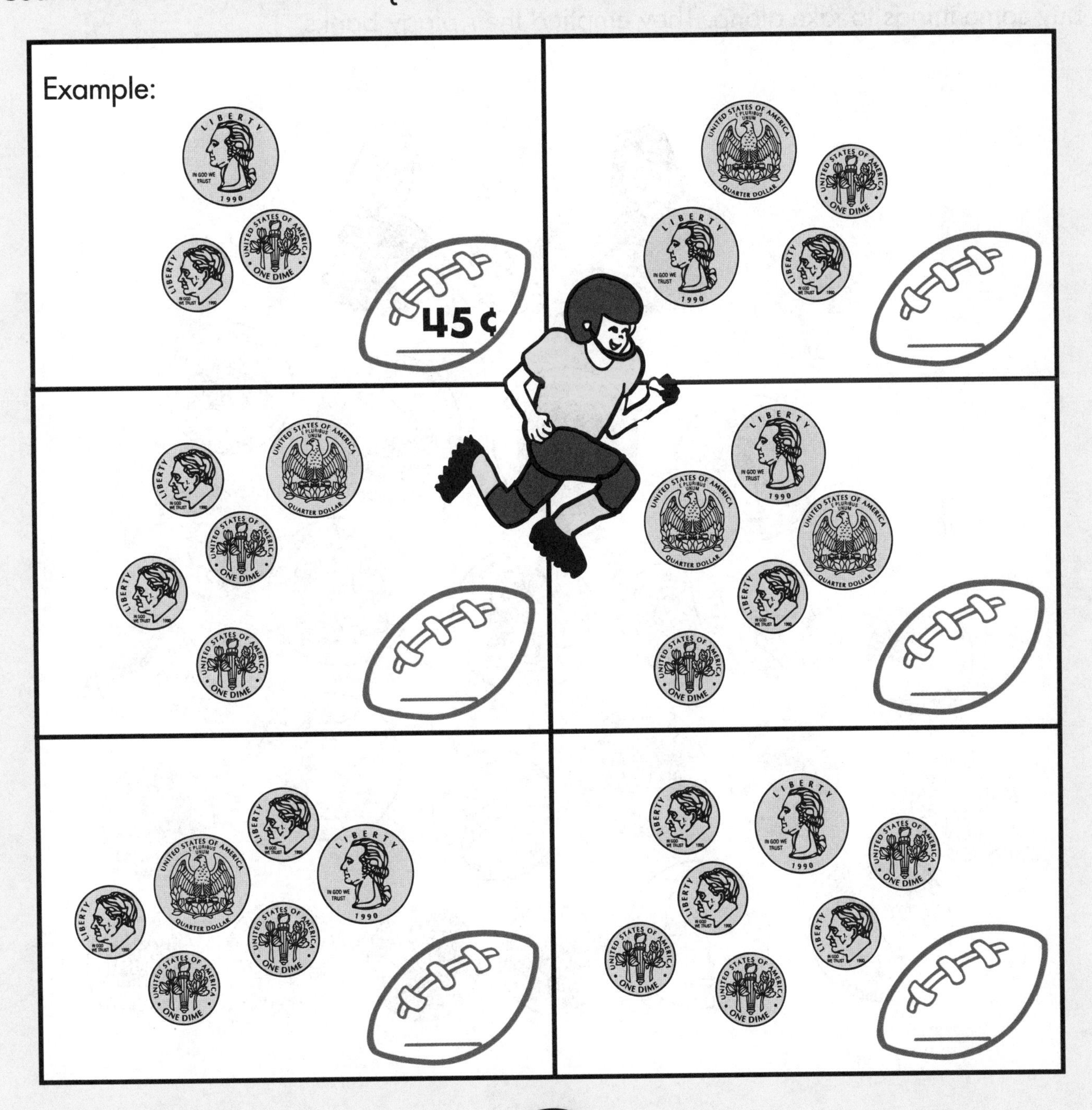

Counting with Quarters, Dimes, Nickels, and Pennies

Carolyn and Marilyn are going to the beach for their vacation. The twins wanted to buy some things to take along. They emptied their piggy banks.

Counting with Quarters, Dimes, Nickels, and Pennies

Use page 146 to help you answer the questions below.

Cross off the money Carolyn and Marilyn used for:

Color the pails **pink**.

Cross off the money they used for:

Color the beach balls **red** and **yellow**.

Cross off the money they used for:

Color the beach towels **blue** and **green**.

Cross off the money they used for:

Color the sunglasses.

Did they have enough money? ____________

Counting with Quarters, Dimes, Nickels, and Pennies

Count the coins. Do you have enough money to buy each toy?

Example:

Toy price	You have...		yes or no
58¢		51¢	no
47¢			
75¢			
43¢			
98¢			
32¢			
26¢			
45¢			

Counting with Quarters, Dimes, Nickels, and Pennies

It is fun to buy things to keep your hair looking great!

How many of each coin do you need? Write **1**, **2**, **3**, or **4**.

	Quarters	Dimes	Nickels	Pennies

Adding and Comparing Amounts of Money

Christopher was a good shopper. He looked for the best prices when he bought school supplies.

Circle and color the one he bought.

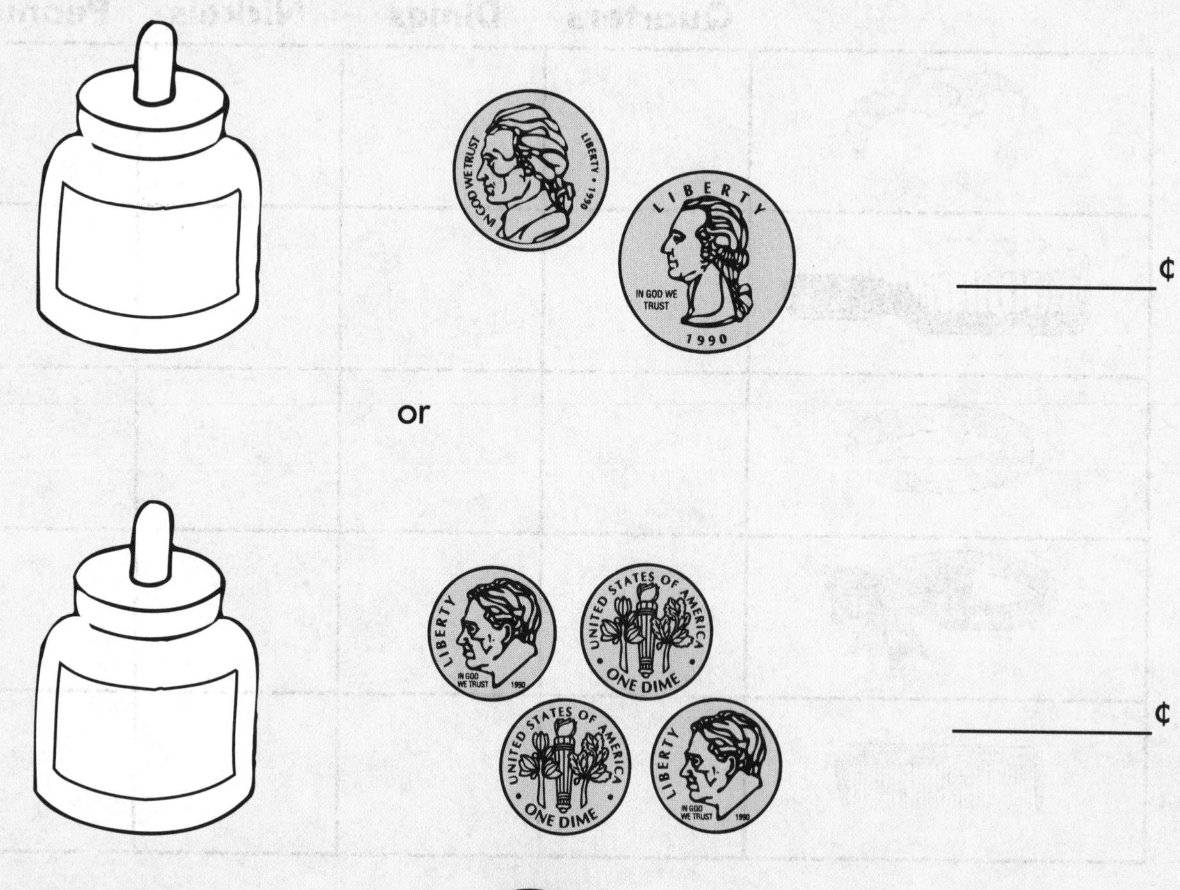

Adding and Comparing Amounts of Money

Circle and color the one Christopher bought.

_____________¢

or

_____________¢

_____________¢

or

_____________¢

Subtracting for Change

Adam wanted to know how much change he would have left when he bought things. He made this picture to help him subtract.

4	dimes
− 1	dime
3	dimes

40¢
− 10¢

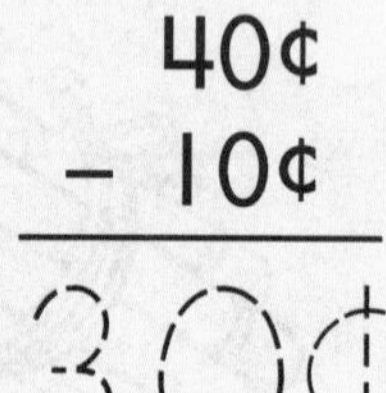

30¢

Cross out the dimes to help you subtract.

6	dimes
− 4	dime
	dimes

60¢
− 40¢

Subtracting for Change

Pay the exact amount for each toy. Cross out the coins you use. How much is left?

Coins left: ___________

Money left: ___________¢

Coins left: ___________

Money left: ___________¢

Coins left: ___________

Money left: ___________¢

Subtracting for Change

Cross out the coins. Write the problem.

Example:

Adam wants:

Adam has:

65¢
- 60¢

5¢

Adam wants:

Adam has:

LIBERTY
IN GOD WE TRUST
1990
LIBERTY
IN GOD WE TRUST
1990
UNITED STATES OF AMERICA
E PLURIBUS UNUM
QUARTER DOLLAR

¢

– ¢

Adam wants:

Adam has:

¢

– ¢

Subtracting from 50 Cents

Maria went to the store to buy a birthday gift for her best friend. Maria took 50¢ to the store. Circle the things she could buy.

Subtracting from 50 Cents

Maria wanted to know how much change she would get back from each toy. Color the toy you think Maria chose.

50¢
– ¢

50¢
– ¢

50¢
– ¢

50¢
– ¢

Making Exact Amounts of Money

Use dimes, nickels, and pennies. Pay the exact amount for each toy.

1. What coins did you use?

__________ dimes __________ nickels

__________ pennies

2. What coins did you use?

__________ dimes __________ nickels

__________ pennies

3. Solve this puzzle.

What coins did Cat use to pay for the ball?

__________ dimes __________ nickels

__________ pennies

Making Exact Amounts of Money

Use dimes, nickels, and pennies. Pay the exact amount for each toy.

1. What coins did you use?

_________ dimes _________ nickels

_________ pennies

2. What coins did you use?

_________ quarters _________ dimes

_________ nickels _________ pennies

3. Solve this puzzle.

What coins did Alligator use to pay for the toothbrush?

_________ dimes

_________ nickels _________ pennies

Making Exact Amounts of Money

Use quarters, dimes, nickels, and pennies. Pay the exact amount for each toy.

1. What coins did you use?

27¢

__________ quarters __________ dimes

__________ nickels __________ pennies

2. What coins did you use?

40¢

__________ quarters __________ dimes

__________ nickels __________ pennies

3. Solve this puzzle.

What coins did Bird use to pay for the pilot wings?

I used six coins to pay.

PILOT WINGS 30¢

__________ quarters __________ dimes

__________ nickels __________ pennies

Making Exact Amounts of Money and Change

Use the coins shown. Pay the exact amount for each toy. How much do you have left?

Coins left: ___________

Money left: ___________¢

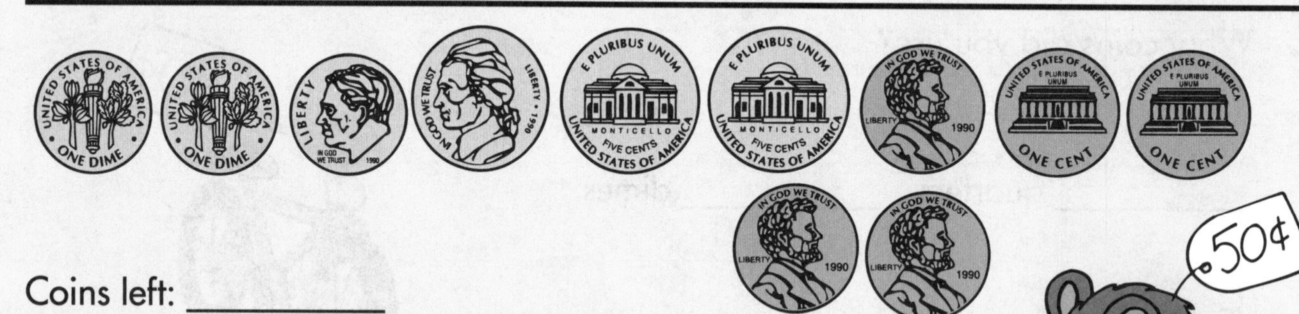

Coins left: ___________

Money left: ___________¢

Choose a price between 42¢ and 58¢. Write the price on the tag.

Coins left: ___________

Money left: ___________¢

Incredible!

Incredible!

Incredible!

Incredible!

BRAVO!

BRAVO!

BRAVO!

WOW!

WOW!

WOW!

GOOD!

GOOD!

GOOD!

Making Exact Amounts of Money and Change

Use the coins shown. Pay the exact amount for each toy.

Coins left: ___________

Money left: ___________¢

Coins left: ___________

Money left: ___________¢

Solve this puzzle.

How much money does Turtle have left?

Coins left: ___________

Money left: ___________¢

Problem-Solving with Money

To be a good problem-solver, you must read the problem carefully.

Solve these problems.

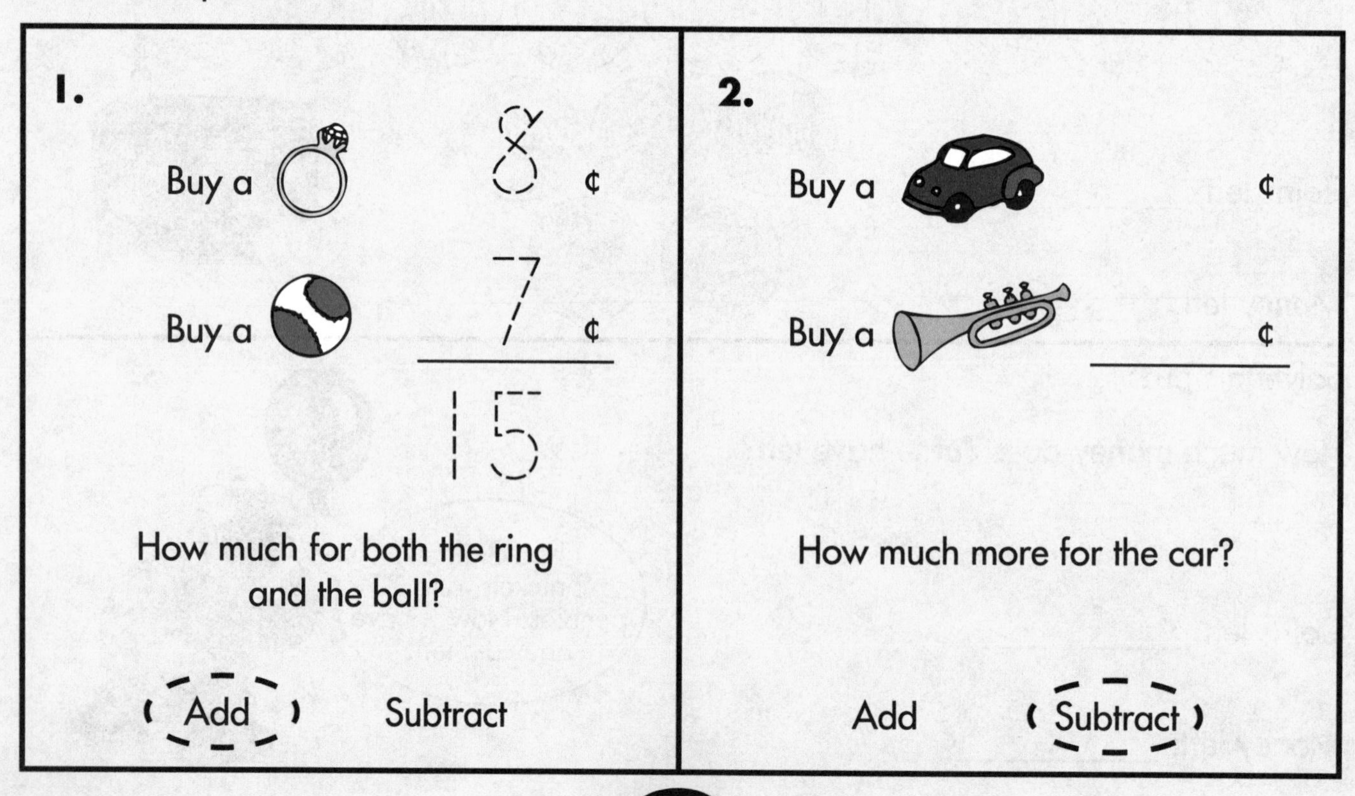

Problem-Solving with Money

Use page 162 to help you answer the questions below.

3. Buy a ¢ Buy a ______ ¢ How much more for the plant? Add Subtract	**4.** Buy a ¢ Buy a ______ ¢ How much for both the horn and the ring? Add Subtract
5. Buy a ¢ Buy a ______ ¢ How much for both the ball and car? Add Subtract	**6.** Buy a ¢ Buy a ______ ¢ How much more for the frog? Add Subtract
7. Circle the one that costs more.	**8.** Circle the one that costs more.

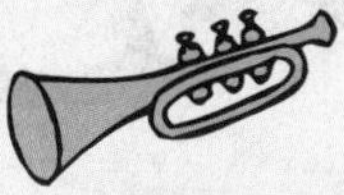

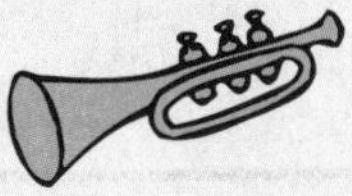

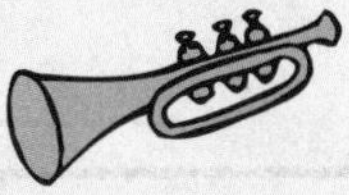

Problem-Solving with Money

Draw the coins you use. Write the number of coins on each blank.

1.  ______ dimes ______ nickels ______ pennies	**2.** 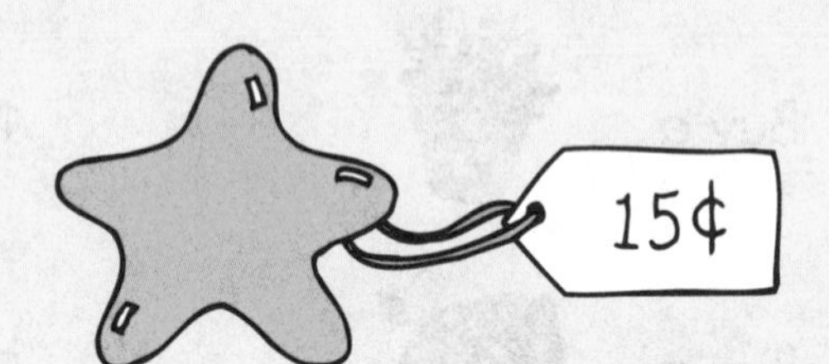 ______ dimes ______ nickels ______ pennies
3. 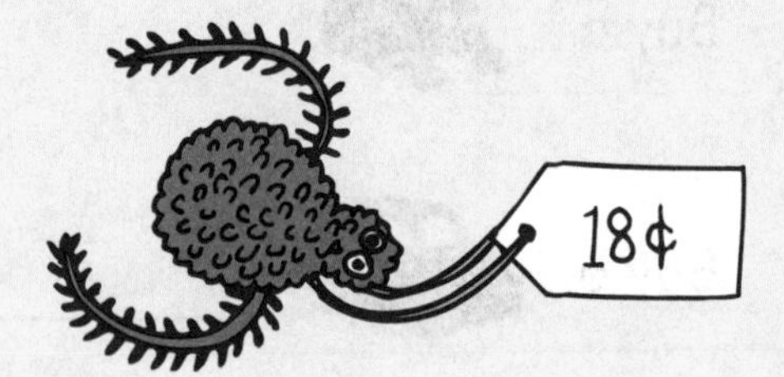 ______ dimes ______ nickels ______ pennies	**4.** Find another way to pay for the 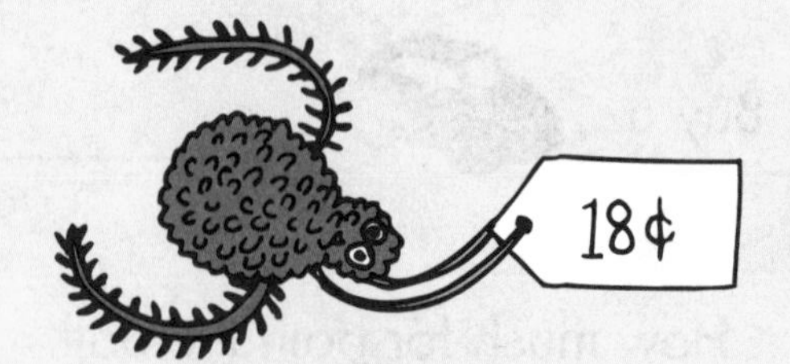 ______ dimes ______ nickels ______ pennies

Problem-Solving with Money

Draw the coins you use. Write the number of coins on each blank.

1.	2.
 35¢	 29¢
_____ quarters _____ dimes _____ nickels _____ pennies	_____ quarters _____ dimes _____ nickels _____ pennies
3.	**4.** Find another way to pay for the
 43¢	 43¢
_____ quarters _____ dimes _____ nickels _____ pennies	_____ quarters _____ dimes _____ nickels _____ pennies

Making Exact Amounts of Money: Two Ways to Pay

Find two ways to pay. Show what coins you use.

1.

_____ quarters

_____ dimes

_____ nickels

_____ pennies

2.

_____ quarters

_____ dimes

_____ nickels

_____ pennies

3.

_____ quarters

_____ dimes

_____ nickels

_____ pennies

4.

_____ quarters

_____ dimes

_____ nickels

_____ pennies

Making Exact Amounts of Money: Two Ways to Pay

Find two ways to pay. Show what coins you use.

1.

_______ quarters

_______ dimes

_______ nickels

_______ pennies

2.

_______ quarters

_______ dimes

_______ nickels

_______ pennies

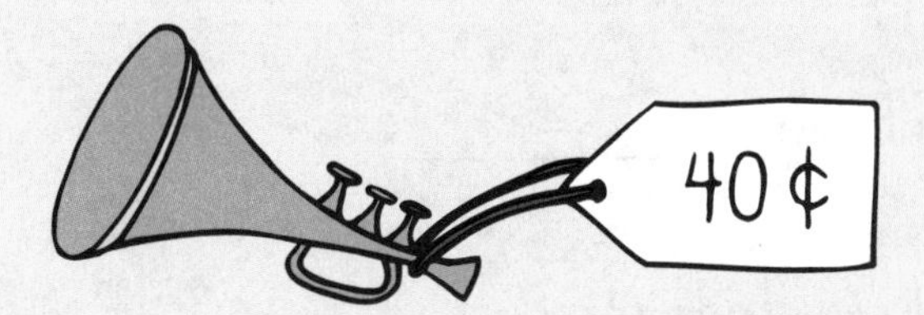

3.

_______ quarters

_______ dimes

_______ nickels

_______ pennies

4.

_______ quarters

_______ dimes

_______ nickels

_______ pennies

Making Exact Amounts of Money: How Much More?

Count the coins. Find out how much more money you need to pay the exact amount.

How much money do you have? __________ ¢

How much more money do you need? __________ ¢

How much money do you have? __________ ¢

How much more money do you need? __________ ¢

Solve this puzzle.

How much more money does Monkey need?

__________ ¢

Half-Dollars: Introduction

This is a half-dollar. The half-dollar is worth 50¢.

front **back**

Look at each side of the half-dollar. Color them **silver**.

1 half-dollar = 50 pennies

1 half-dollar = 50 cents

1 half-dollar = 50 ¢

Half-Dollars: Introduction

These are ways to make a half dollar. Color each coin.

10 nickels

5 dimes

50 pennies

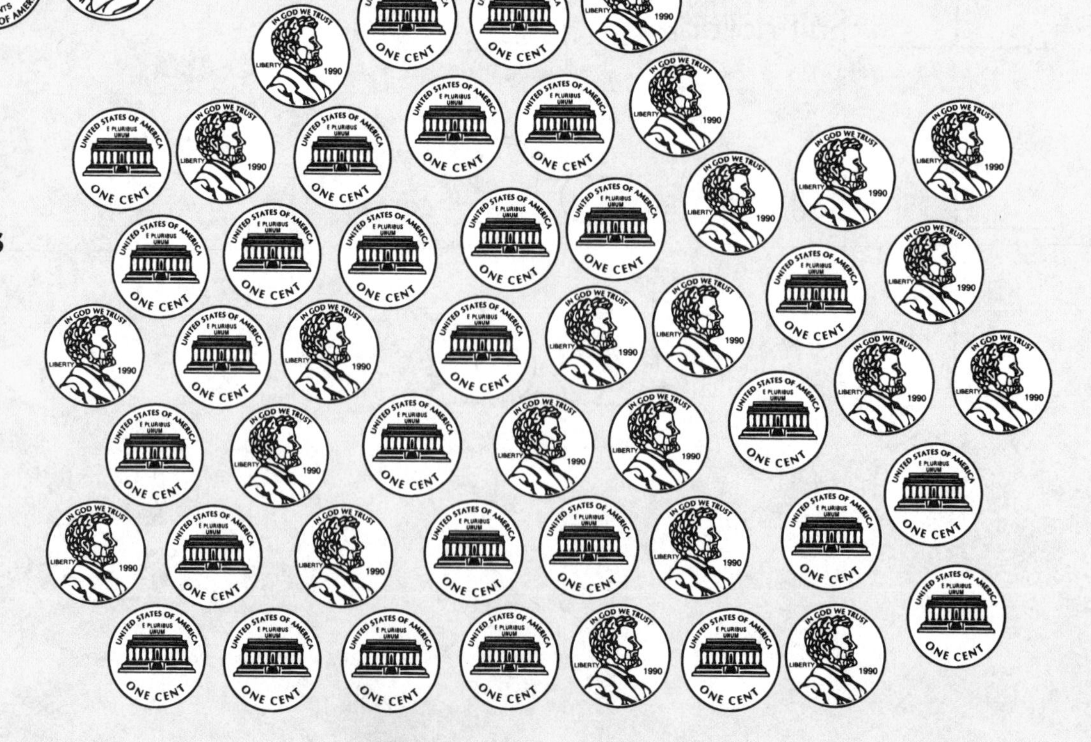

Counting Half-Dollars, Quarters, Dimes, Nickels, and Pennies

Count the money. Write each amount. A half-dollar is worth 50¢ or $.50

1.

________ ________ ________ ________¢

2.

________ ________ ________ ________ ________¢

3. Draw between 50¢ and 90¢ in the jar.

Counting Coins: How Much More?

Count the coins. Find out how much more money you need to pay the exact amount.

How much money do you have? ___________¢

How much more money do you need? ___________¢

How much money do you have? ___________¢

How much more money do you need? ___________¢

Solve this puzzle.

How much more money does Alligator need?

___________¢

Dollar Bills: Introduction

This is a dollar bill. It has two sides. Color both sides **green**.

1 dollar = $1.00

1 dollar = one dollar

1 dollar = 100 pennies

1 dollar = 100 cents

Dollar Bills: Introduction

Long ago, people got tired of carrying heavy coins in their pockets, so dollar bills were made!

This is the dollar sign: $.

It is an **S** with a line through it.

There is also a period between the dollars and the cents: $1.00

Dollar Bills: Introduction

There are many ways to make a dollar.

1 dollar bill

2 half-dollars

4 quarters

100 pennies

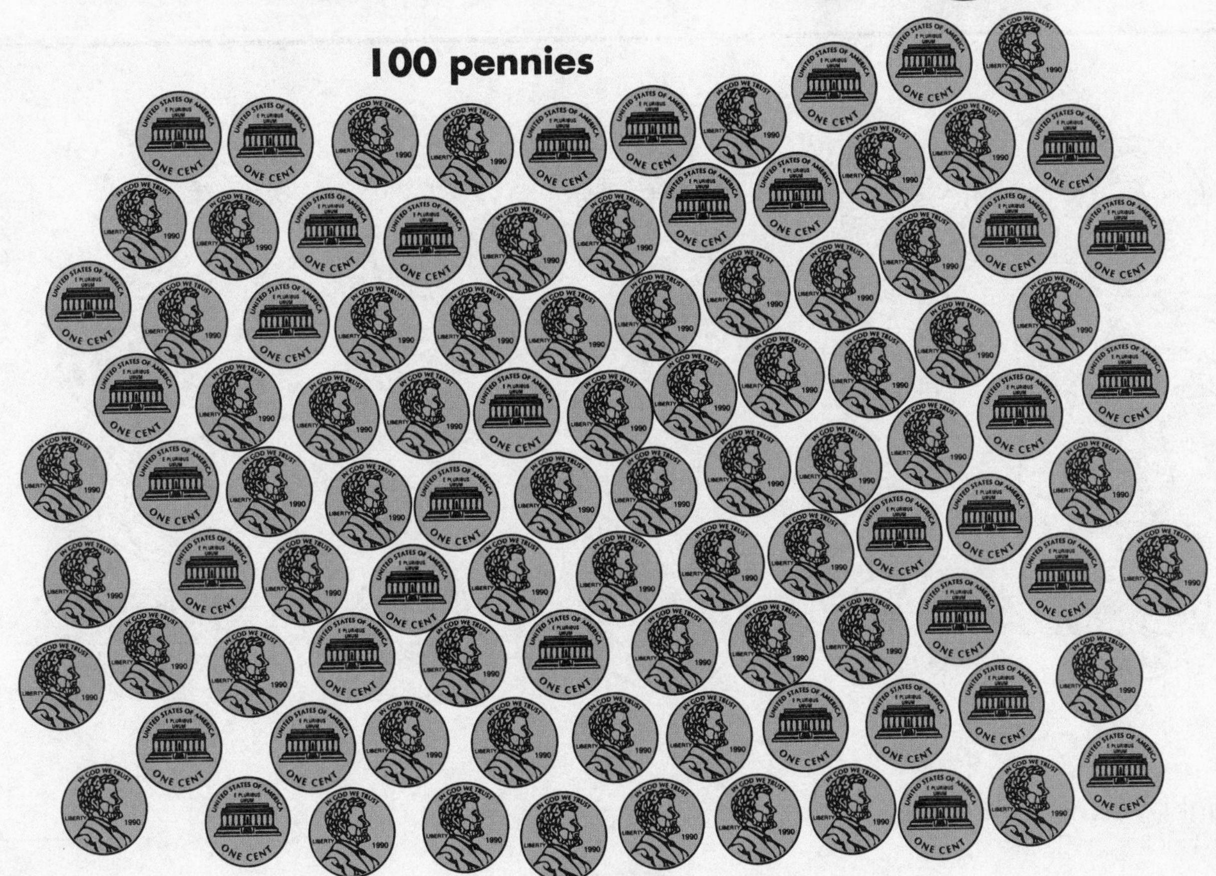

Dollar Bills: Introduction

Count each set of coins. If it equals one dollar, write $1.00 on the line.

Count by tens with dimes. ________

Count by fives with nickels. ________

Counting with Dollar Bills and Coins

A few dollar tips for you:

1. Drop the ¢ sign.
2. Add the $ sign.
3. Use a . (period) between the dollars and cents.

Write the amount of dollars and cents.

$ 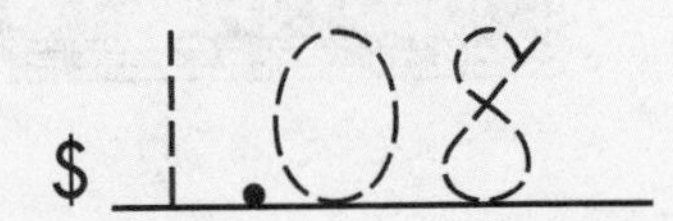

$ _____._______

Counting with Dollar Bills and Coins

Count the money. Write each amount.

A one-dollar bill  is worth 100¢ or $1.00.

1.

______ ______ $ 1.25

2.

______ ______ ______ $ ______

3. Draw $2.00 in the bank. Use a one-dollar bill.

Counting with Dollar Bills and Coins

Count the money. Write each amount.

$ ____._____

$ ____._____

$ ____._____

$ ____._____

Matching Dollar Amounts

Count the money. Draw a line to match.

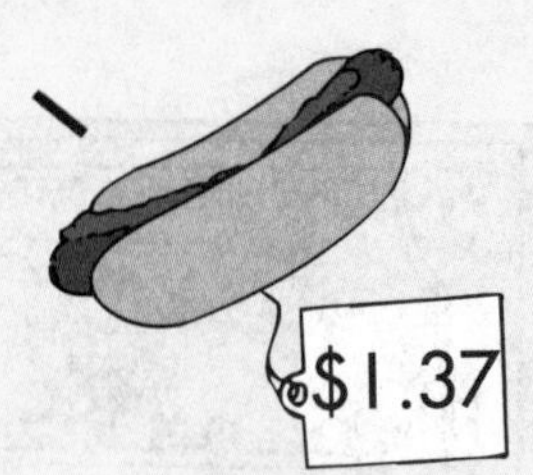

Matching Dollar Amounts

Count the money. Draw a line to match.

Example:

$1.26

$.86

$1.75

$1.27

$1.21

$1.81

$1.25

$1.02

$1.01

$1.65

$1.06

$.78

Counting Dollar Bills and Coins: How Much More?

Count the coins and bills. Find out how much more money you need to pay the exact amount.

How much money do you have? __________¢

How much more money do you need? __________¢

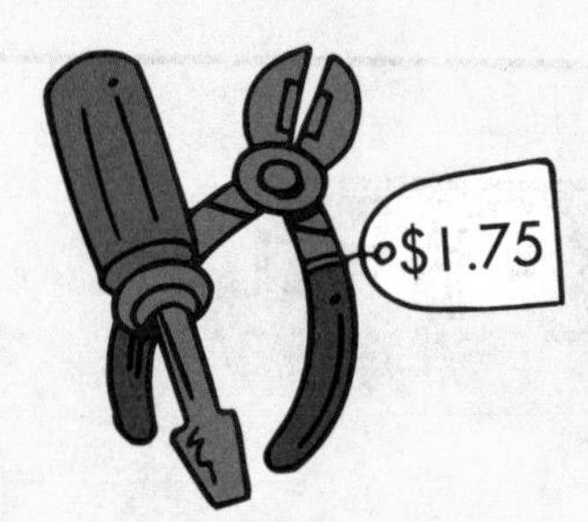

How much money do you have? __________¢

How much more money do you need? __________¢

Solve this puzzle.

How much more money does Anteater need?

__________¢

Estimating Amounts of Money

We estimate, or round up or down, to make a quick guess about money.

Circle the amount that is closer to the amount on the tag. This is an estimate.

about 30¢

about 30¢

about 40¢

about 30¢

about 40¢

about 50¢

Estimating Amounts of Money

Circle the best estimate.

about 50¢

about $1.40

about $1.50

about $2.00

about $3.00

about $4.00

about $1.00

about $2.00

about $3.00

about $3.00

about $4.00

Adding and Subtracting Amounts of Money: Using Estimation

Using estimation makes it much easier to add or subtract in your head. These foods are for sale in the lunchroom.

You have this much money:

You want the .

Round or estimate the cost. ___________¢

Do you have enough money? ___________

The and look good.

Add the estimated prices.

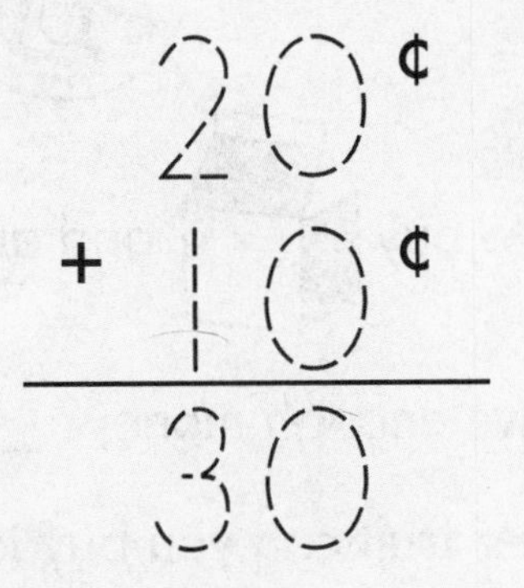

You probably have enough!

Adding and Subtracting Amounts of Money: Using Estimation

Use page 185 to help you answer the questions below.

You have this money:     

You have __________ cents.

If you buy , will you have enough left to buy a 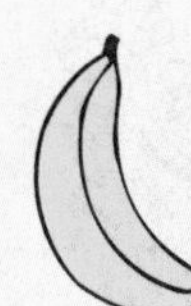? **yes** **no**

money you have = ¢

estimated milk = – ¢

____

You have this money:   

You want to buy  and an . Estimate.

Do you have enough money? __________

Which other fruit can you buy to have with your milk? ______________

Adding and Subtracting Amounts of Money: Making Change

How much change should you get?

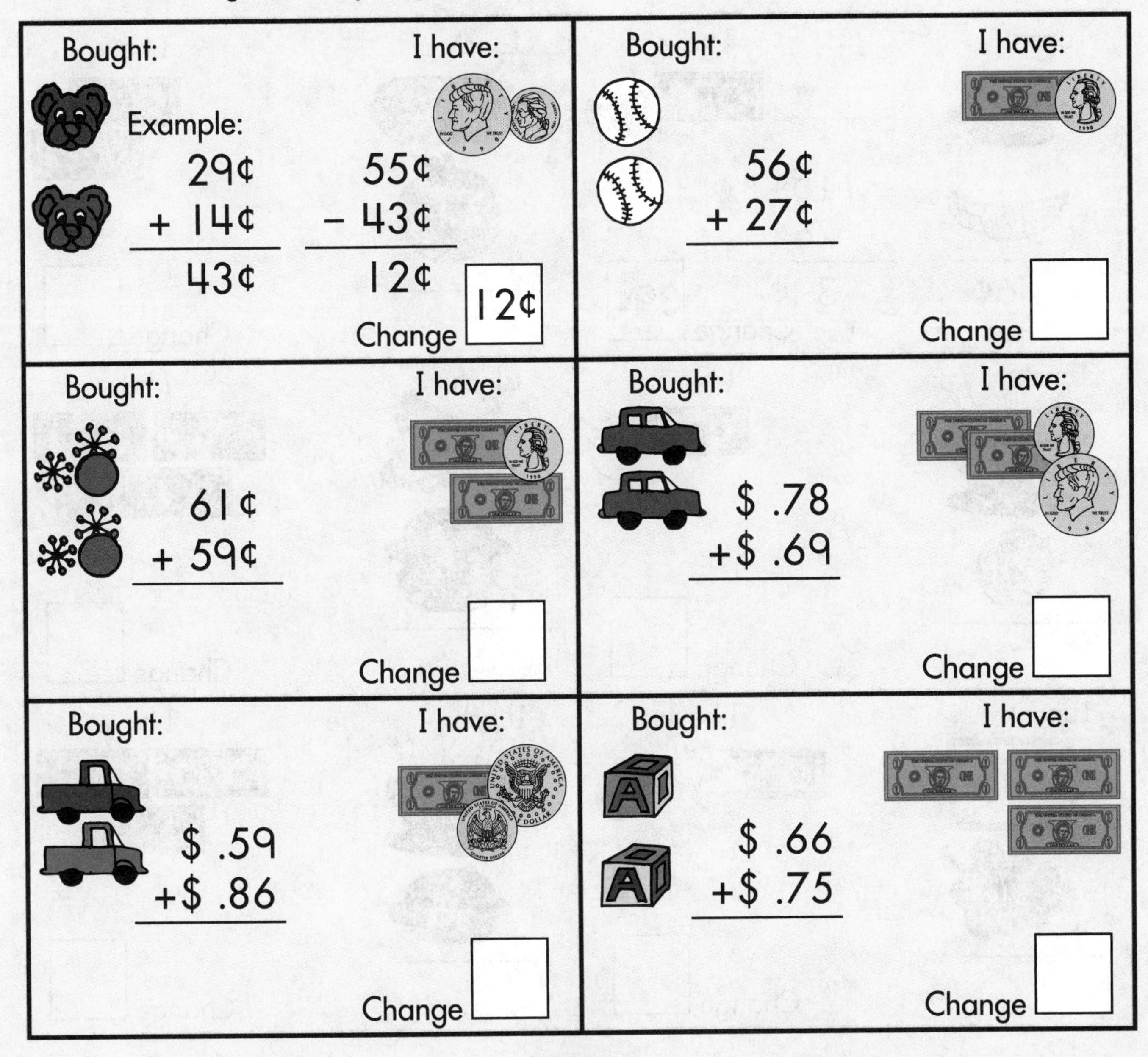

Adding and Subtracting Amounts of Money: Making Change

How much change should you get?

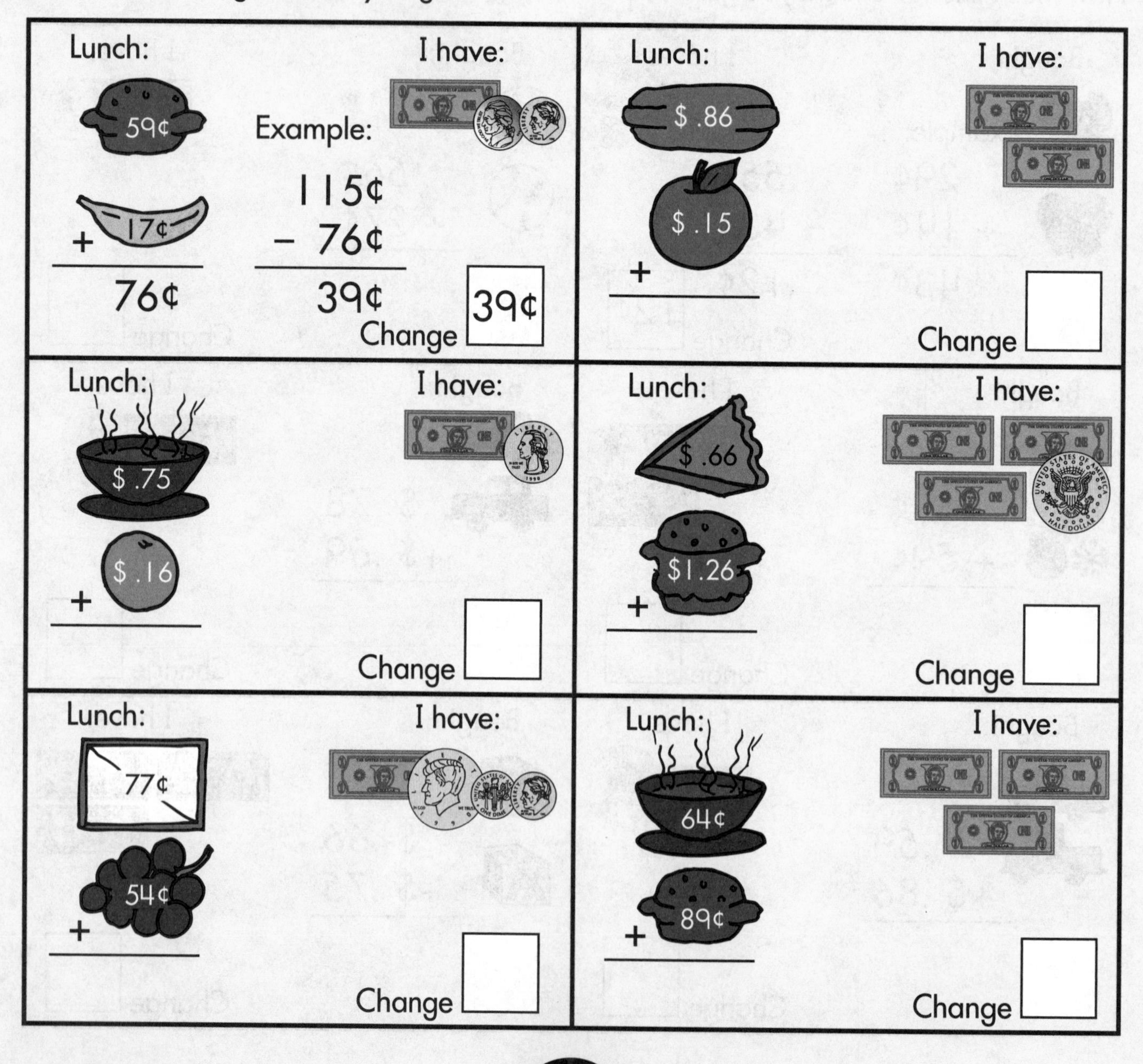

Making Change: Money Puzzles

Solve the puzzles. Show how much change you get.

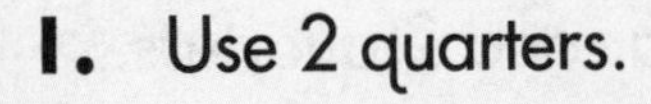

1. Use 2 quarters.

Pay 

What change will you get? _______

2. Use 1 quarter, 2 dimes, and 2 nickels.

Pay 

What change will you get? _______

3. Use 3 quarters and 1 dime.

Pay 

What change will you get? _______

4. Use 3 quarters and 2 nickels.

Pay 

What change will you get? _______

Making Change: Money Puzzles

Solve the puzzles. Show how much change you get.

1. Use 1 one-dollar bill.

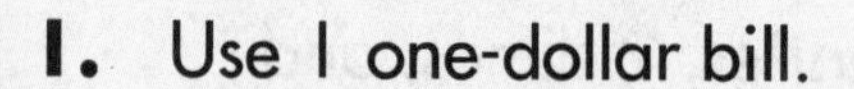

Pay

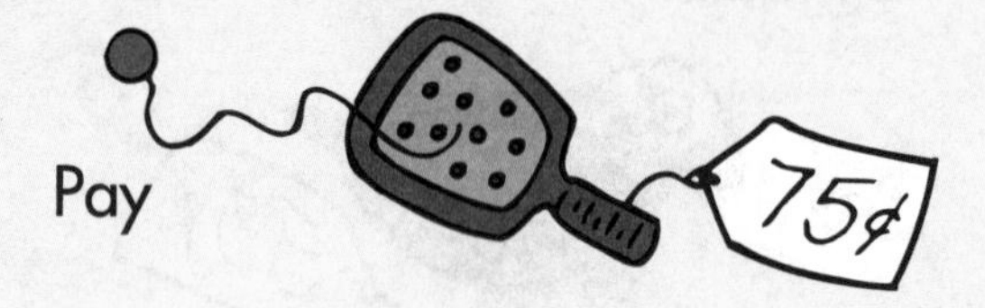

What change will you get? _______

2. Use 1 half-dollar and 2 quarters.

Pay

What change will you get? _______

3. Use 1 one-dollar bill and 1 quarter.

Pay

What change will you get? _______

4. Use 2 half-dollars, 1 quarter, and 1 dime.

Pay

What change will you get? _______

Making Change: Money Puzzles

Solve the puzzles. Show how much change you get.

1. Use 3 half-dollars.

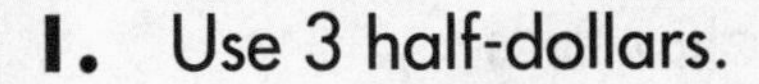

Pay 

What change will you get? ______

2. Use 1 one-dollar bill, 2 quarters, and 1 dime.

Pay 

What change will you get? ______

3. Use 1 one-dollar bill, 1 half-dollar, and 1 quarter.

Pay 

What change will you get? ______

4. Use 1 one-dollar bill and 2 half-dollars.

Pay 

What change will you get? ______

Making Change: Money Puzzles

Solve the puzzles. Show how much change you get.

1. Use 2 one-dollar bills.

Pay

What change will you get? ______

2. Use 2 one-dollar bills.

Pay

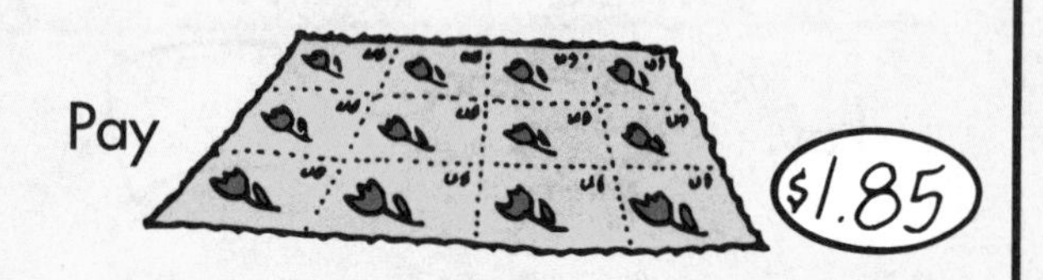

What change will you get? ______

3. Use 3 one-dollar bills.

Pay

What change will you get? ______

4. Use 3 one-dollar bills.

Pay

What change will you get? ______

Making Change: Money Puzzles

Solve the puzzles. Show how much change you get.

<table>
<tr>
<td>

1. Use 4 one-dollar bills.

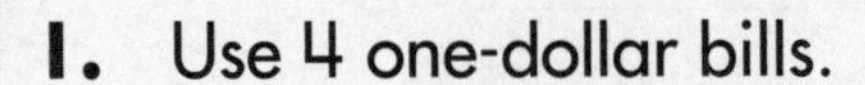

Pay 

What change will you get? _______

</td>
<td>

2. Use 5 one-dollar bills.

Pay 

What change will you get? _______

</td>
</tr>
<tr>
<td>

3. Use 3 one-dollar bills.

Pay 

What change will you get? _______

</td>
<td>

4. Use 2 one-dollar bills.

Pay

What change will you get? _______

</td>
</tr>
</table>

Making Exact Amounts of Money

Pay for each toy. Show what coins you use.

_______ quarters

_______ dimes

_______ nickels

_______ pennies

_______ quarters

_______ dimes

_______ nickels

_______ pennies

Choose the price. Write it on the tag.

_______ quarters

_______ dimes

_______ nickels

_______ pennies

Making Exact Amounts of Money

Pay for each snack. Show what coins you use.

_______ quarters

_______ dimes

_______ nickels

_______ pennies

_______ quarters

_______ dimes

_______ nickels

_______ pennies

Choose the price. Write it on the tag.

_______ quarters

_______ dimes

_______ nickels

_______ pennies

Making Exact Amounts of Money

Pay for each robot. Show what coins you use.

_______ half-dollars

_______ quarters

_______ dimes

_______ nickels

_______ pennies

_______ half-dollars

_______ quarters

_______ dimes

_______ nickels

_______ pennies

Choose the price. Write it on the tag.

_______ half-dollars

_______ quarters

_______ dimes

_______ nickels

_______ pennies

Making Exact Amounts of Money

Pay for each animal. Show what coins you use.

__________ half-dollars

__________ quarters

__________ dimes

__________ nickels

__________ pennies

__________ half-dollars

__________ quarters

__________ dimes

__________ nickels

__________ pennies

Choose the price. Write it on the tag.

__________ half-dollars

__________ quarters

__________ dimes

__________ nickels

__________ pennies

Making Exact Amounts of Money

Pay for each toy. Show what money you use.

Making Exact Amounts of Money

Pay for each game. Show what money you use.

_____ dollars

_____ half-dollars

_____ quarters

_____ dimes

_____ nickels

_____ pennies

_____ dollars

_____ half-dollars

_____ quarters

_____ dimes

_____ nickels

_____ pennies

Choose the price. Write it on the tag.

_____ dollars

_____ half-dollars

_____ quarters

_____ dimes

_____ nickels

_____ pennies

Using Combinations of Coins to Pay

Pay for each cookie. Use as few coins as you can.

					Number of Coins Used
28¢	1			3	4
39¢					
49¢					
Choose the price. ¢					

Using Combinations of Coins to Pay

Pay for each toy. Use as few coins as you can.

					Number of Coins Used
22¢					
37¢					
52¢					
Choose the price. ¢					

Using Combinations of Coins to Pay

Pay for each book. Use as few coins as you can.

	 Quarter	 Dime	 Nickel	 Penny	Number of Coins Used
 SUPER 75¢					
 SPORT 80¢					
 Monster 97¢					
Choose the price.  MAGIC ¢					

Using Combinations of Coins to Pay

Pay for each snack. Use as few coins as you can.

					Number of Coins Used
$1.05					
95¢					
85¢					
Choose the price.					

Using Combinations of Coins to Pay

Pay for each mask. Use as few coins and bills as you can.

					Number of Coins Used
 $1.75					
 $1.95					
 $2.50					
Choose the price. 					

Making Exact Amounts of Money Two Ways

Find two ways to pay for each thing. Pay the exact amount.

1.

	Dimes	Nickels	Pennies
Way 1	4		
Way 2		8	

2.

	Dimes	Nickels	Pennies
Way 1			
Way 2			

3. Choose a price for the magnifying glass.

	Dimes	Nickels	Pennies
Way 1			
Way 2			

Making Exact Amounts of Money Two Ways

Find two ways to pay for each thing. Pay the exact amount.

1. 52¢ MARBLE MAGNETS

	Quarters	Dimes	Nickels	Pennies
Way 1				
Way 2				

2. 75¢ INK STAMP PAD

	Quarters	Dimes	Nickels	Pennies
Way 1				
Way 2				

3. Choose a price for the game.

	Quarters	Dimes	Nickels	Pennies
Way 1				
Way 2				

MONEY MYSTERIES

Making Exact Amounts of Money Two Ways

Find two ways to pay for each thing. Pay the exact amount.

1.

	Half-Dollars	Quarters	Dimes	Nickels	Pennies
Way 1					
Way 2					

2.

	Half-Dollars	Quarters	Dimes	Nickels	Pennies
Way 1					
Way 2					

3. Choose a price for the robot.

	Half-Dollars	Quarters	Dimes	Nickels	Pennies
Way 1					
Way 2					

Making Exact Amounts of Money Two Ways

Find two ways to pay for each thing. Pay the exact amount.

1.

	$1 Bills	Half-Dollars	Quarters	Dimes	Nickels
Way 1					
Way 2					

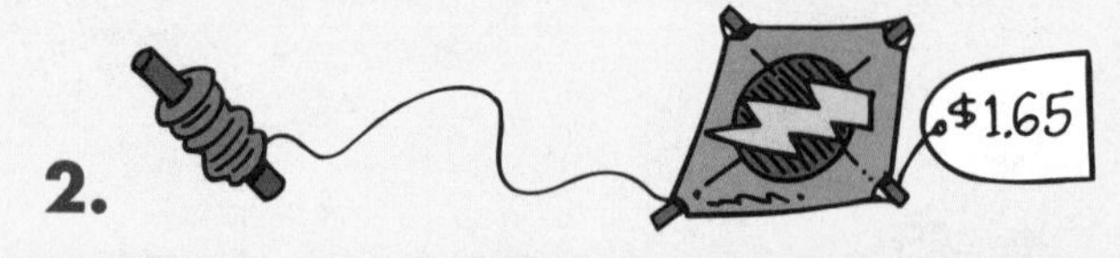

2.

	$1 Bills	Half-Dollars	Quarters	Dimes	Nickels
Way 1					
Way 2					

3. Solve this puzzle. What's missing in each way?

	$1 Bills	Half-Dollars	Quarters	Dimes	Nickels
Way 1	2			2	
Way 2		4	1		

Making Exact Amounts of Money Two Ways

Find two ways to pay for each thing. Pay the exact amount.

$5.60

1.

	$1 Bills	Half-Dollars	Quarters	Dimes	Nickels	Pennies
Way 1						
Way 2						

$5.95

JUMBO MARKERS

2.

	$1 Bills	Half-Dollars	Quarters	Dimes	Nickels	Pennies
Way 1						
Way 2						

$6.72

WHITE SHARK ACTION VIDEO

3. Solve this puzzle. What's missing in each way?

	$1 Bills	Half-Dollars	Quarters	Dimes	Nickels	Pennies
Way 1	5	1				12
Way 2	4		1			7

Estimating Amounts of Money

Use the coins shown. If you spend all your money, which snacks can you buy? First, estimate. Then, check.

1.

I think I can buy: ______________________________

I can buy: ______________________________

2. 

I think I can buy: ______________________________

I can buy: ______________________________

3. Solve this puzzle.

Ahmad had 1 quarter, 1 dime, 1 nickel, and 10 pennies.
He bought two snacks. He has less than 10 cents left.

What snacks did he buy? ______________________________

Estimating Amounts of Money

Use the coins shown. If you spend all your money, which pet treats can you buy? First, estimate. Then, check.

1. 

I think I can buy: ______________________________

I can buy: ______________________________

2. 

I think I can buy: ______________________________

I can buy: ______________________________

3. Solve this puzzle.

Ismelda had 3 half-dollars. She bought 3 pet treats.
She has less than 20 cents left.

What treats did she buy? ______________________________

Estimating Amounts of Money

Use the coins and bills shown. If you spend all your money, what tickets can you buy? First, estimate. Then, check.

1.

I think I can buy: ______________________________

I can buy: ______________________________

2.

I think I can buy: ______________________________

I can buy: ______________________________

3. Solve this puzzle.

Larry and Leticia had 2 one-dollar bills and 3 half-dollars. They bought 6 tickets. They used all of their money.

What tickets did they buy? ______________________________

Estimating Amounts of Money

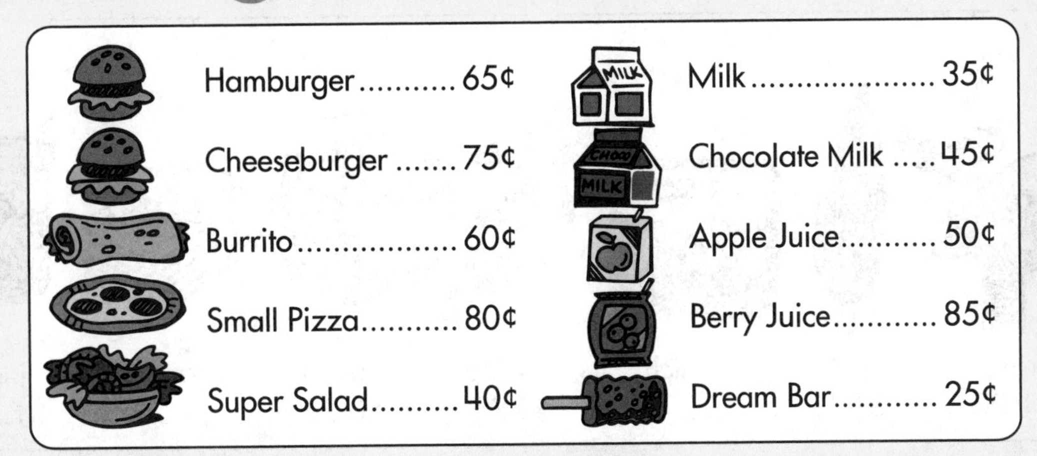

Use the coins and bills shown. If you spend all your money, what can you buy? First, estimate. Then, check.

1.

I think I can buy: ______________________________

I can buy: ______________________________

2.

I think I can buy: ______________________________

I can buy: ______________________________

3. Solve this puzzle.

Tina had 1 one-dollar bill, 1 half-dollar, and 2 quarters. She bought three things. She has less than 25 cents left.

What did Tina buy? ______________________________

Estimating Amounts of Money

Use the coins and bills shown. If you spend all your money, what can you buy? First, estimate. Then, check.

1.

I think I can buy: ______________________________

I can buy: ______________________________

2.

I think I can buy: ______________________________

I can buy: ______________________________

3. Solve this puzzle.

Martin had 3 one-dollar bills. He bought three gifts.
He has less than 25 cents left.

What did Martin buy? ______________________________

Making Exact Amounts and Change

Pay the exact amount. What change do you get back?

Amount you get back:

__________¢

Amount you get back:

__________¢

Amount you get back:

__________¢

Making Exact Amounts and Change

Pay the exact amount. What change do you get back?

Amount you get back:

__________ ¢

Amount you get back:

__________ ¢

Choose a price between 75¢ and 90¢.
Write the price.

Amount you get back: __________ ¢

Making Exact Amounts and Change

Pay the exact amount. What change do you get back?

Amount you get back:

__________¢

Amount you get back:

__________¢

Choose a price between $1.15 and $1.28.
Write the price.

Amount you get back: __________¢

Making Exact Amounts and Change

Pay the exact amount. What change do you get back?

Amount you get back: ___________¢

Amount you get back: ___________¢

Solve this puzzle.

What did Abby pay?
Write the amount on the tag.

I had 2 one-dollar bills. I paid for the kite. I got back 1 quarter, 1 dime, and 1 penny.

Making Exact Amounts and Change

Pay the exact amount. What change do you get back?

Amount you get back: $__________

Amount you get back: $__________

Solve this puzzle.

What did Dominic pay?
Write the amount on the tag.

Money Puzzles

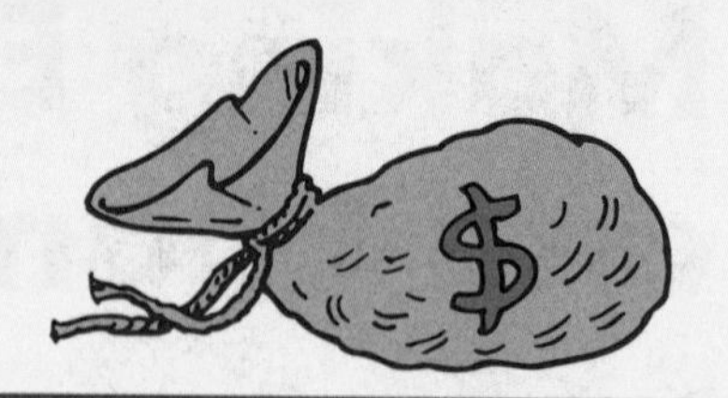

Solve the puzzles. Draw the coins.

1. There are 4 coins in the bag. Together, they are worth less than 50¢. What coins could they be?	**2.** There are 4 coins in the bag. Two are worth more than 25¢ each. Two are worth less than 10¢ each. What coins could they be?
3. There are 5 coins in the bag. Together, they are worth more than 90¢. What coins could they be?	**4.** There are 6 coins in the bag. Together, they are worth between 75¢ and $1.00. What coins could they be?

Money Puzzles

Solve the puzzles. Draw the coins.

1. There are 5 coins in the bank. Together, they are worth $1.00 exactly. What coins could they be?	**2.** There are 6 coins in the bank. Together, they are worth between 80¢ and $1.20. What coins could they be?
3. There are 6 coins in the bank. Two are worth more than 10¢ each. Four are worth less than 10¢ each. All together, they are worth more than $1.00. What coins could they be?	**4.** There are 6 coins in the bank. Four are worth more than 10¢ each. Two are worth less than 25¢ each. All together, they are worth less than $1.50. What coins could they be?

Using Combinations of Coins to Pay

Use the coins shown to make each amount.

Use 3 of the coins to make 25¢. What coins did you use?			2	1	
Use 4 of the coins to make 50¢. What coins did you use?					
Use 4 of the coins to make 66¢. What coins did you use?					
Use 5 of the coins to make 96¢. What coins did you use?					

Using Combinations of Coins to Pay

Use the coins shown to make each amount.

Use 3 of the coins to make 60¢. What coins did you use?				
What other way can you do it?				
Use 4 of the coins to make 40¢. What coins did you use?				
What other way can you do it?				
Use 4 of the coins to make 80¢. What coins did you use?				
What other way can you do it?				

Money Story Puzzles

Solve the money story puzzles.

Sean sees a box of magnets on sale for 50 cents. He takes 10 coins out of his pocket and buys the magnets.

What coins could they be?

Tonia sees a small bag of jacks for 58 cents. She takes 9 coins out of her pocket to pay.

What coins could they be?

Dustin sees a toy hammer. He wants to buy it for his little brother. He pulls six coins out of his pocket and pays 75 cents.

What coins could they be?

Money Story Puzzles

Solve the money story puzzles.

Matt buys a box of things for doing magic tricks. He takes an even number of coins out of his pocket and pays 65 cents.

What coins could they be?

Stacey buys a poster for 70 cents. She uses an odd number of coins to buy it.

What coins could they be?

Write a money story puzzle about buying the stuffed whale.

Money Story Puzzles

Solve the money story puzzles.

Amber put coins into her bank for a long time. She saved $6.25 in all. Amber saved $3.55 more than her sister Holly.

How much did Holly save?

Collin and Jason each bought a watch. Jason paid $4.99 for his Flip-up Crocodile Watch. That was $1.20 more than Collin paid for his Dinosaur Watch.

How much did Collin pay?

Write a money story puzzle about yourself and a friend.

Money Story Puzzles

Solve the money story puzzles.

Darci and Kara fed the horses at the fair. Kara's mother gave the girls 3 one-dollar bills, 3 quarters, 5 dimes, and 3 nickels. Darci and Kara divided the money equally.

How much money did each of them get?

Josh and Ben washed cars one Saturday. When they finished, they had 3 one-dollar bills, 11 half-dollars, 3 quarters, 2 dimes, and 1 nickel in their money box. The boys divided the money fairly.

How much money did each of them get?

Write a money story puzzle about earning money and dividing it equally.

Money Story Puzzles

Solve the money story puzzles.

Eric and Alicia took all the coins out of their pockets. They put the coins together and paid 65 cents for a bag of corn chips. Alicia paid 15 cents more than Eric.

How much did each of them pay?

Two friends put their money together and bought a package of stickers for $1.60. Rachel paid 20 cents more than Amanda.

How much did each girl pay?

Write a money story puzzle about buying something with a friend.

Coins and Dollar Bills

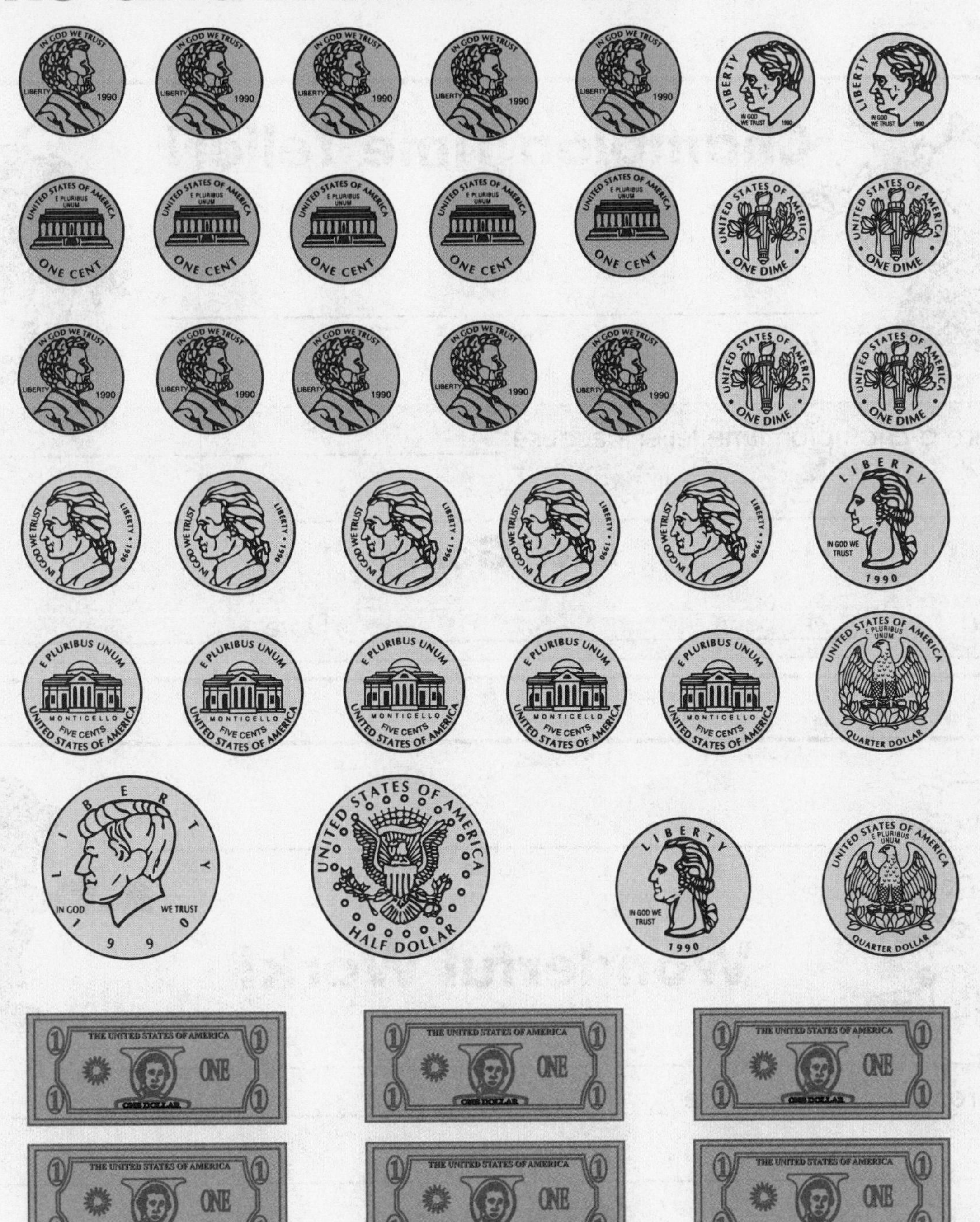

Time Award Certificates

Champion Time Teller!

____
name

You are a champion time teller because ______________________________

____

Nice Going!

Signed ____________________ Date ____________

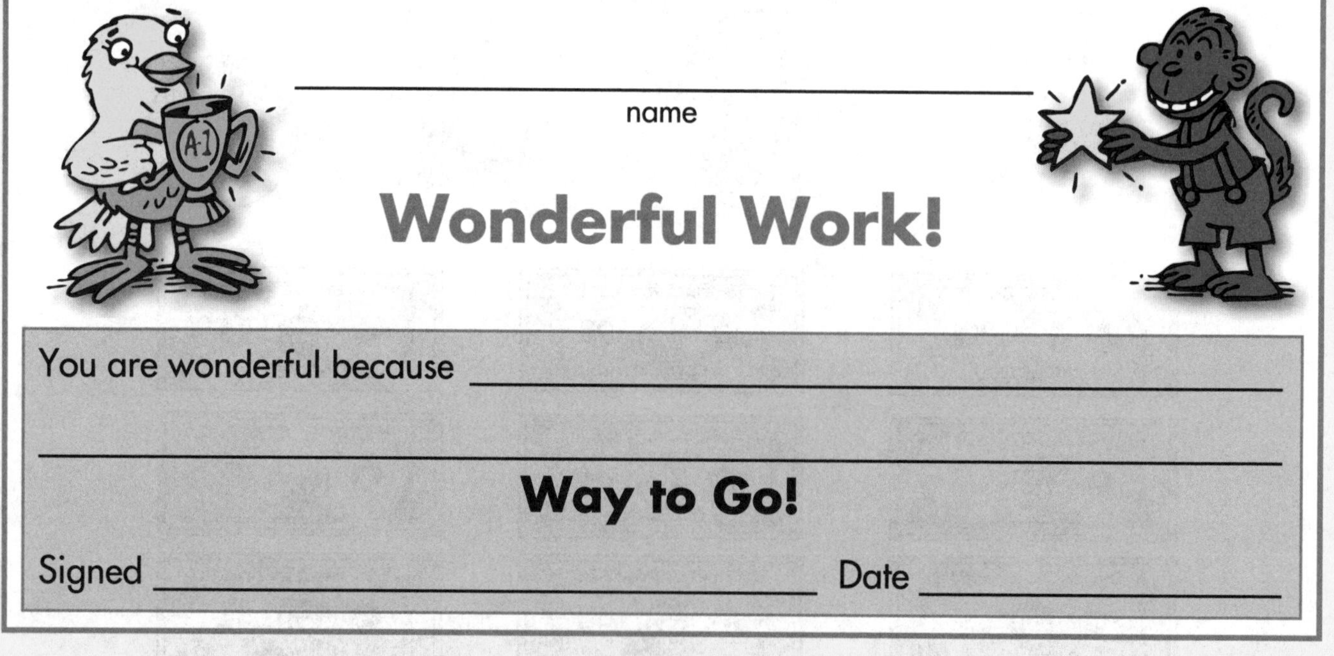

____
name

Wonderful Work!

You are wonderful because ______________________________

____

Way to Go!

Signed ____________________ Date ____________

Money Award Certificates

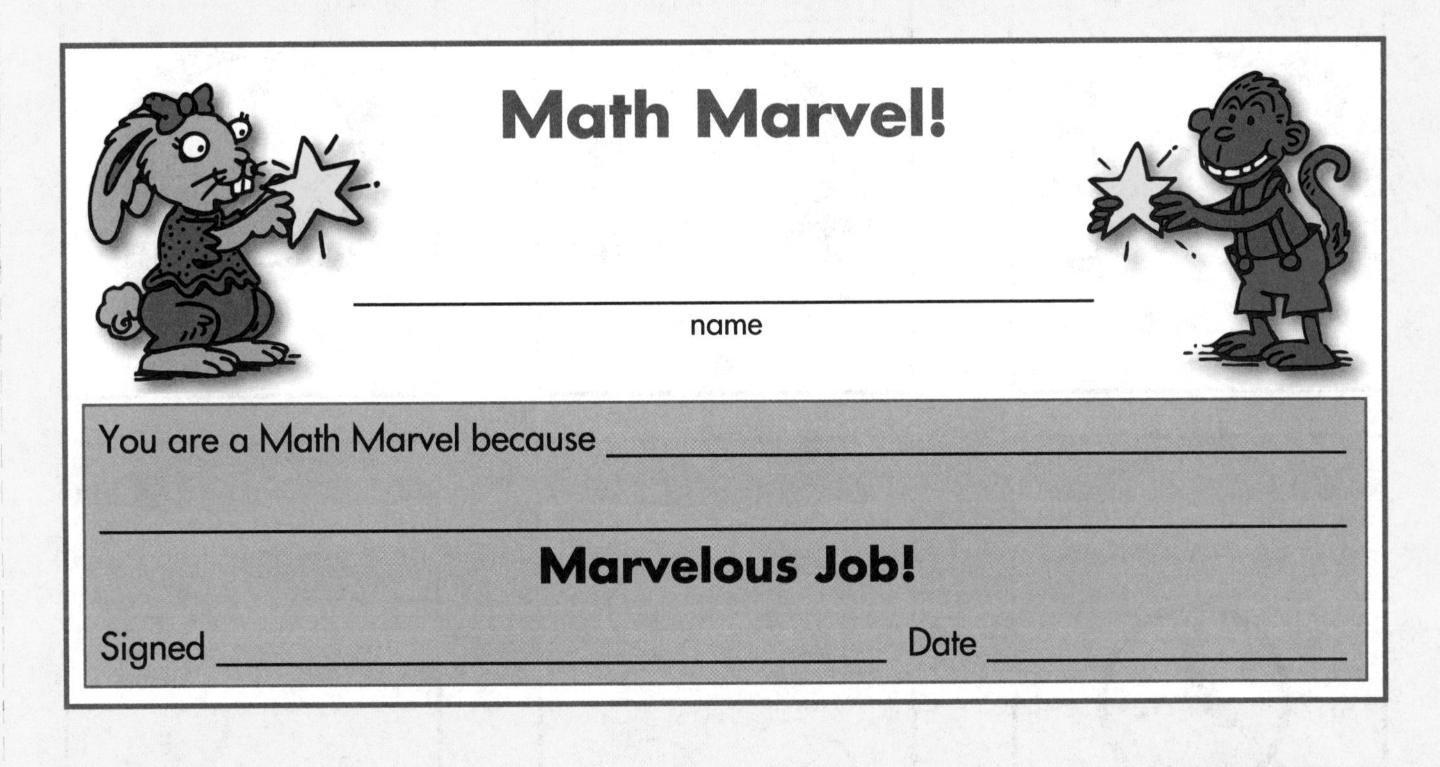

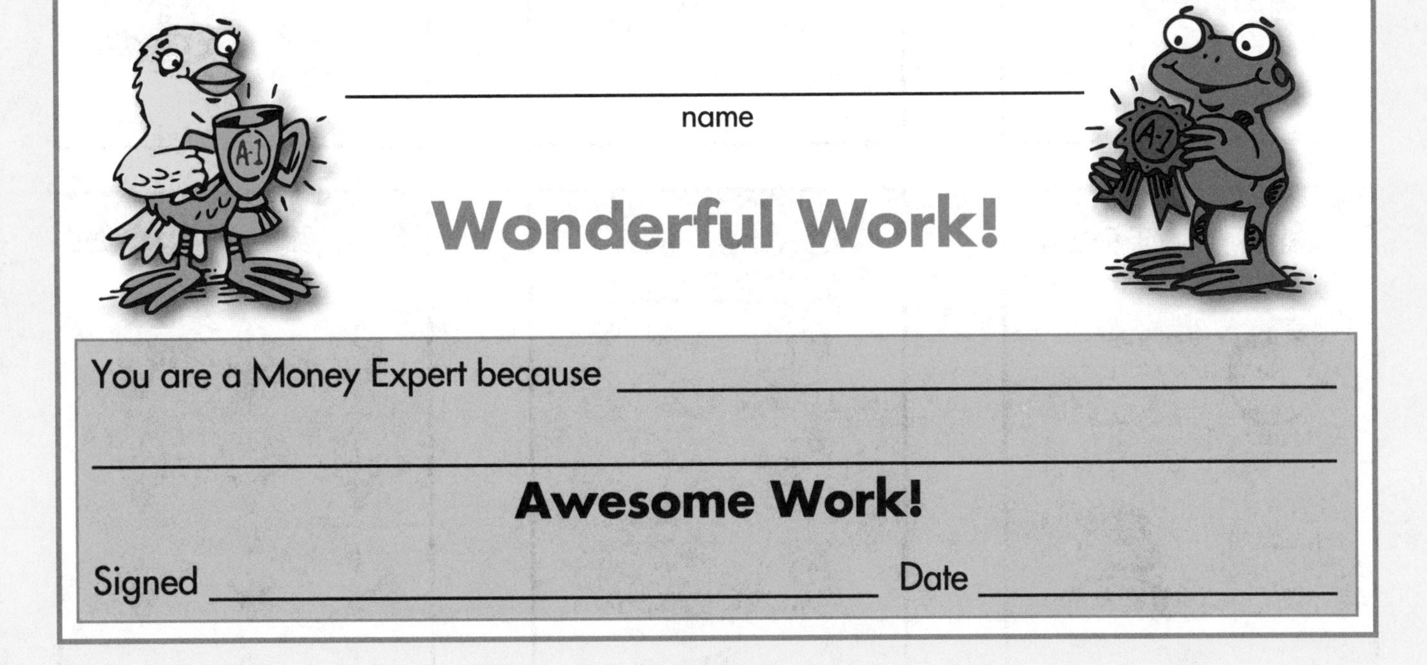

ANSWER KEY

TIME TO THE HOUR

Face Clocks: Introduction

What is the best way to tell what time it is? A clock! There are all kinds of clocks.

Circle the ones you have seen.

Answers will vary.

8:00

8

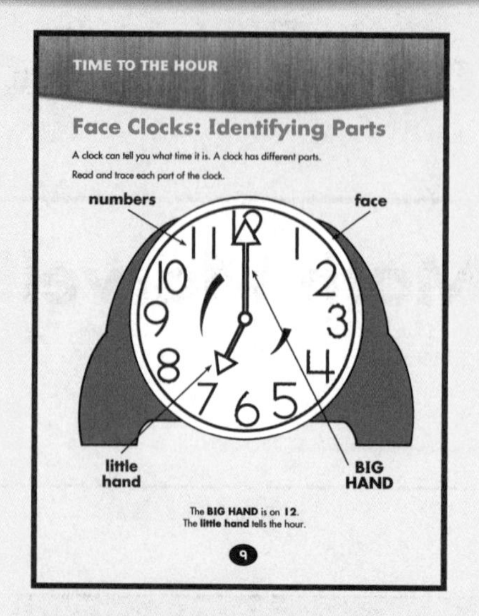
TIME TO THE HOUR

Face Clocks: Identifying Parts

A clock can tell you what time it is. A clock has different parts.

Read and trace each part of the clock.

numbers

face

little hand

BIG HAND

The **BIG HAND** is on **12**.
The **little hand** tells the hour.

9

TIME TO THE HOUR

Writing the Time

Write the numbers on the clock face. Draw the BIG HAND to 12. Draw the little hand to 5.

What time is it? 5 o'clock

10

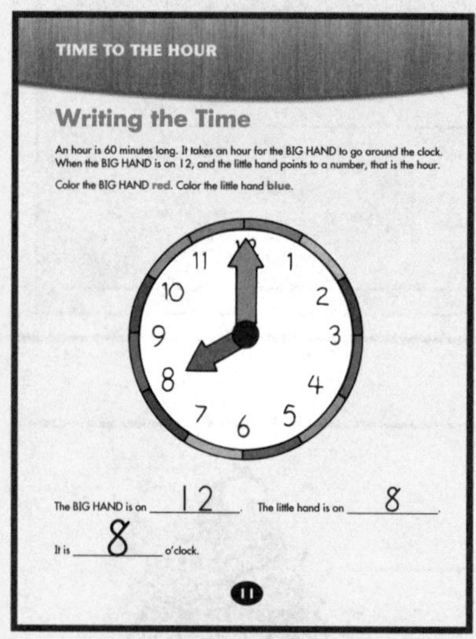
TIME TO THE HOUR

Writing the Time

An hour is 60 minutes long. It takes an hour for the BIG HAND to go around the clock. When the BIG HAND is on 12, and the little hand points to a number, that is the hour.

Color the BIG HAND red. Color the little hand blue.

The BIG HAND is on 12. The little hand is on 8.

It is 8 o'clock.

11

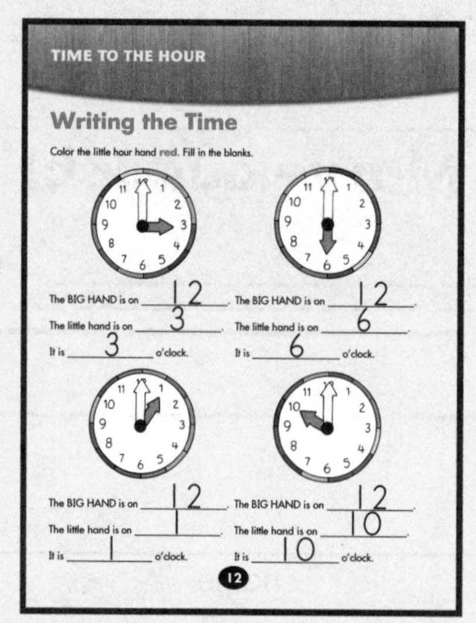
TIME TO THE HOUR

Writing the Time

Color the little hour hand red. Fill in the blanks.

The BIG HAND is on 12. The little hand is on 3. It is 3 o'clock.

The BIG HAND is on 12. The little hand is on 6. It is 6 o'clock.

The BIG HAND is on 12. The little hand is on 1. It is 1 o'clock.

The BIG HAND is on 12. The little hand is on 10. It is 10 o'clock.

12

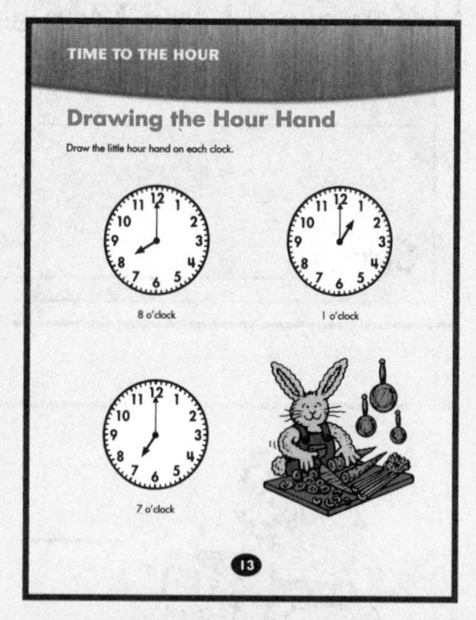
TIME TO THE HOUR

Drawing the Hour Hand

Draw the little hour hand on each clock.

8 o'clock

1 o'clock

7 o'clock

13

TIME TO THE HOUR

Drawing the Hour Hand

Draw the little hour hand on each clock.

2 o'clock

10 o'clock

9 o'clock

14

TIME TO THE HOUR

Circling the Hour Hand

Circle the little hour hand on each clock. What time is it? Write the time below.

3 o'clock

8 o'clock

4 o'clock

12 o'clock

10 o'clock

5 o'clock

15

TIME TO THE HOUR

Practice

Draw the little hour hand on each clock.

8 o'clock

4 o'clock

2 o'clock

6 o'clock

11 o'clock

3 o'clock

1 o'clock

5 o'clock

7 o'clock

16

ANSWER KEY

TIME TO THE HOUR

Practice

What is the time?

7 o'clock | 12 o'clock | 3 o'clock
6 o'clock | 11 o'clock | 1 o'clock
8 o'clock | 4 o'clock | 2 o'clock
10 o'clock | 9 o'clock | 5 o'clock

17

TIME TO THE HOUR

Writing the Time: One Hour Later

Write the original time and 1 hour later.

7:00 — one hour later — 8:00

4:00 — one hour later — 5:00

18

TIME TO THE HOUR

Time Poems

Read each poem. Draw a line to the clock that matches.

1. It is 7 o'clock.
   Time to rise and shine.
   First it will rain,
   Then turn out fine.
2. It is 10 o'clock.
   We are at the pool.
   We're happy today
   Because there is no school!
3. It is 4 o'clock.
   It is time to play!
   We will see friends
   Outside today.

19

TIME TO THE HOUR

Digital Clocks: Introduction

A digital clock tells time with numbers. First, it tells the hour, then the minutes.

10:00

Draw the little hour hand on this face clock below to read 10 o'clock.

Both clocks show that it is 10 o'clock. Make a green circle around the kinds of clocks you have at home.

Answers will vary.

20

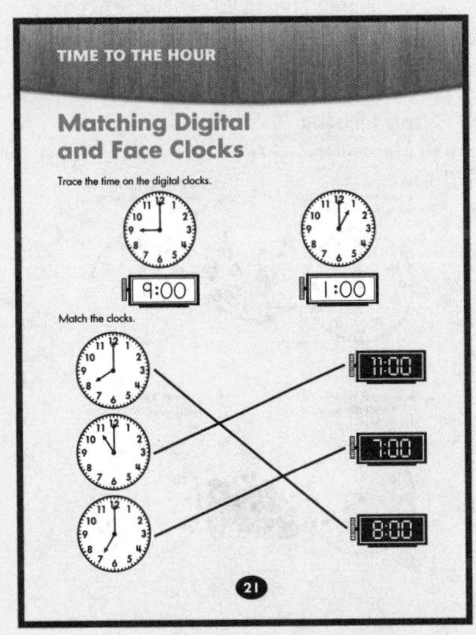
TIME TO THE HOUR

Matching Digital and Face Clocks

Trace the time on the digital clocks.

9:00 | 1:00

Match the clocks.

11:00
7:00
8:00

21

TIME TO THE HOUR

Matching Digital and Face Clocks

Long ago, there were only wind-up clocks. Today, we also have electric and battery clocks. We even have solar clocks!

Match these digital and face clocks.

6:00
9:00
3:00
1:00

22

TIME TO THE HOUR

Digital Clocks

Write the time on the digital clocks.

5:00 | 12:00
8:00 | 3:00

23

TIME TO THE HOUR

Drawing the Hour Hand: Matching Digital and Face Clocks

Look at the digital clock. Say the time. Draw the little hour hand on each face clock.

4:00 | 2:00
8:00 | 6:00

24

TIME TO THE HOUR

Time Two Ways

Show each time two ways. Draw the hands on each clock face. Then, write the time on each digital clock.

1. Bessie Bear gets up at **6 o'clock.** 6:00
2. Bernie Bear eats breakfast at **7 o'clock.** 7:00
3. What time do you get up for school? Draw it below!

Answers will vary.

25

ANSWER KEY

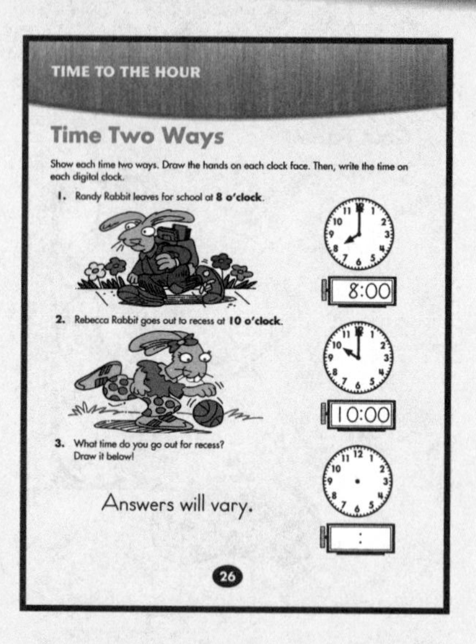
TIME TO THE HOUR

Time Two Ways

Show each time two ways. Draw the hands on each clock face. Then, write the time on each digital clock.

1. Randy Rabbit leaves for school at **8 o'clock**.

8:00

2. Rebecca Rabbit goes out to recess at **10 o'clock**.

10:00

3. What time do you go out for recess? Draw it below!

Answers will vary.

:

26

TIME TO THE HOUR

Time Two Ways

Show each time two ways. Draw the hands on each clock face. Then, write the time on each digital clock.

1. Fernando Frog eats lunch at **12 o'clock**.

12:00

2. Fanny Frog goes to the library at **1 o'clock**.

1:00

3. What time do you eat lunch? Draw it below!

Answers will vary.

:

27

TIME TO THE HOUR

Time Two Ways

Show each time two ways. Draw the hands on each clock face. Then, write the time.

1. At **9 o'clock**, Frog goes for a swim.

9:00

2. At **11 o'clock**, Frog sits on a lily pad.

11:00

3. At **12 o'clock**, Frog eats a sandwich.

12:00

28

TIME TO THE HOUR

Time Stories

Read each story. Draw the hands on each clock face.

1. At **11:00**, Mouse starts to cook. Yum! Cheese soup is good.
2. At **12 o'clock**, Mouse sets the table. Oh no! He drops a spoon.
3. At **7:00**, Mouse reads a book. What a funny story!
4. Time for bed. It is **9 o'clock**, and Mouse is sleepy.

29

TIME TO THE HOUR

Time Stories

Read each story. Draw the hands on each clock face.

1. Rabbit is hungry. It is **6 o'clock**—time for supper and some carrot stew.
2. At **8:00**, Rabbit washes the dishes. Scrub, scrub, the pot is sticky.
3. Rabbit works in his garden. It is **4 o'clock**, and he is picking lettuce.
4. At **5:00**, Rabbit makes a lettuce salad. What a tasty meal!

30

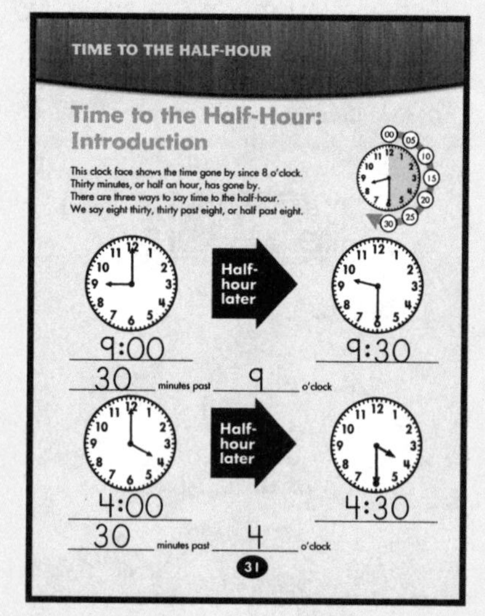
TIME TO THE HALF-HOUR

Time to the Half-Hour: Introduction

This clock face shows the time gone by since 8 o'clock. Thirty minutes, or half an hour, has gone by. There are three ways to say time to the half-hour. We say eight thirty, thirty past eight, or half past eight.

00 05 10 15 20 25 30

Half-hour later

9:00 9:30

30 minutes past 9 o'clock

Half-hour later

4:00 4:30

30 minutes past 4 o'clock

31

TIME TO THE HALF-HOUR

Writing Time on the Half-Hour

Trace the big minute hand green. Trace the little hour hand yellow. Write the time on the line.

5:30

11:30

6:30

2:30

32

TIME TO THE HALF-HOUR

Matching Digital and Face Clocks

These digital numbers got lost. Write them in the correct clocks on this page and page 34.

12:30

5:30

6:30	12:30	3:30	8:30	9:30	5:30

33

TIME TO THE HALF-HOUR

Matching Digital and Face Clocks

8:30

3:30

6:30

9:30

34

ANSWER KEY

TIME TO THE HALF-HOUR

Drawing the Hour Hand

Say the time. Draw the little hour hand on each clock.

3:30 6:30

2:30 9:30

35

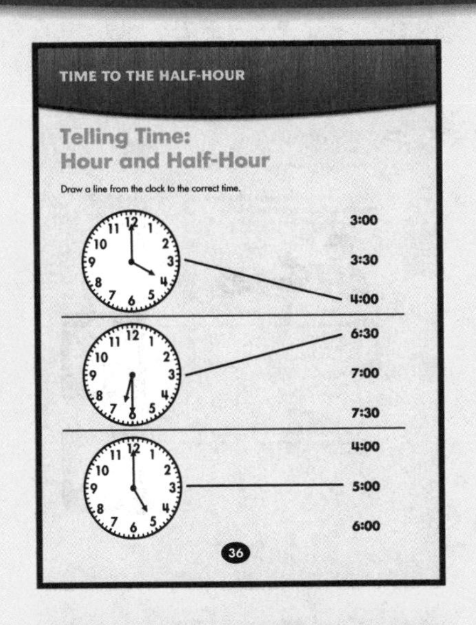
TIME TO THE HALF-HOUR

Telling Time: Hour and Half-Hour

Draw a line from the clock to the correct time.

3:00
3:30
4:00

6:30
7:00
7:30

4:00
5:00
6:00

36

TIME TO THE HALF-HOUR

Writing the Time: Practice

Draw the hands on the sock clocks.

3:00 1:30 7:00

4:30 10:00 3:30

9:30 4:00 2:30

37

TIME TO THE HALF-HOUR

Writing the Time: Practice

What time is it?

3:00 9:30 8:00 7:30

1:30 6:30 10:30 12:00

7:00 11:00 2:00 4:30

38

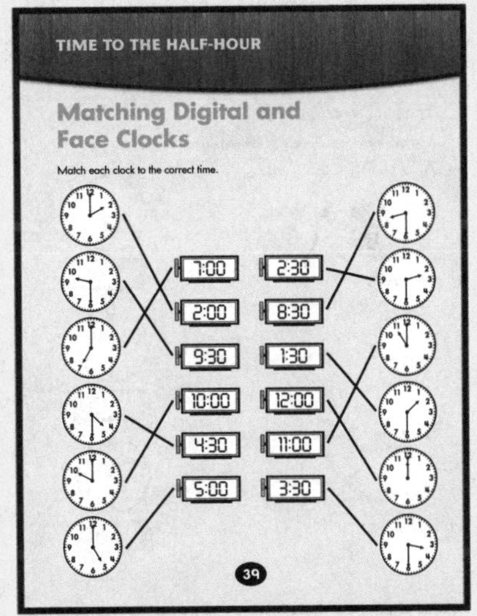
TIME TO THE HALF-HOUR

Matching Digital and Face Clocks

Match each clock to the correct time.

7:00 2:30

2:00 8:30

9:30 1:30

10:00 12:00

4:30 11:00

5:00 3:30

39

TIME TO THE HALF-HOUR

Time Stories

Read each story. Draw the hands on each clock face.

1. It is **5:30**, and the sun is coming up. Bird is ready for the day.

2. At **6:30**, Bird is looking for breakfast. Watch out, worms!

3. Bird is resting after breakfast. It is **9:30** and almost time for flying practice.

4. At **12:30**, Bird naps before lunch. Flying is hard work!

40

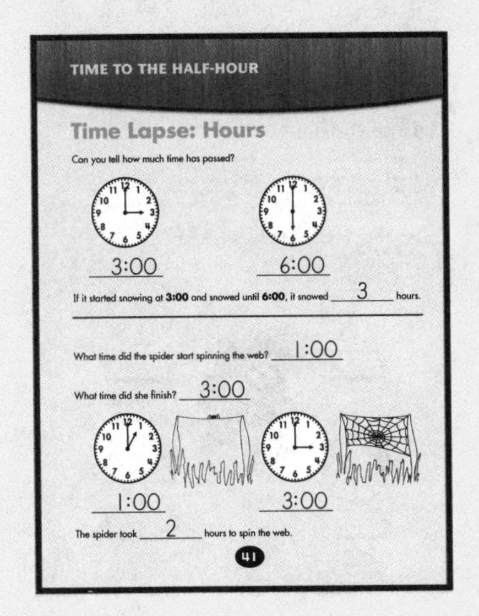
TIME TO THE HALF-HOUR

Time Lapse: Hours

Can you tell how much time has passed?

3:00 6:00

If it started snowing at **3:00** and snowed until **6:00**, it snowed 3 hours.

What time did the spider start spinning the web? 1:00

What time did she finish? 3:00

1:00 3:00

The spider took 2 hours to spin the web.

41

TIME TO THE HALF-HOUR

Time Lapse: Hours

1. Steve went to play baseball at **3:30**. Mom told him to be home in **2 hours**.

He should be home at 5:30.

Show the time on this watch.

2. Tiffany went to Latonia's house to ride bikes at **10:00**. Dad asked her to be home in **3 hours**.

She should be home at 1:00.

Show the time on this watch.

42

TIME TO THE HALF-HOUR

Time Lapse: Hours

1. Kristen took her sister to the movies at **7:30**. Mom said she would meet them in **2 hours**.

She will meet them at 9:30.

Show the time on this watch.

2. Latrissa went to the library for story hour. She got there at **1:00**. She stayed **1 hour**.

Story hour should be over at 2:00.

Show the time on this watch.

43

ANSWER KEY

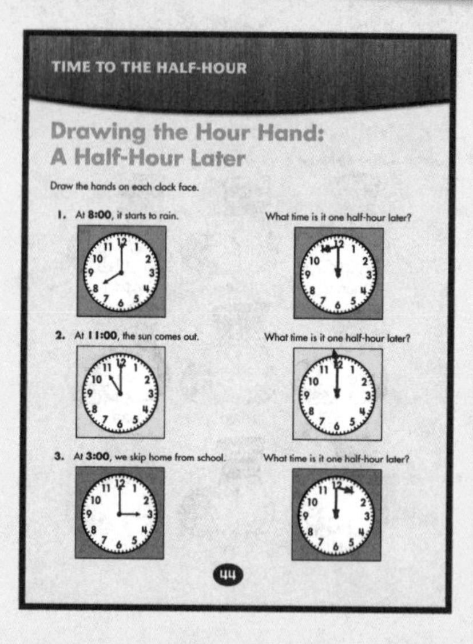
TIME TO THE HALF-HOUR

Drawing the Hour Hand: A Half-Hour Later

Draw the hands on each clock face.

1. At **8:00**, it starts to rain. What time is it one half-hour later?
2. At **11:00**, the sun comes out. What time is it one half-hour later?
3. At **3:00**, we skip home from school. What time is it one half-hour later?

44

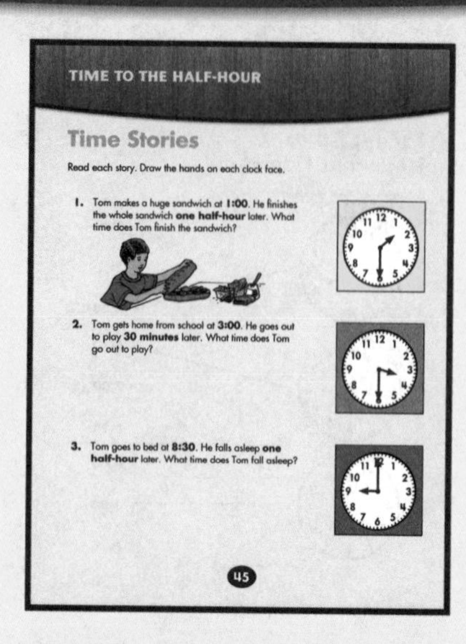
TIME TO THE HALF-HOUR

Time Stories

Read each story. Draw the hands on each clock face.

1. Tom makes a huge sandwich at **1:00**. He finishes the whole sandwich **one half-hour** later. What time does Tom finish the sandwich?
2. Tom gets home from school at **3:00**. He goes out to play **30 minutes** later. What time does Tom go out to play?
3. Tom goes to bed at **8:30**. He falls asleep **one half-hour** later. What time does Tom fall asleep?

45

TIME TO THE HALF-HOUR

Time Stories

Read each story. Draw the hands on each clock face.

1. Maria makes lunch at **7:00**. She gets on the bus **30 minutes** later. What time does she get on the bus?
2. Maria helps make dinner at **5:30**. Everyone eats it **one half-hour** later. What time does everyone eat?
3. Maria's family plays a game at **8:30**. They stop playing **30 minutes** later. What time do they stop playing?

46

TIME TO THE HALF-HOUR

Time Two Ways

Draw the hands on each clock face. Write the time on the digital clock.

1. At **1:30**, Squirrel hides seven nuts. 1:30
2. At **2:00**, Squirrel runs down the tree to find more nuts. 2:00
3. By **3:30**, Squirrel is ready for a long rest. 3:30

47

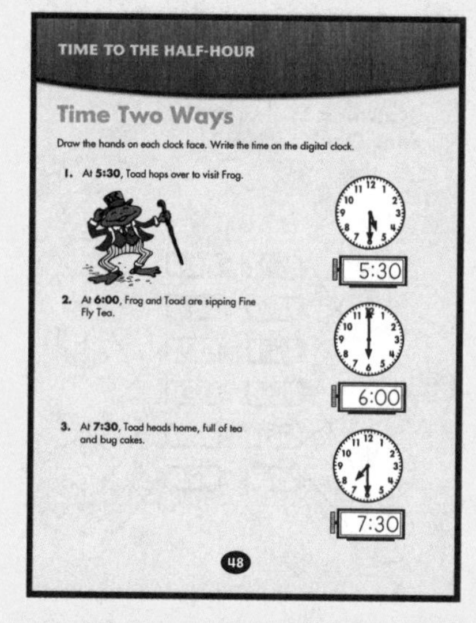
TIME TO THE HALF-HOUR

Time Two Ways

Draw the hands on each clock face. Write the time on the digital clock.

1. At **5:30**, Toad hops over to visit Frog. 5:30
2. At **6:00**, Frog and Toad are sipping Fine Fly Tea. 6:00
3. At **7:30**, Toad heads home, full of tea and bug cakes. 7:30

48

TIME TO THE HALF-HOUR

Time Two Ways

Draw the hands on each clock face. Write the time on the digital clock.

1. Ricardo Raccoon starts his lunch at **12:00**. He finishes his lunch **30 minutes after 12:00**.

Starts lunch 12:00 — Finishes lunch 12:30

2. Rachel Raccoon sits down at the computer at **7:00**. She gets up from the computer a **half-hour after 7:00**.

Sits down 7:00 — Gets up 7:30

49

TIME TO THE HALF-HOUR

Time Stories

Read the story. Write the time two ways. Choose a time for everyone to eat lunch!

Bear is going on a picnic today with his brother and sister. They leave for the park at **9:00**. They get to the park at **10:00**. Bear helps carry the food to a picnic table. Then, he gets out his kite. Bear flies his kite at **10:30**. Later, at __________, everyone has a picnic lunch! Answers will vary.

Put the story in order by writing what time Bear did each thing.

1. **Leave for the park** 9:00
2. **Get to the park** 10:00
3. **Fly kite** 10:30
4. **Eat lunch** Answers will vary.

50

TIME TO THE HALF-HOUR

Time Stories

Read the story. Write the time two ways. Choose a time for everyone to go home!

Pig wakes up at **7:00**. Pig's grandmother is taking her to the zoo today! They get to the zoo at **10:30**. They walk and walk. They stop to eat at **12:30**. They walk some more. Pig and her grandmother don't get home until __________. They had a wonderful day! Answers will vary.

Put the story in order by writing what time Pig did each thing.

1. Wakes up 7:00
2. Get to zoo 10:30
3. Stop to eat 12:30
4. Answers will vary.

51

TIME TO THE HALF-HOUR

Time Stories

Read the story. Write the time two ways. Choose a time for everyone to wake up!

It's a hot summer day. Frog and Turtle begin to walk to the lake at **11:00**. They jump into the cold water at **12:30**. They swim and dive. Then, they enjoy lunch at **1:30**. They fall asleep after lunch. Later, at __________, Frog and Turtle wake up. They hurry home! Answers will vary.

Put the story in order by writing what time Frog and Turtle did each thing.

1. Walk to the lake 11:00
2. Jump into water 12:30
3. Have lunch 1:30
4. Answers will vary.

52

ANSWER KEY

TIME TO THE HALF-HOUR
Time Puzzles
Read each clue and guess what time it might be. Draw the hands on each clock. Write the time.
Answers will vary.
It's dark outside. Everyone is asleep.
Ring, ring! Time to get up.
Here comes the school bus. Run, so you won't be late!
I'm hungry! Soon it will be time for lunch.
53

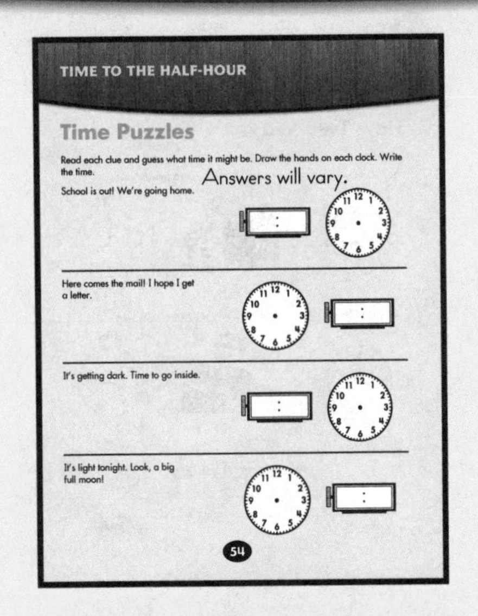
TIME TO THE HALF-HOUR
Time Puzzles
Read each clue and guess what time it might be. Draw the hands on each clock. Write the time.
Answers will vary.
School is out! We're going home.
Here comes the mail! I hope I get a letter.
It's getting dark. Time to go inside.
It's light tonight. Look, a big full moon!
54

TIME TO THE HALF-HOUR
Time Puzzles
Read each clue and guess what time it might be. Draw the hands on each clock. Write the time.
Answers will vary.
Sometimes, I have homework to do.
Sometimes, I have jobs to do.
The best time is when I can do just what I want to do.
On Saturday and Sunday, I play with friends.
55

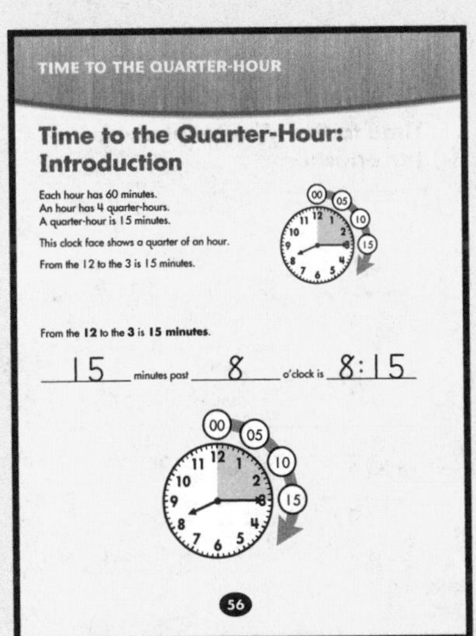
TIME TO THE QUARTER-HOUR
Time to the Quarter-Hour: Introduction
Each hour has 60 minutes.
An hour has 4 quarter-hours.
A quarter-hour is 15 minutes.
This clock face shows a quarter of an hour.
From the 12 to the 3 is 15 minutes.
From the 12 to the 3 is 15 minutes.
15 minutes past 8 o'clock is 8:15
56

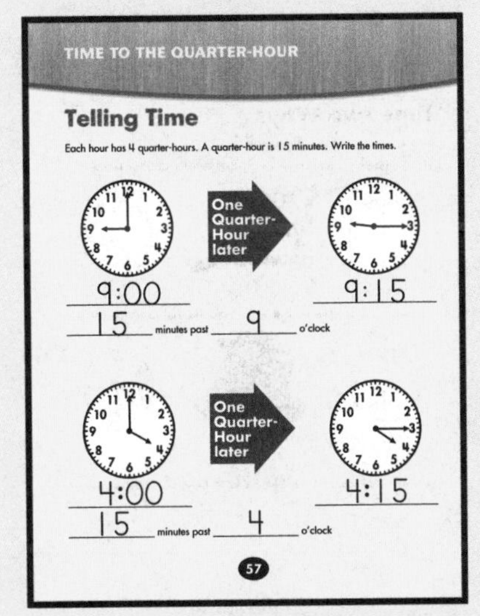
TIME TO THE QUARTER-HOUR
Telling Time
Each hour has 4 quarter-hours. A quarter-hour is 15 minutes. Write the times.
One Quarter-Hour later
9:00
9:15
15 minutes past 9 o'clock
One Quarter-Hour later
4:00
4:15
15 minutes past 4 o'clock
57

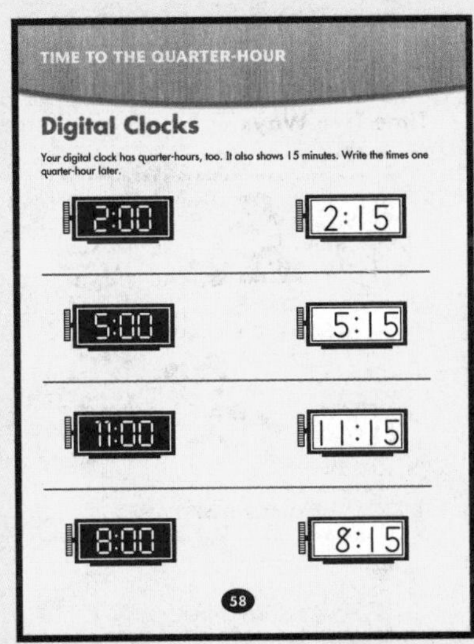
TIME TO THE QUARTER-HOUR
Digital Clocks
Your digital clock has quarter-hours, too. It also shows 15 minutes. Write the times one quarter-hour later.
2:00
2:15
5:00
5:15
11:00
11:15
8:00
8:15
58

TIME TO THE QUARTER-HOUR
Telling Time
Count by fives to see how many minutes have passed.
15 minutes after 12
30 minutes after 12
45 minutes after 12
59

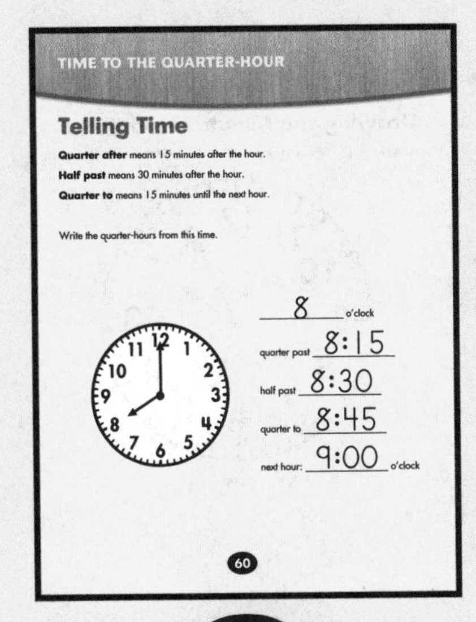
TIME TO THE QUARTER-HOUR
Telling Time
Quarter after means 15 minutes after the hour.
Half past means 30 minutes after the hour.
Quarter to means 15 minutes until the next hour.
Write the quarter-hours from this time.
8 o'clock
quarter past 8:15
half past 8:30
quarter to 8:45
next hour: 9:00 o'clock
60

TIME TO THE QUARTER-HOUR
Telling Time
Circle the time.
5:15
7:15
11:30
9:30
10:45
12:45
9:45
3:45
7:30
6:45
10:00
2:00
6:15
6:45
10:30
10:45
This pie bakes until a quarter past 4.
4:45
4:15
61

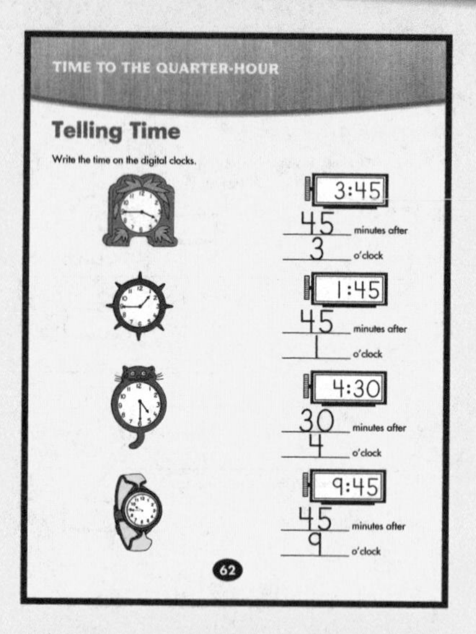
TIME TO THE QUARTER-HOUR

Telling Time

Write the time on the digital clocks.

3:45 — 45 minutes after 3 o'clock

1:45 — 45 minutes after 1 o'clock

4:30 — 30 minutes after 4 o'clock

9:45 — 45 minutes after 9 o'clock

62

TIME TO THE QUARTER-HOUR

Time Two Ways

Draw the hands on each clock face. Write the time.

1. Marta begins writing a letter at **3:30**. She stops **30 minutes later**.
   Begins 3:30 — Stops 4:00
2. Arnold begins drying dishes at **8:00**. He stops **15 minutes later**.
   Begins 8:00 — Stops 8:15
3. Write your own time story.
   Answers will vary.
   Begins : — Stops :

63

TIME TO THE QUARTER-HOUR

Time Two Ways

Draw the hands on each clock face. Write the time.

1. Darius begins throwing balls for the dog at **5:00**. He stops **15 minutes later**.
   Begins 5:00 — Stops 5:15
2. Olga begins playing frisbee at **4:15**. She stops **15 minutes later**.
   Begins 4:15 — Stops 4:30
3. Write your own time story.
   Answers will vary.
   Begins : — Stops :

64

TIME TO THE QUARTER-HOUR

Time Two Ways

Draw the hands on each clock face. Write the time.

1. Alberto begins working in the yard at **10:30**. He stops **45 minutes later**.
   Begins 10:30 — Stops 11:15
2. Darlene begins playing catch at **2:30**. She stops **15 minutes later**.
   Begins 2:30 — Stops 2:45
3. Write your own time story.
   Answers will vary.
   Begins : — Stops :

65

TIME TO THE QUARTER-HOUR

Time Two Ways

Draw the hands on each clock face. Write the time.

1. Lucia begins practicing for the play at **3:00**. She stops **45 minutes later**.
   Begins 3:00 — Stops 3:45
2. Ann begins sorting her baseball cards at **7:30**. She stops **15 minutes later**.
   Begins 7:30 — Stops 7:45
3. Solve this puzzle.
   When did Ray begin biking? Ray biked for **30 minutes**. He stopped biking at **5:30**.
   Began 5:00 — Stopped 5:30

66

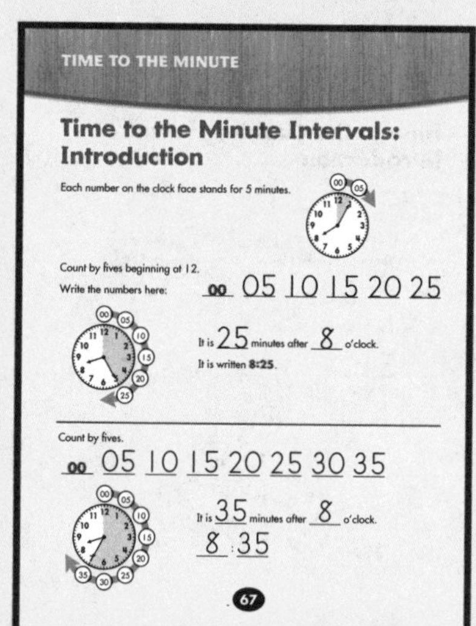
TIME TO THE MINUTE

Time to the Minute Intervals: Introduction

Each number on the clock face stands for 5 minutes.

Count by fives beginning at 12.
Write the numbers here: 00 05 10 15 20 25

It is 25 minutes after 8 o'clock.
It is written **8:25**.

Count by fives.
00 05 10 15 20 25 30 35

It is 35 minutes after 8 o'clock.
8:35

67

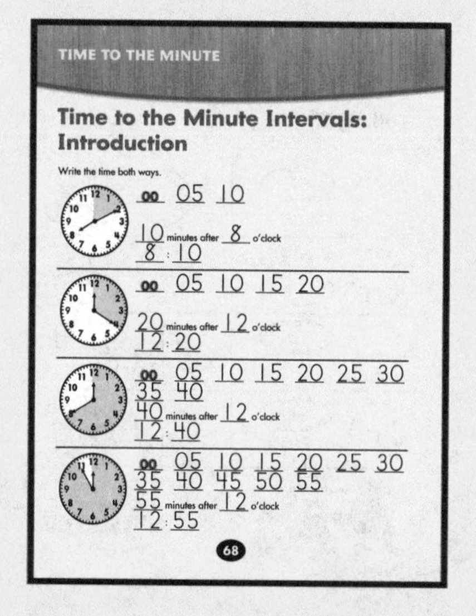
TIME TO THE MINUTE

Time to the Minute Intervals: Introduction

Write the time both ways.

00 05 10
10 minutes after 8 o'clock
8:10

00 05 10 15 20
20 minutes after 12 o'clock
12:20

00 05 10 15 20 25 30 35 40
40 minutes after 12 o'clock
12:40

00 05 10 15 20 25 30 35 40 45 50 55
55 minutes after 12 o'clock
12:55

68

TIME TO THE MINUTE

Drawing the Minute Hand

Read the time. Draw the minute hand with a pencil. Color over it with a red crayon.

2:05

5 minutes after 2 o'clock

69

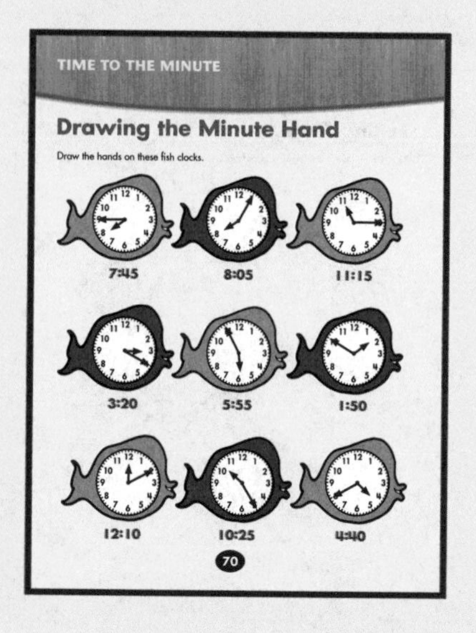
TIME TO THE MINUTE

Drawing the Minute Hand

Draw the hands on these fish clocks.

7:45 8:05 11:15
3:20 5:55 1:50
12:10 10:25 4:40

70

ANSWER KEY

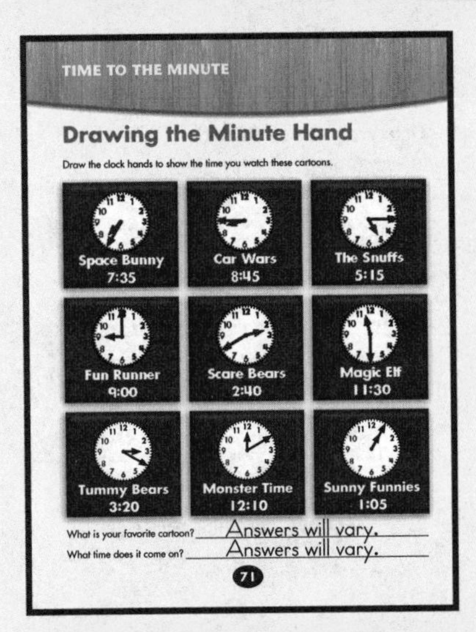

TIME TO THE MINUTE

Drawing the Minute Hand

Draw the clock hands to show the time you watch these cartoons.

Space Bunny 7:35
Car Wars 8:45
The Snuffs 5:15
Fun Runner 9:00
Scare Bears 2:40
Magic Elf 11:30
Tummy Bears 3:20
Monster Time 12:10
Sunny Funnies 1:05

What is your favorite cartoon? Answers will vary.
What time does it come on? Answers will vary.

71

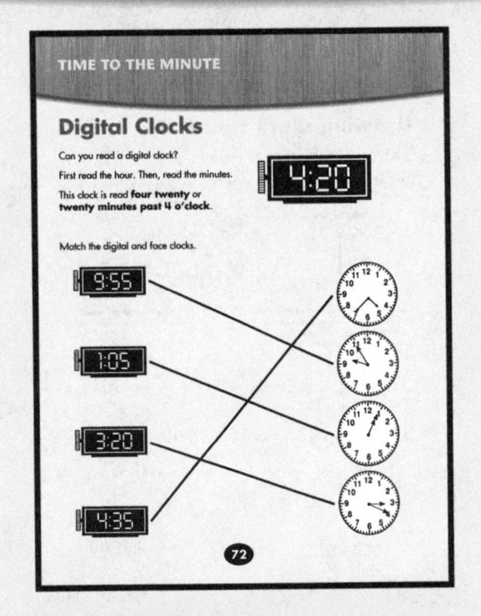

TIME TO THE MINUTE

Digital Clocks

Can you read a digital clock?
First read the hour. Then, read the minutes.
This clock is read **four twenty** or **twenty minutes past 4 o'clock.**

4:20

Match the digital and face clocks.

9:55
1:05
3:20
4:35

72

TIME TO THE MINUTE

Digital Clocks

Circle the words to match the times.

five twenty | 5:20 | five fifty
six twenty-five | 6:35 | six thirty-five
seven ten | 7:10 | seven twenty
one fifty-five | 11:55 | eleven fifty-five

73

TIME TO THE MINUTE

Writing the Time

What time is it?

9:10 8:25
10:05 8:20 1:45
7:55 8:15 3:50
2:35 7:30 2:40

74

TIME TO THE MINUTE

Drawing Clock Hands

Draw the hands. Write the time.

Three thirty 3:30
Five forty-five 5:45
Eleven twenty 11:20
Eight ten 8:10
Two fifty-five 2:55
Nine forty 9:40

75

TIME TO THE MINUTE

Time Two Ways

Draw the hands on each clock face. Write the time.

1. 30 minutes after 6:00 — 6:30
2. 20 minutes before 6:00 — 5:40
3. Exactly 6 o'clock — 6:00
4. 20 minutes after 6:00 — 6:20

76

TIME TO THE MINUTE

Time Two Ways

Draw the hands on each clock face. Write the time.

1. Exactly noon — 12:00
2. Quarter past 12:00 — 12:15
3. 15 minutes before 12:00 — 11:45
4. Half past 12:00 — 12:30

77

TIME TO THE MINUTE

Writing Familiar Times: Family "Time Tree"

Write the time. Draw the hands on each clock. Answers will vary.

I get up at ____. I go to bed at ____. Lunch is at ____.
Dinner is at ____. School starts at ____. School ends at ____.
Recess is at ____. I play at ____.

78

TIME TO THE MINUTE

Time Lapse: Minutes

How much time did each activity take?

1. Jimmy played darts from 1:20 to 1:40.
   He played for 20 minutes.
2. Marietta rode a pony for 15 minutes. She began at 1:00.
   She finished at 1 : 15.
3. She had so much fun, she rode another 15 minutes.
   She finished at 1 : 30.

79

ANSWER KEY

TIME TO THE MINUTE

Time Lapse: Minutes

How much time did each activity take?

1. Tim worked at the snow cone booth. The first clock shows the time he started. He worked 1 hour and 30 minutes.

   Show the time he finished on the second clock.

2. Andrea won the juggling contest. She kept the balls in the air for 5 minutes. She began juggling at 1:25.

   She finished at 1 : 30.

   Circle the clock that shows the correct time.

80

TIME TO THE MINUTE

Drawing Clock Hands

Read each story. Draw the hands on each clock face.

1. Rabbit hops into his garden at **6:00**. He finishes working in the garden **one and one-half hours later.**

   Hops in garden — Finishes work

2. Rabbit gets out lettuce and carrots at **8:30**. He finishes eating **45 minutes later.**

   Gets out lettuce and carrots — Finishes eating

3. Rabbit lies down for a nap at **4:00**. He wakes up **55 minutes later.**

   Lies down — Wakes up

81

TIME TO THE MINUTE

Drawing Clock Hands

Read each story. Draw the hands on each clock face.

1. Pig takes a mud bath at **9:00**. She showers off **15 minutes later.**

   Takes mud bath — Showers off

2. On Monday, Pig begins cleaning at **noon**. Her house is clean and neat **90 minutes later.**

   Begins cleaning — House is clean

3. On Tuesday, Pig goes to the market at **12:45**. She comes home with a basket full of goodies **30 minutes later.**

   Goes to market — Comes home

82

TIME REVIEW

Time Stories

Read the story. Write the times on each digital clock.

Val and Phil go out to the backyard at **6:00**. They put up their tent. This takes them **1 hour and 30 minutes**. They get in the tent and talk for **1 hour**. Then, they fall asleep. They sleep for **2 hours**, until a dog barks and wakes them up.

1. **Go to backyard** 6:00
2. **Finish putting up tent** 7:30
3. **Fall asleep** 8:30
4. **Dog barks** 10:30
5. How long are Val and Phil in the yard before the dog wakes them up? 4 hours 30 minutes

83

TIME REVIEW

Time Stories

Read the story. Write the times on each digital clock.

Joe and José put on roller skates at **8:30**. They skate for **2 hours**, then stop to rest. They rest for **one half-hour**, then start skating again. They reach the park **1 hour and 45 minutes later.**

1. **Put on roller skates** 8:30
2. **Stop to rest** 10:30
3. **Start skating again** 11:00
4. **Get to park** 12:45
5. How long does Joe and José's trip to the park take? 4 hours 15 minutes

84

TIME REVIEW

Time Stories

Read each time story. Write the times on each digital clock.

1. Andrea took her dog for a walk. They left home at **5:30**. They walked for **20 minutes.** What time did they get home?

   Leave home 5:30 — **Get home** 5:50

2. Rhiannon and her mother were making cookies. They put the cookies in the oven at **7:15**. After **10 minutes** they took the cookies out of the oven. Yum! What time did they take them out?

   Cookies in oven 7:15 — **Cookies out of oven** 7:25

3. Solve the time puzzle.

   When did Anita begin playing ping-pong? Anita played ping-pong with her brother for **30 minutes.** They stopped playing at **4:30.**

   Begin playing 4:00 — **Stop playing** 4:30

85

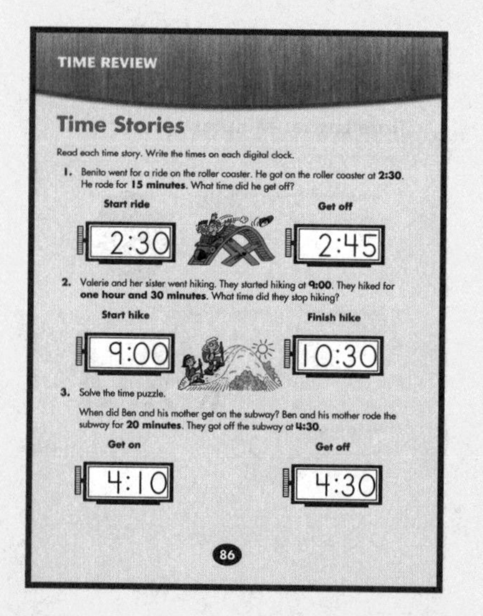

TIME REVIEW

Time Stories

Read each time story. Write the times on each digital clock.

1. Benito went for a ride on the roller coaster. He got on the roller coaster at **2:30**. He rode for **15 minutes.** What time did he get off?

   Start ride 2:30 — **Get off** 2:45

2. Valerie and her sister went hiking. They started hiking at **9:00**. They hiked for **one hour and 30 minutes.** What time did they stop hiking?

   Start hike 9:00 — **Finish hike** 10:30

3. Solve the time puzzle.

   When did Ben and his mother get on the subway? Ben and his mother rode the subway for **20 minutes.** They got off the subway at **4:30.**

   Get on 4:10 — **Get off** 4:30

86

TIME REVIEW

Time Puzzles

Answers will vary.

Write any time that fits the time clues.

1. Between 11:00 and 12:00.
2. Between 30 minutes after 2:00 and 3:00.
3. After quarter-past 7:00 and before 8:00.
4. Make up your own time clues. Ask a friend to solve your time puzzle!

87

TIME REVIEW

Time Puzzles

Answers will vary.

Write any time that fits the time clues.

1. Between 4:15 and 5:15.
2. After 6:00 and before quarter to 7:00.
3. Between noon and 1:00.
4. Make up your own time clues. Ask a friend to solve your time puzzle!

88

TIME REVIEW

Time Stories

Read the story. Write the time on each clock.

Erin and her brother Harry were shopping for dinner. First, they went into the bakery at **5:00** to buy fresh bread. This took **5 minutes**. Next, they walked to the market for vegetables and cereal. This took them **20 minutes**. Then, they walked next door for a treat at Fanny's Famous Fudge. This took them **15 minutes**. Then, they met their brother Andrew outside.

1. Go into bakery — 5:00
2. Leave bakery — 5:05
3. Leave market — 5:25
4. See Andrew — 5:40
5. How long had Erin and Harry been shopping when they saw Andrew? 40 minutes
6. Make up your own story about shopping. What do you do, and how long does each thing take? Make up a starting time. Use your clock to find the ending time.

89

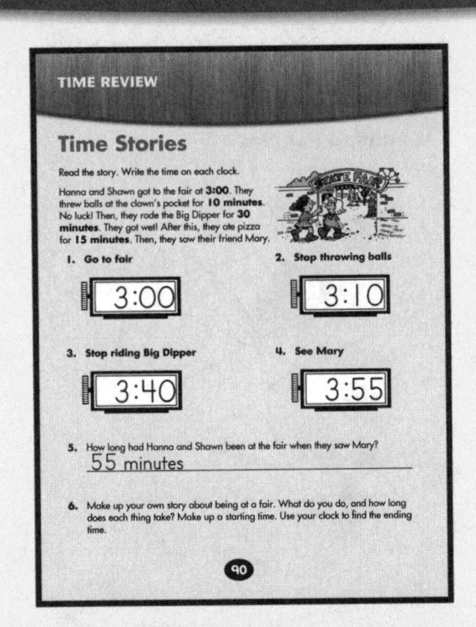
TIME REVIEW

Time Stories

Read the story. Write the time on each clock.

Hanna and Shawn got to the fair at **3:00**. They threw balls at the clown's pocket for **10 minutes**. No luck! Then, they rode the Big Dipper for **30 minutes**. They got wet! After this, they ate pizza for **15 minutes**. Then, they saw their friend Mary.

1. Go to fair — 3:00
2. Stop throwing balls — 3:10
3. Stop riding Big Dipper — 3:40
4. See Mary — 3:55
5. How long had Hanna and Shawn been at the fair when they saw Mary? 55 minutes
6. Make up your own story about being at a fair. What do you do, and how long does each thing take? Make up a starting time. Use your clock to find the ending time.

90

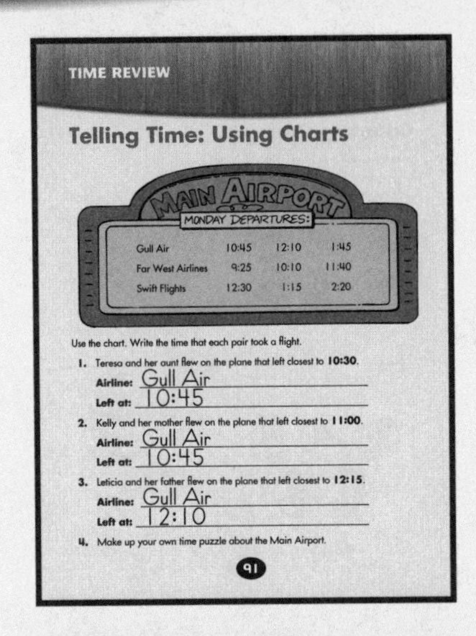
TIME REVIEW

Telling Time: Using Charts

MAIN AIRPORT

MONDAY DEPARTURES:

Gull Air	10:45	12:10	1:45
Far West Airlines	9:25	10:10	11:40
Swift Flights	12:30	1:15	2:20

Use the chart. Write the time that each pair took a flight.

1. Teresa and her aunt flew on the plane that left closest to **10:30**.
   Airline: Gull Air
   Left at: 10:45
2. Kelly and her mother flew on the plane that left closest to **11:00**.
   Airline: Gull Air
   Left at: 10:45
3. Leticia and her father flew on the plane that left closest to **12:15**.
   Airline: Gull Air
   Left at: 12:10
4. Make up your own time puzzle about the Main Airport.

91

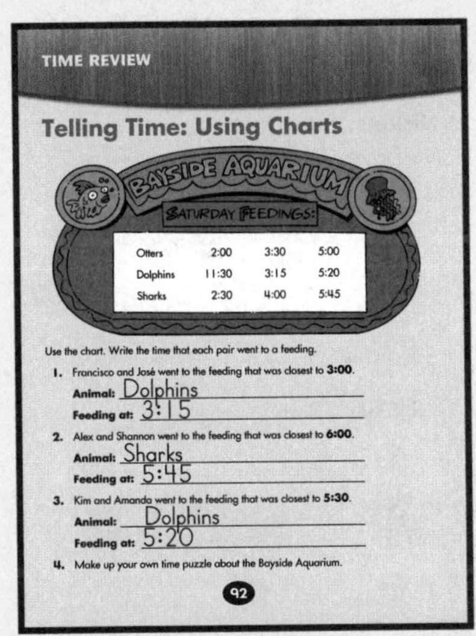
TIME REVIEW

Telling Time: Using Charts

BAYSIDE AQUARIUM

SATURDAY FEEDINGS:

Otters	2:00	3:30	5:00
Dolphins	11:30	3:15	5:20
Sharks	2:30	4:00	5:45

Use the chart. Write the time that each pair went to a feeding.

1. Francisco and José went to the feeding that was closest to **3:00**.
   Animal: Dolphins
   Feeding at: 3:15
2. Alex and Shannon went to the feeding that was closest to **6:00**.
   Animal: Sharks
   Feeding at: 5:45
3. Kim and Amanda went to the feeding that was closest to **5:30**.
   Animal: Dolphins
   Feeding at: 5:20
4. Make up your own time puzzle about the Bayside Aquarium.

92

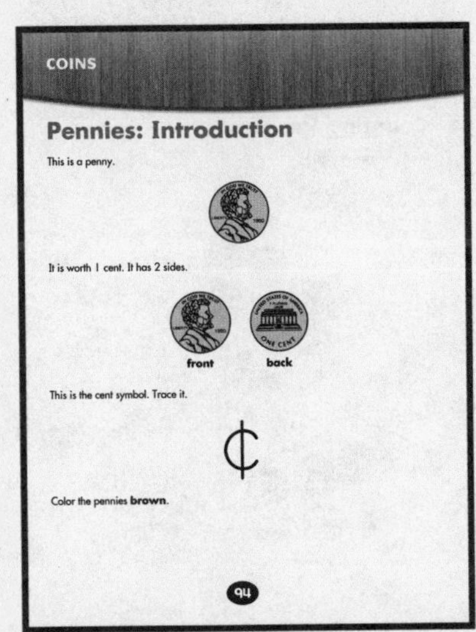
COINS

Pennies: Introduction

This is a penny.

It is worth 1 cent. It has 2 sides.

front back

This is the cent symbol. Trace it.

¢

Color the pennies **brown**.

94

COINS

Pennies: Introduction

Find each penny. Color it **brown**.

How many pennies did you find? 4

95

COINS

Counting Pennies

Count the pennies.

3 pennies = 3¢

5 pennies = 5¢

1 penny = 1¢

96

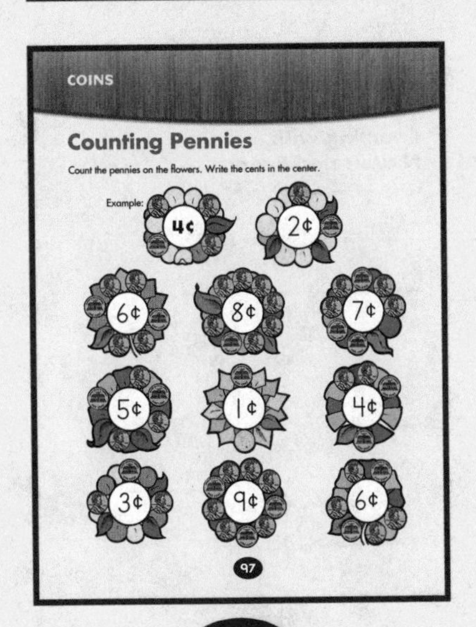
COINS

Counting Pennies

Count the pennies on the flowers. Write the cents in the center.

Example: 4¢ 2¢

6¢ 8¢ 7¢

5¢ 1¢ 4¢

3¢ 9¢ 6¢

97

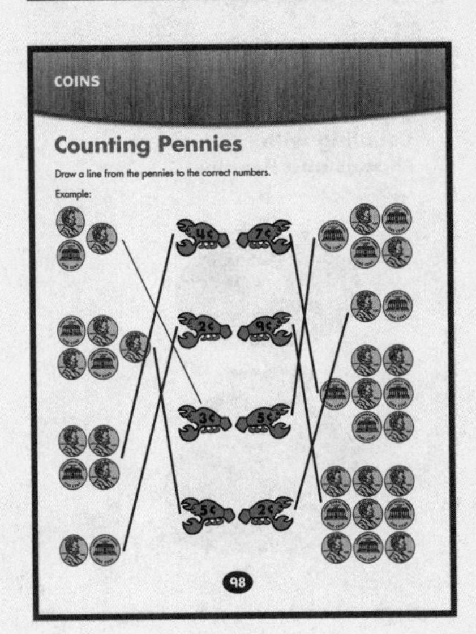
COINS

Counting Pennies

Draw a line from the pennies to the correct numbers.

Example:

98

ANSWER KEY

COINS

Counting Pennies

Write the number of pennies on each bag. Color each penny.

6¢

5¢

99

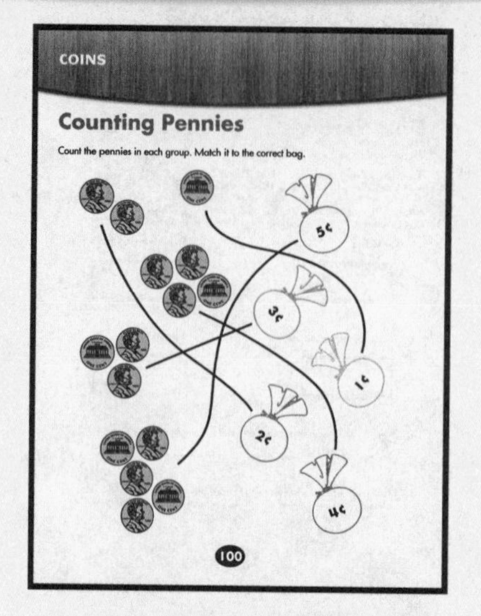
COINS

Counting Pennies

Count the pennies in each group. Match it to the correct bag.

5¢ 3¢ 1¢ 2¢ 4¢

100

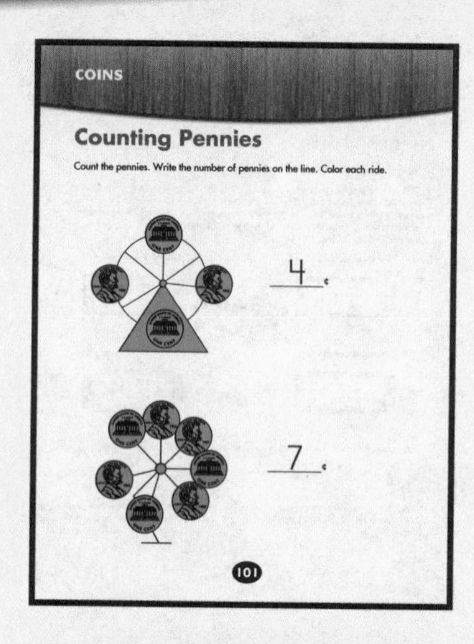
COINS

Counting Pennies

Count the pennies. Write the number of pennies on the line. Color each ride.

4 ¢

7 ¢

101

COINS

Counting Pennies

Count the pennies. Write the number of pennies on the line. Color each ride.

3 ¢

5 ¢

5 ¢

102

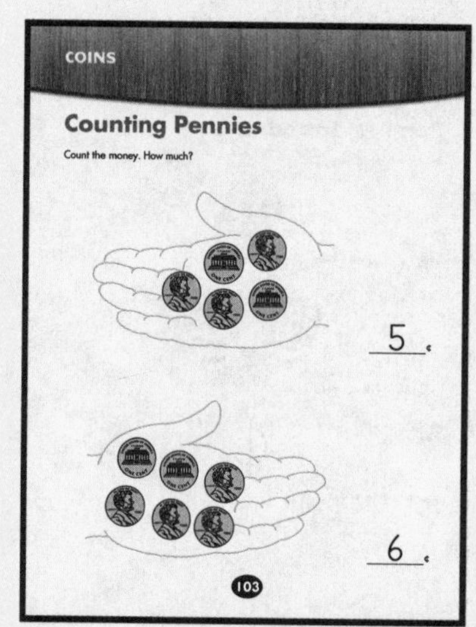
COINS

Counting Pennies

Count the money. How much?

5 ¢

6 ¢

103

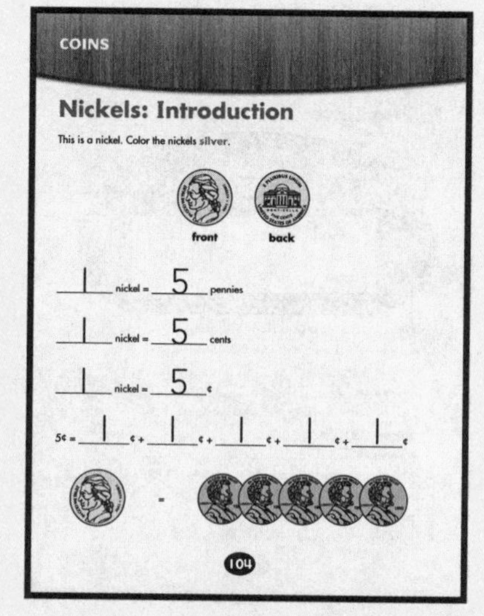
COINS

Nickels: Introduction

This is a nickel. Color the nickels silver.

front back

1 nickel = 5 pennies

1 nickel = 5 cents

1 nickel = 5 ¢

5¢ = 1 ¢ + 1 ¢ + 1 ¢ + 1 ¢ + 1 ¢

104

COINS

Counting with Nickels and Pennies

A nickel is worth 5¢. Count the money.

5 ¢

5 ¢

105

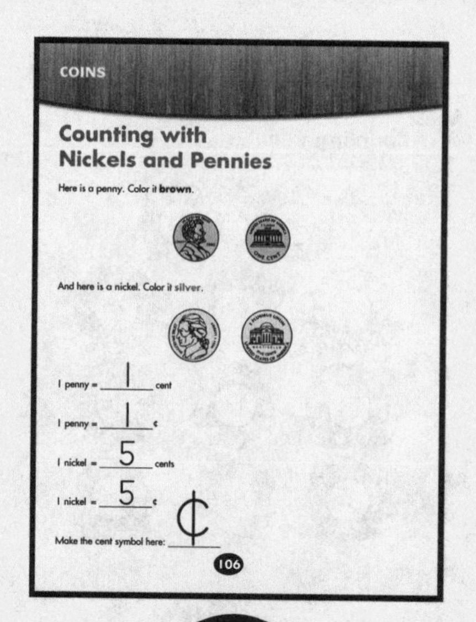
COINS

Counting with Nickels and Pennies

Here is a penny. Color it **brown**.

And here is a nickel. Color it silver.

1 penny = 1 cent

1 penny = 1 ¢

1 nickel = 5 cents

1 nickel = 5 ¢

Make the cent symbol here: ¢

106

COINS

Counting with Nickels and Pennies

Count the money. Start with the nickel. Then, count the pennies. Write the amount.

5 ¢

8 ¢

4 ¢

7 ¢

10 ¢

4 ¢

107

ANSWER KEY

COINS
Counting with Nickels and Pennies
Who has more money? Count the money. Write the amount.
10¢
8¢
Who has more money? Circle the answer.
108

COINS
Counting with Nickels and Pennies
Each nickel is worth 5 cents. Show how much these nickels are worth.
= 5¢
= 5¢
= 5¢ = 10¢
= 5¢
= 5¢
= 5¢ = 15¢
= 5¢
= 5¢
= 5¢
= 5¢ = 20¢
109

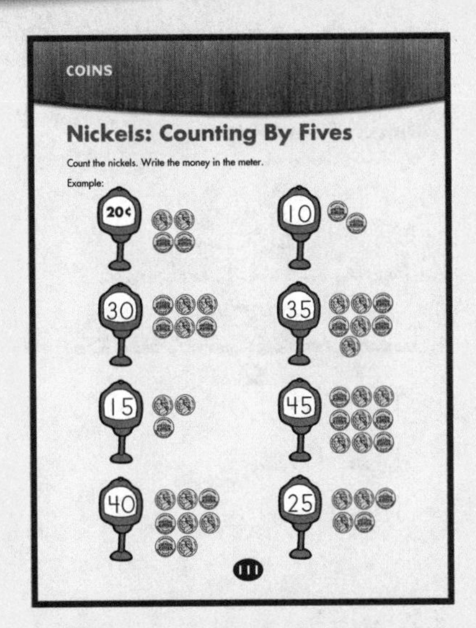

COINS
Nickels: Counting By Fives
Count the nickels. Write the money in the meter.
Example:
20¢
10
30
35
15
45
40
25
111

COINS
Nickels: Counting By Fives
How much money is in each hive?
Example:
20¢
25¢
10¢
30¢
15¢
5¢
35¢
45¢
40¢
112

COINS
Counting with Nickels and Pennies
Count the coins. Write the amount under each bunny's carrot.
Example:
7¢
11¢
17¢
21¢
12¢
14¢
113

COINS
Counting with Nickels and Pennies
Look at the price on each toy. Color it if there are enough nickels.
25¢
30¢
20¢
35¢
114

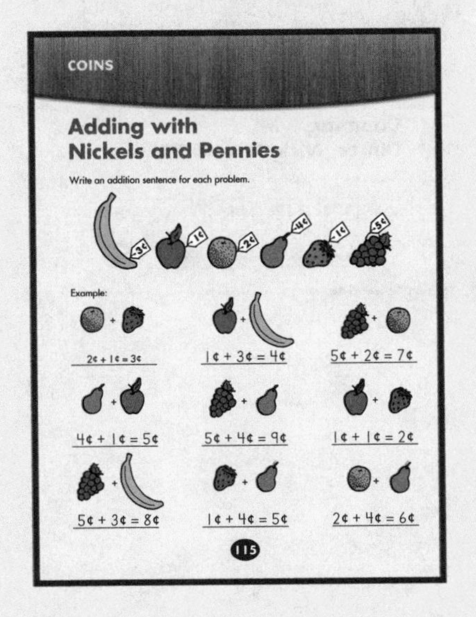

COINS
Adding with Nickels and Pennies
Write an addition sentence for each problem.
3¢
1¢
2¢
4¢
1¢
5¢
Example:
2¢ + 1¢ = 3¢
1¢ + 3¢ = 4¢
5¢ + 2¢ = 7¢
4¢ + 1¢ = 5¢
5¢ + 4¢ = 9¢
1¢ + 1¢ = 2¢
5¢ + 3¢ = 8¢
1¢ + 4¢ = 5¢
2¢ + 4¢ = 6¢
115

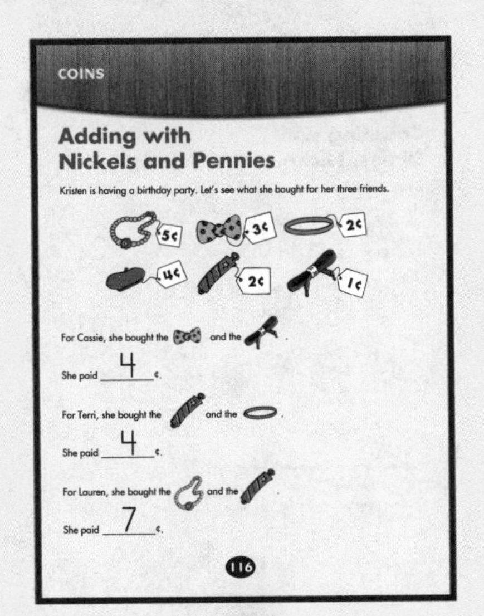

COINS
Adding with Nickels and Pennies
Kristen is having a birthday party. Let's see what she bought for her three friends.
5¢
3¢
2¢
4¢
2¢
1¢
For Cassie, she bought the and the.
She paid 4¢.
For Terri, she bought the and the.
She paid 4¢.
For Lauren, she bought the and the.
She paid 7¢.
116

COINS
Adding with Nickels and Pennies
Use page 116 to help you answer the questions below.
Every birthday party needs balloons. Draw one for each girl, including Kristen.
They cost 5¢ each. Count by fives. She paid 20¢.
She also bought bubble wands. Draw one for each girl.
They cost 2¢ each. Count by twos. She paid 8¢.
Finally! The presents! Color the presents.
117

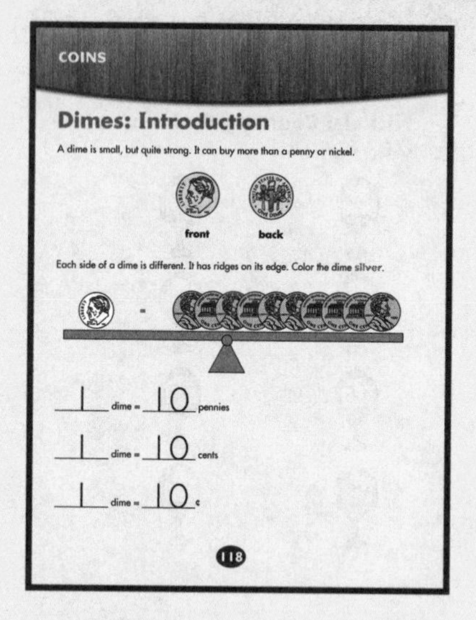
COINS

Dimes: Introduction

A dime is small, but quite strong. It can buy more than a penny or nickel.

front back

Each side of a dime is different. It has ridges on its edge. Color the dime silver.

1 dime = 10 pennies

1 dime = 10 cents

1 dime = 10¢

118

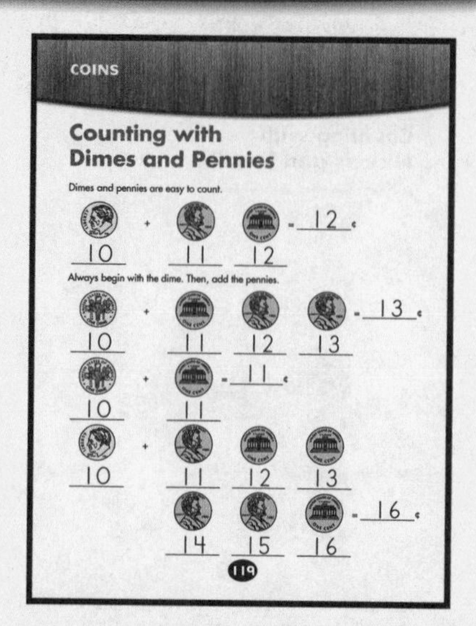
COINS

Counting with Dimes and Pennies

Dimes and pennies are easy to count.

10 + 11 12 = 12¢

Always begin with the dime. Then, add the pennies.

10 + 11 12 13 = 13¢

10 + 11 = 11¢

10 + 11 12 13 14 15 16 = 16¢

119

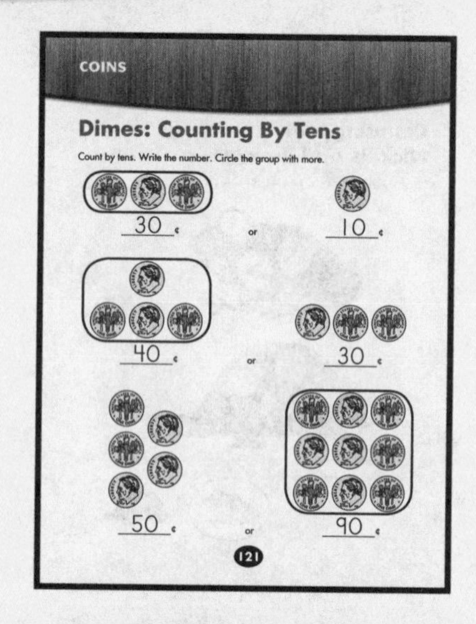
COINS

Dimes: Counting By Tens

Count by tens. Write the number. Circle the group with more.

30¢ or 10¢

40¢ or 30¢

50¢ or 90¢

121

COINS

Counting with Dimes and Pennies

Count the dimes by tens. Then, count the pennies. How much?

Example:

33¢ 24¢ 41¢

52¢ 36¢ 64¢

15¢ 27¢ 18¢

122

COINS

Counting with Dimes and Nickels

Do you like to do tricks? Here is a trick for counting dimes and nickels.

Look carefully at these dimes and nickels. Circle two nickels, then two more, until all the nickels are circled. Then, count by tens to see how much money is here.

I see 90¢

123

COINS

Counting with Dimes, Nickels, and Pennies

Count the money. Start with the dime. Write the amount.

12¢

16¢

Who has more money? Circle the answer.

124

COINS

Counting with Dimes, Nickels, and Pennies

Count the money. Start with the dime. Write the amount.

20¢

15¢

125

COINS

Counting with Dimes, Nickels, and Pennies

Write how many cents.

1. 12¢

2. 16¢

3. 13¢

If you add 1 more penny to number 1, you will have 13¢

If you add 1 more penny to number 2, you will have 17¢

If you add 1 more penny to number 3, you will have 14¢

126

COINS

Counting with Dimes, Nickels, and Pennies

There is a bake sale at school today.

19¢ 12¢ 15¢ 9¢ 8¢

Decide which one you want. In the space below, draw enough money to pay for it.

Answers will vary.

127

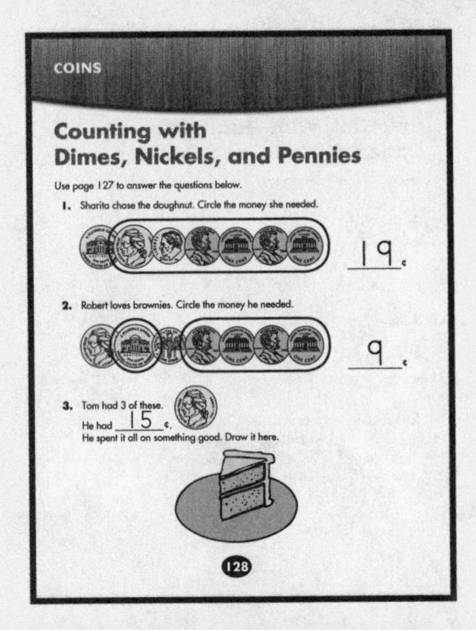
COINS

Counting with Dimes, Nickels, and Pennies

Use page 127 to answer the questions below.

1. Sharita chose the doughnut. Circle the money she needed. 19¢

2. Robert loves brownies. Circle the money he needed. 9¢

3. Tom had 3 of these. He had 15¢. He spent it all on something good. Draw it here.

128

COINS

Counting with Dimes, Nickels, and Pennies

Circle the coins to equal the right amount.

Example:

32¢ 26¢ 21¢ 14¢ 54¢ 31¢ 44¢ 42¢

129

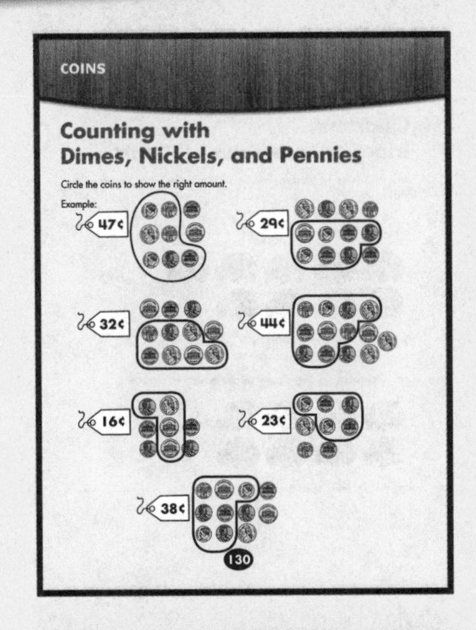
COINS

Counting with Dimes, Nickels, and Pennies

Circle the coins to show the right amount.

Example:

47¢ 29¢ 32¢ 44¢ 16¢ 23¢ 38¢

130

COINS

Subtracting with Dimes, Nickels, and Pennies

Earning money is fun! So is spending it! See what the children buy with their money. Draw an X on the coins needed. Write how much money is left.

José wants: 10¢ He has: 2¢ is left

Catherine wants: 12¢ She has: 10¢ is left

131

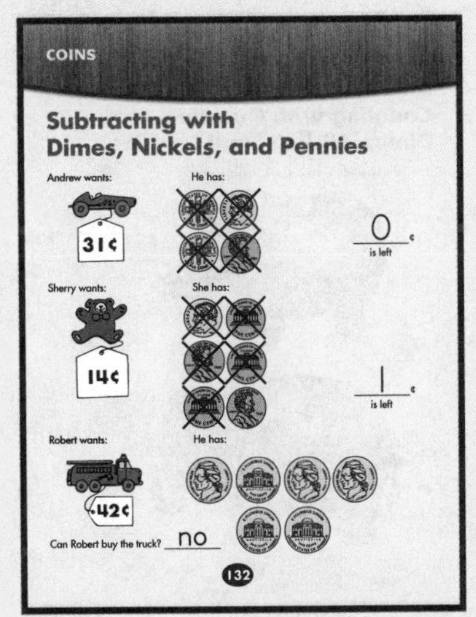
COINS

Subtracting with Dimes, Nickels, and Pennies

Andrew wants: 31¢ He has: 0¢ is left

Sherry wants: 14¢ She has: 1¢ is left

Robert wants: 42¢ He has:

Can Robert buy the truck? no

132

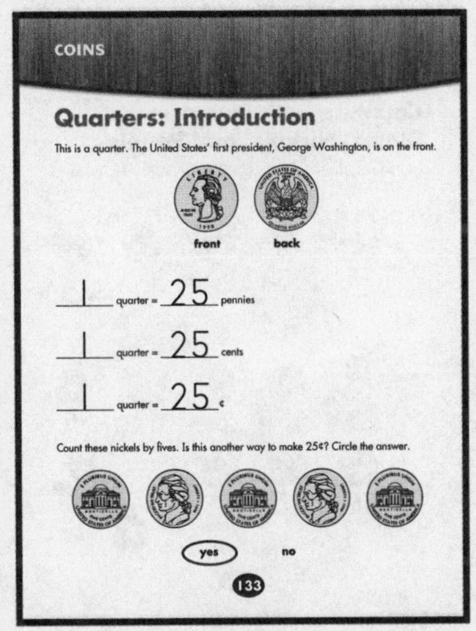
COINS

Quarters: Introduction

This is a quarter. The United States' first president, George Washington, is on the front.

front back

1 quarter = 25 pennies

1 quarter = 25 cents

1 quarter = 25¢

Count these nickels by fives. Is this another way to make 25¢? Circle the answer.

yes no

133

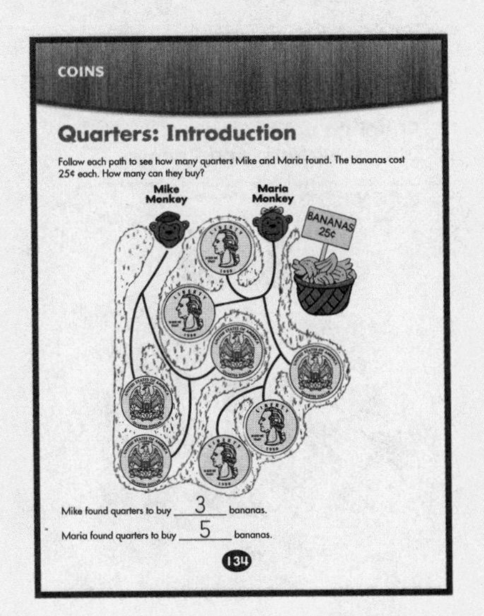
COINS

Quarters: Introduction

Follow each path to see how many quarters Mike and Maria found. The bananas cost 25¢ each. How many can they buy?

Mike Monkey Maria Monkey BANANAS 25¢

Mike found quarters to buy 3 bananas.

Maria found quarters to buy 5 bananas.

134

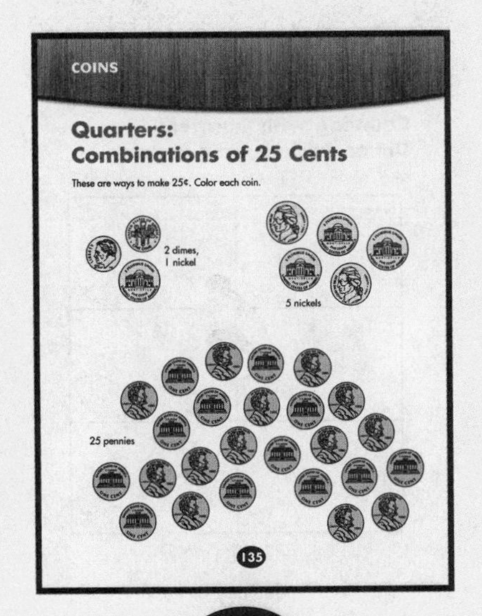
COINS

Quarters: Combinations of 25 Cents

These are ways to make 25¢. Color each coin.

2 dimes, 1 nickel

5 nickels

25 pennies

135

COINS

Quarters: More or Less Than 50 Cents

The tooth fairy left 2 quarters for your shiny baby tooth.

How much money do you have?
Each quarter is worth 25¢.
Two quarters = 50¢

Color each toy you can buy.

49¢ 25¢ 72¢ 60¢ 45¢ 39¢ 5¢

136

COINS

Quarters: More or Less Than 50 Cents

Some children had fun spending the allowance they earned. The boys bought some cars.

Terry paid 5¢ for each blue car. Color Terry's cars blue.

5¢ each

How much did Terry pay for the blue cars? 45 ¢

Lucas liked the red cars. They were the same price. Color his cars red.

5¢ each

How much did Lucas pay for the red cars? 40 ¢

Which boy paid more? Terry

137

COINS

Quarters: More or Less Than 50 Cents

Patty bought some pears at the store. She paid 25¢ for each pear. Color the pears.

25¢ each

Draw the quarters she spent.

How much money did she spend? 50 ¢

Jennifer bought these bananas. She paid 10¢ for each one. Color the bananas.

10¢ each

Draw the dimes she spent.

How much money did she spend? 70 ¢

Which girl spent less? Patty

138

COINS

Counting with Quarters, Dimes, Nickels, and Pennies

Count the money. Write the amount.

1. 25 ¢ 35 ¢ 45 ¢ — 45 ¢ Total

2. 25 ¢ 50 ¢ 55 ¢ — 55 ¢ Total

3. Put more than 50¢ in the bank. Show the coins.

Answers will vary.

___ ¢ Total

140

COINS

Counting with Quarters, Dimes, Nickels, and Pennies

Count the money. Start with the quarters. Then, count the dimes, nickels, and pennies.

1. 25 ¢ 35 ¢ 40 ¢ 41 ¢ 42 ¢ Total

2. 25 ¢ 35 ¢ 45 ¢ 50 ¢ 55 ¢

56 ¢ 57 ¢ 58 ¢ Total

141

COINS

Counting with Quarters, Dimes, Nickels, and Pennies

Count the money. Start with the quarter. Write the amount.

36 ¢

31 ¢

142

COINS

Counting with Quarters, Dimes, Nickels, and Pennies

Count the money. Start with the quarter. Write the amount.

40 ¢

35 ¢

143

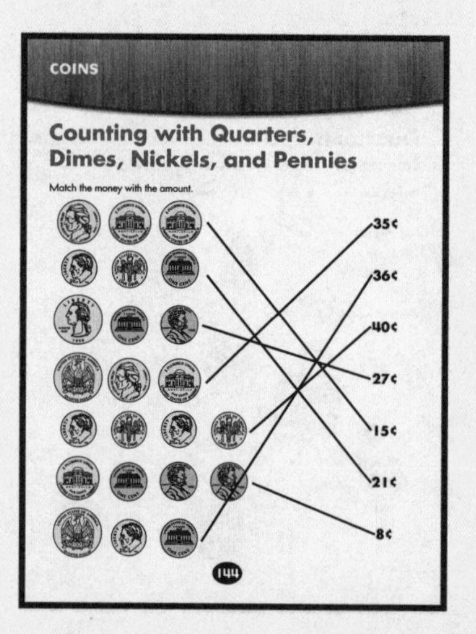
COINS

Counting with Quarters, Dimes, Nickels, and Pennies

Match the money with the amount.

35¢

36¢

40¢

27¢

15¢

21¢

8¢

144

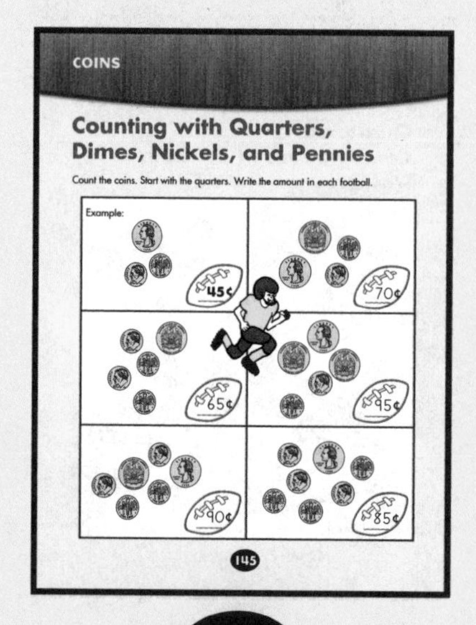
COINS

Counting with Quarters, Dimes, Nickels, and Pennies

Count the coins. Start with the quarters. Write the amount in each football.

Example: 45¢

70¢

65¢

95¢

90¢

85¢

145

COINS

Counting with Quarters, Dimes, Nickels, and Pennies

Carolyn and Marilyn are going to the beach for their vacation. The twins wanted to buy some things to take along. They emptied their piggy banks.

146

ANSWER KEY

COINS

Counting with Quarters, Dimes, Nickels, and Pennies

Use page 146 to help you answer the questions below.

Cross off the money Carolyn and Marilyn used for:

45¢ 45¢

Color the pails pink.

Cross off the money they used for:

26¢ 26¢

Color the beach balls red and yellow.

Cross off the money they used for:

35¢ 35¢

Color the beach towels blue and green.

Cross off the money they used for:

47¢ 47¢

Color the sunglasses.

Did they have enough money? no

147

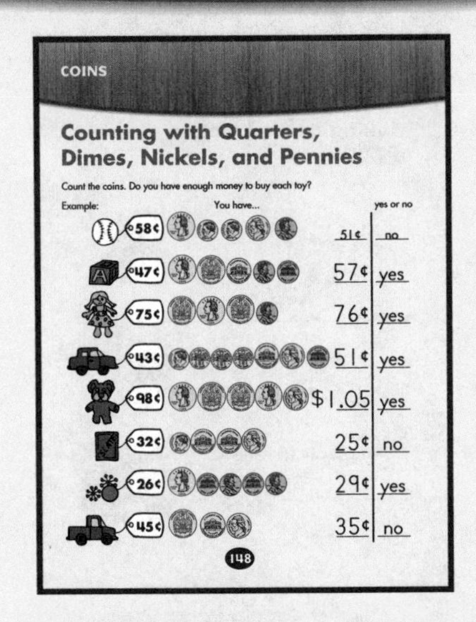
COINS

Counting with Quarters, Dimes, Nickels, and Pennies

Count the coins. Do you have enough money to buy each toy?

Price	You have...	yes or no
Example: 58¢	51¢	no
47¢	57¢	yes
75¢	76¢	yes
43¢	51¢	yes
98¢	$1.05	yes
32¢	25¢	no
26¢	29¢	yes
45¢	35¢	no

148

COINS

Counting with Quarters, Dimes, Nickels, and Pennies

It is fun to buy things to keep your hair looking great!

29¢ 20¢ 13¢ 35¢ 32¢

How many of each coin do you need? Write 1, 2, 3, or 4.

	Quarters	Dimes	Nickels	Pennies
(32¢)	1		1	2
(35¢)	1	1		
(29¢)	1			4
(13¢)		1		3
(20¢)		2		

149

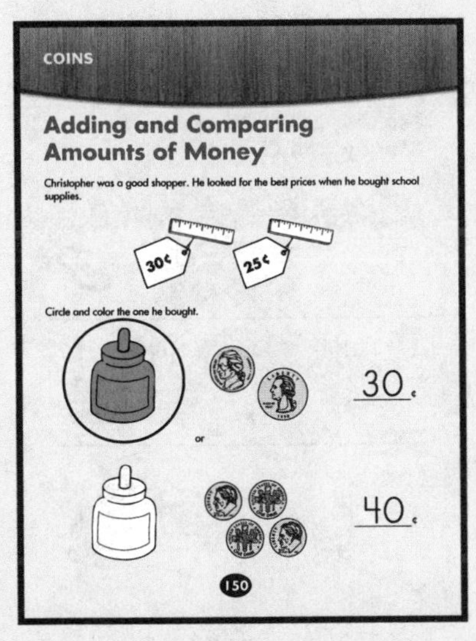
COINS

Adding and Comparing Amounts of Money

Christopher was a good shopper. He looked for the best prices when he bought school supplies.

30¢ 25¢

Circle and color the one he bought.

30¢

or

40¢

150

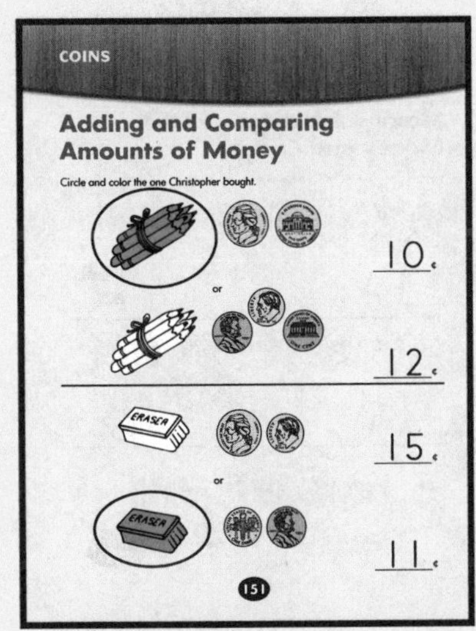
COINS

Adding and Comparing Amounts of Money

Circle and color the one Christopher bought.

10¢

or

12¢

15¢

or

11¢

151

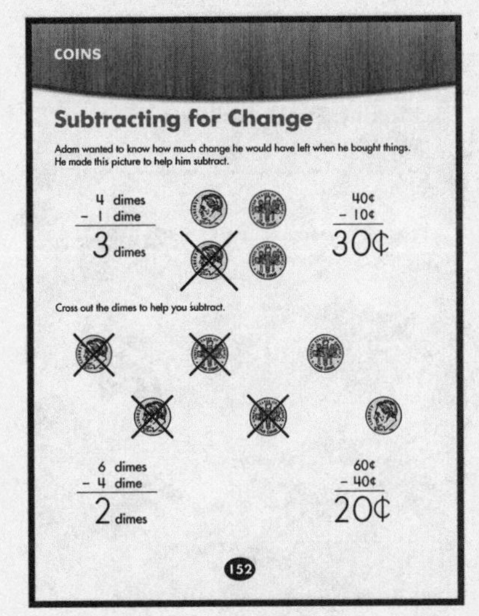
COINS

Subtracting for Change

Adam wanted to know how much change he would have left when he bought things. He made this picture to help him subtract.

4 dimes − 1 dime = 3 dimes

40¢ − 10¢ = 30¢

Cross out the dimes to help you subtract.

6 dimes − 4 dime = 2 dimes

60¢ − 40¢ = 20¢

152

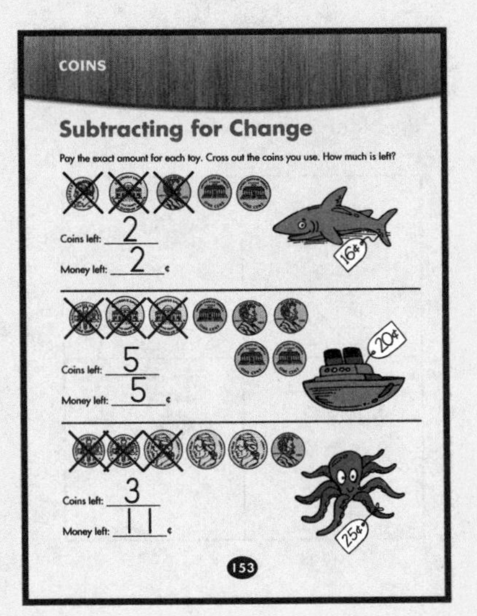
COINS

Subtracting for Change

Pay the exact amount for each toy. Cross out the coins you use. How much is left?

16¢ — Coins left: 2 — Money left: 2¢

20¢ — Coins left: 5 — Money left: 5¢

25¢ — Coins left: 3 — Money left: 11¢

153

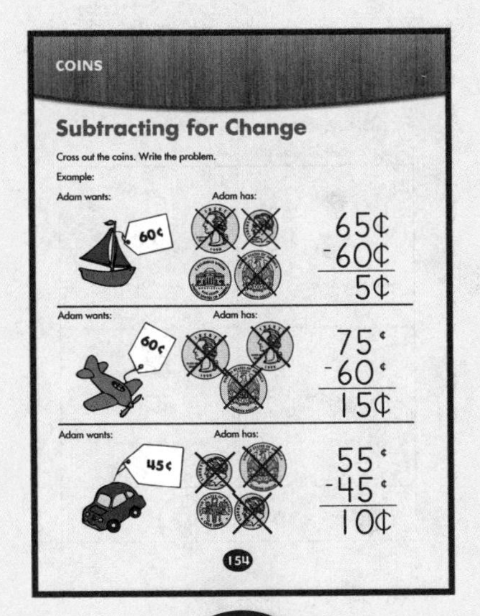
COINS

Subtracting for Change

Cross out the coins. Write the problem.

Example:

Adam wants: 60¢ — Adam has: 65¢ − 60¢ = 5¢

Adam wants: 60¢ — Adam has: 75¢ − 60¢ = 15¢

Adam wants: 45¢ — Adam has: 55¢ − 45¢ = 10¢

154

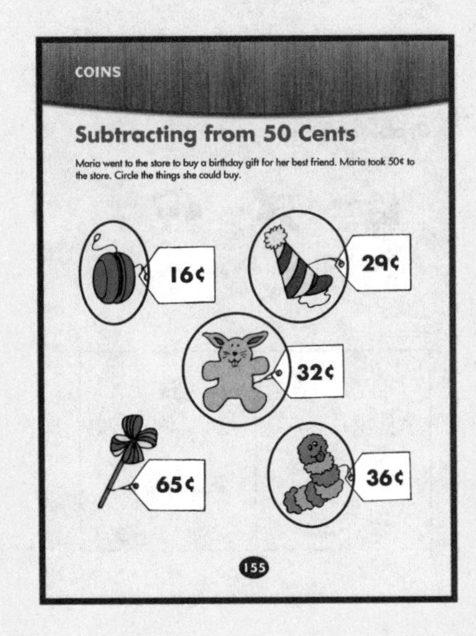
COINS

Subtracting from 50 Cents

Maria went to the store to buy a birthday gift for her best friend. Maria took 50¢ to the store. Circle the things she could buy.

16¢ 29¢ 32¢ 65¢ 36¢

155

ANSWER KEY

COINS

Subtracting from 50 Cents

Maria wanted to know how much change she would get back from each toy. Color the toy you think Maria chose.

Answers will vary.

16¢ — 50¢ − 16¢ = 34¢

29¢ — 50¢ − 29¢ = 21¢

32¢ — 50¢ − 32¢ = 18¢

36¢ — 50¢ − 36¢ = 14¢

156

COINS

Making Exact Amounts of Money

Use dimes, nickels, and pennies. Pay the exact amount for each toy.

1. What coins did you use?
1 dimes ___ nickels ___ pennies (10¢)

2. What coins did you use?
1 dimes 1 nickels 4 pennies (19¢)

3. Solve this puzzle. What coins did Cat use to pay for the ball?
1 dimes 1 nickels ___ pennies

157

COINS

Making Exact Amounts of Money

Use dimes, nickels, and pennies. Pay the exact amount for each toy.

1. What coins did you use?
2 dimes ___ nickels 1 pennies (21¢)

2. What coins did you use?
1 quarters 1 dimes ___ nickels 2 pennies (37¢)

3. Solve this puzzle. What coins did Alligator use to pay for the toothbrush?
1 dimes 2 nickels ___ pennies

158

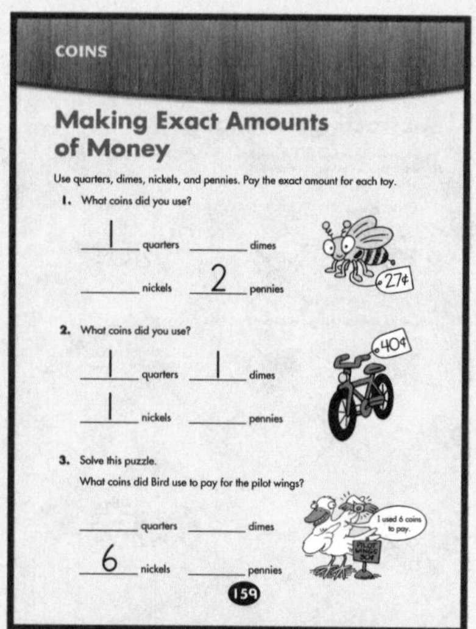
COINS

Making Exact Amounts of Money

Use quarters, dimes, nickels, and pennies. Pay the exact amount for each toy.

1. What coins did you use?
1 quarters ___ dimes ___ nickels 2 pennies (27¢)

2. What coins did you use?
1 quarters 1 dimes 1 nickels ___ pennies (40¢)

3. Solve this puzzle. What coins did Bird use to pay for the pilot wings?
___ quarters ___ dimes 6 nickels ___ pennies

159

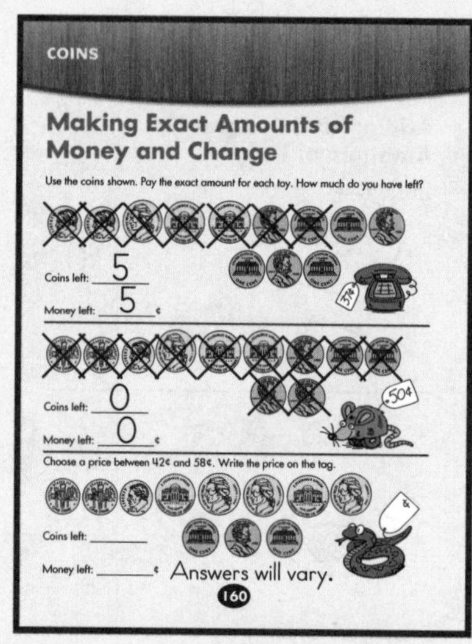
COINS

Making Exact Amounts of Money and Change

Use the coins shown. Pay the exact amount for each toy. How much do you have left?

Coins left: 5
Money left: 5¢ (37¢)

Coins left: 0
Money left: 0¢ (50¢)

Choose a price between 42¢ and 58¢. Write the price on the tag.

Coins left: ___
Money left: ___¢

Answers will vary.

160

COINS

Making Exact Amounts of Money and Change

Use the coins shown. Pay the exact amount for each toy.

Coins left: 2
Money left: 2¢ (40¢)

Coins left: 6
Money left: 10¢ (53¢)

Solve this puzzle. How much money does Turtle have left?

Coins left: 1
Money left: 5¢

161

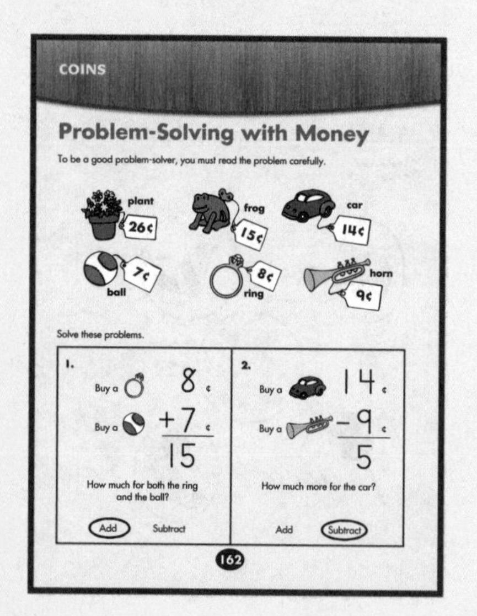
COINS

Problem-Solving with Money

To be a good problem-solver, you must read the problem carefully.

Solve these problems.

1. Buy a ring 8¢. Buy a ball +7¢. 15. How much for both the ring and the ball? (Add) Subtract

2. Buy a car 14¢. Buy a horn −9¢. 5. How much more for the car? Add (Subtract)

162

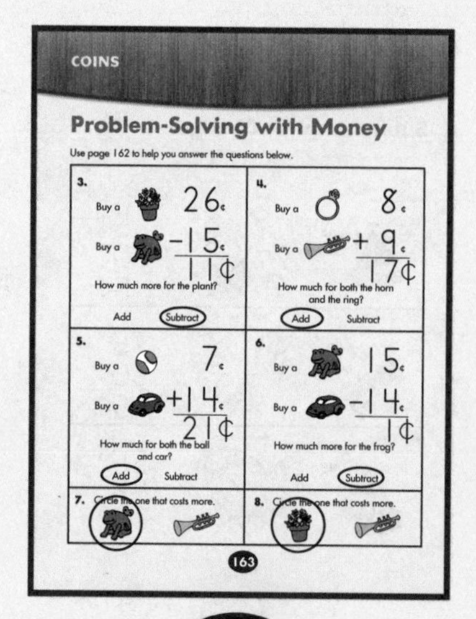
COINS

Problem-Solving with Money

Use page 162 to help you answer the questions below.

3. Buy a plant 26¢. Buy a frog −15¢. 11¢. How much more for the plant? Add (Subtract)

4. Buy a ring 8¢. Buy a horn +9¢. 17¢. How much for both the horn and the ring? (Add) Subtract

5. Buy a ball 7¢. Buy a car +14¢. 21¢. How much for both the ball and car? (Add) Subtract

6. Buy a frog 15¢. Buy a car −14¢. 1¢. How much more for the frog? Add (Subtract)

7. Circle the one that costs more. (frog)

8. Circle the one that costs more. (plant)

163

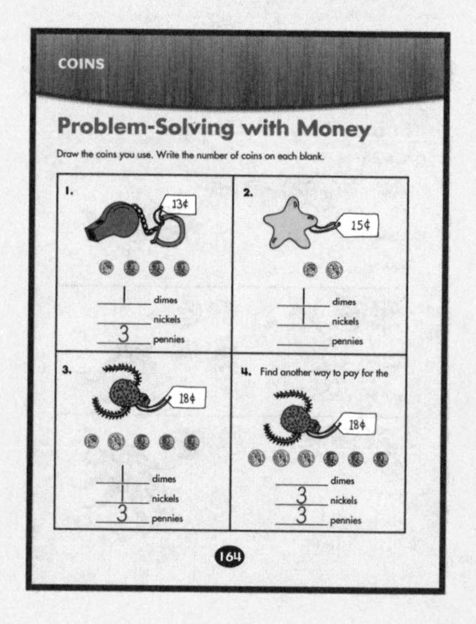
COINS

Problem-Solving with Money

Draw the coins you use. Write the number of coins on each blank.

1. 13¢ — 1 dimes ___ nickels 3 pennies

2. 15¢ — 1 dimes 1 nickels ___ pennies

3. 18¢ — 1 dimes 1 nickels 3 pennies

4. Find another way to pay for the 18¢ — ___ dimes 3 nickels 3 pennies

164

ANSWER KEY

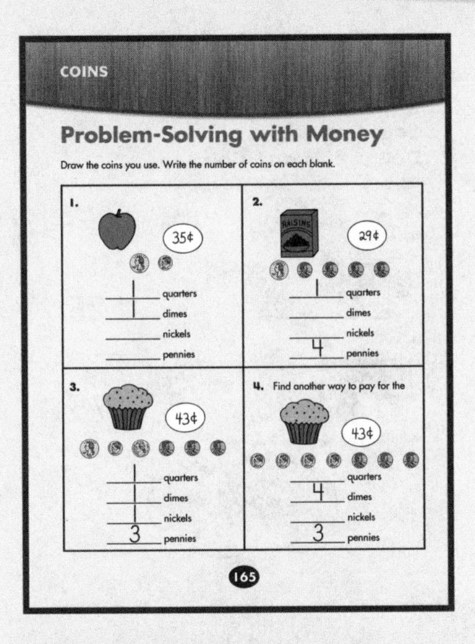
COINS

Problem-Solving with Money

Draw the coins you use. Write the number of coins on each blank.

1. 35¢ — 1 quarters, 1 dimes, ___ nickels, ___ pennies
2. 29¢ — 1 quarters, ___ dimes, ___ nickels, 4 pennies
3. 43¢ — 1 quarters, 1 dimes, 1 nickels, 3 pennies
4. Find another way to pay for the 43¢ — ___ quarters, 4 dimes, ___ nickels, 3 pennies

165

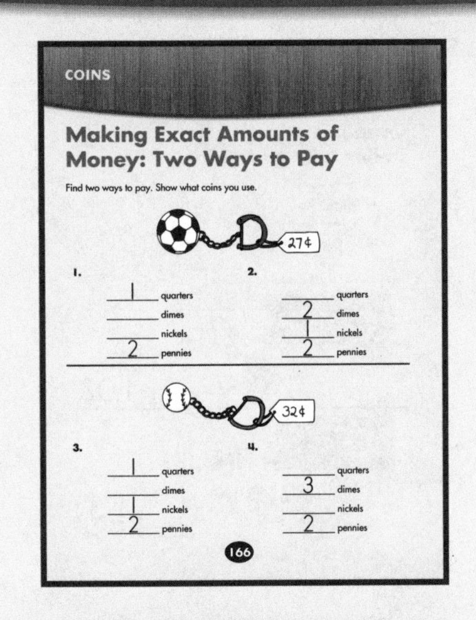
COINS

Making Exact Amounts of Money: Two Ways to Pay

Find two ways to pay. Show what coins you use.

27¢

1. 1 quarters, ___ dimes, ___ nickels, 2 pennies
2. ___ quarters, 2 dimes, 1 nickels, 2 pennies

32¢

3. 1 quarters, ___ dimes, 1 nickels, 2 pennies
4. ___ quarters, 3 dimes, ___ nickels, 2 pennies

166

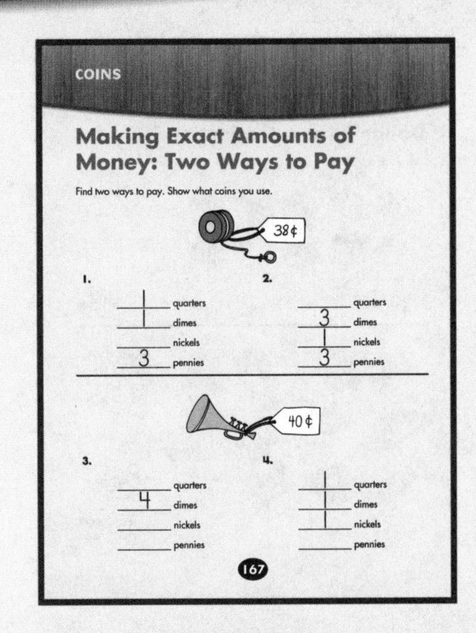
COINS

Making Exact Amounts of Money: Two Ways to Pay

Find two ways to pay. Show what coins you use.

38¢

1. 1 quarters, 1 dimes, ___ nickels, 3 pennies
2. ___ quarters, 3 dimes, 1 nickels, 3 pennies

40¢

3. ___ quarters, 4 dimes, ___ nickels, ___ pennies
4. 1 quarters, 1 dimes, 1 nickels, ___ pennies

167

COINS

Making Exact Amounts of Money: How Much More?

Count the coins. Find out how much more money you need to pay the exact amount.

How much money do you have? 25¢

How much more money do you need? 25¢

How much money do you have? 11¢

How much more money do you need? 49¢

Solve this puzzle.

How much more money does Monkey need? 10¢

168

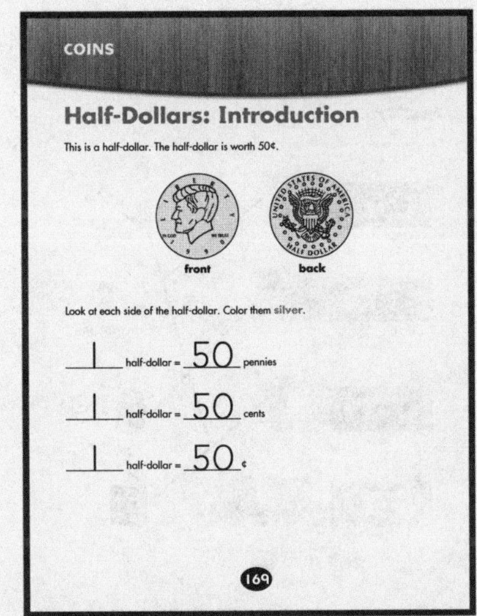
COINS

Half-Dollars: Introduction

This is a half-dollar. The half-dollar is worth 50¢.

front back

Look at each side of the half-dollar. Color them silver.

1 half-dollar = 50 pennies

1 half-dollar = 50 cents

1 half-dollar = 50¢

169

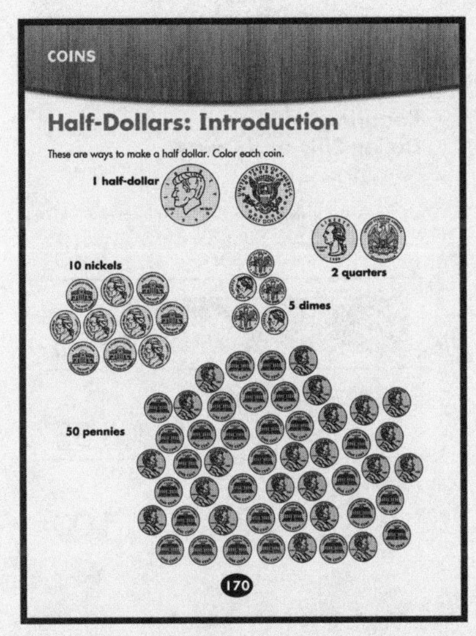
COINS

Half-Dollars: Introduction

These are ways to make a half dollar. Color each coin.

1 half-dollar

2 quarters

10 nickels

5 dimes

50 pennies

170

COINS

Counting Half-Dollars, Quarters, Dimes, Nickels, and Pennies

Count the money. Write each amount. A half-dollar is worth 50¢ or $.50

1. 50 60 70 — 70¢
2. 50 75 85 90 — 90¢
3. Draw between 50¢ and 90¢ in the jar.

Answers will vary.

171

COINS

Counting Coins: How Much More?

Count the coins. Find out how much more money you need to pay the exact amount.

How much money do you have? 75¢

How much more money do you need? 15¢

How much money do you have? 70¢

How much more money do you need? 29¢

Solve this puzzle.

How much more money does Alligator need? 1¢

172

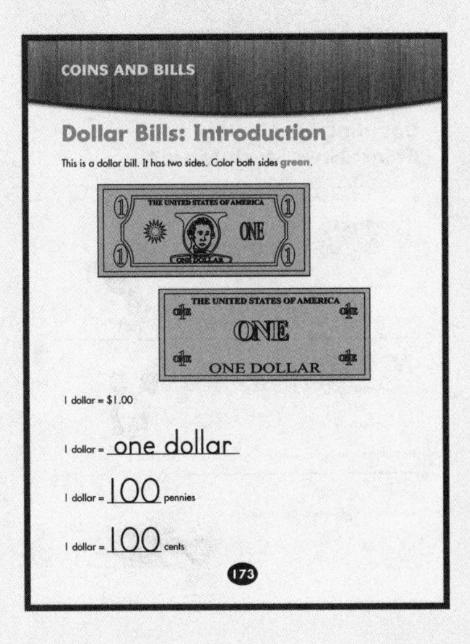
COINS AND BILLS

Dollar Bills: Introduction

This is a dollar bill. It has two sides. Color both sides green.

1 dollar = $1.00

1 dollar = one dollar

1 dollar = 100 pennies

1 dollar = 100 cents

173

ANSWER KEY

COINS AND BILLS

Dollar Bills: Introduction

Count each set of coins. If it equals one dollar, write $1.00 on the line.

Count by tens with dimes. $1.00

Count by fives with nickels. $1.00

176

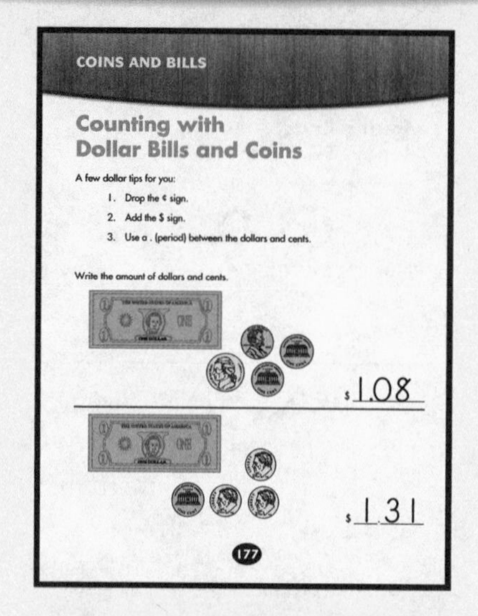

COINS AND BILLS

Counting with Dollar Bills and Coins

A few dollar tips for you:

1. Drop the ¢ sign.
2. Add the $ sign.
3. Use a . (period) between the dollars and cents.

Write the amount of dollars and cents.

$ 1.08

$ 1.31

177

COINS AND BILLS

Counting with Dollar Bills and Coins

Count the money. Write each amount.

A one-dollar bill is worth 100¢ or $1.00.

1. $1.00 25 $ 1.25

2. $1.00 50 25 $ 1.75

3. Draw $2.00 in the bank. Use a one-dollar bill.

Answers will vary.

178

COINS AND BILLS

Counting with Dollar Bills and Coins

Count the money. Write each amount.

$ 1.25

$ 2.00

$ 1.35

$ 1.00

179

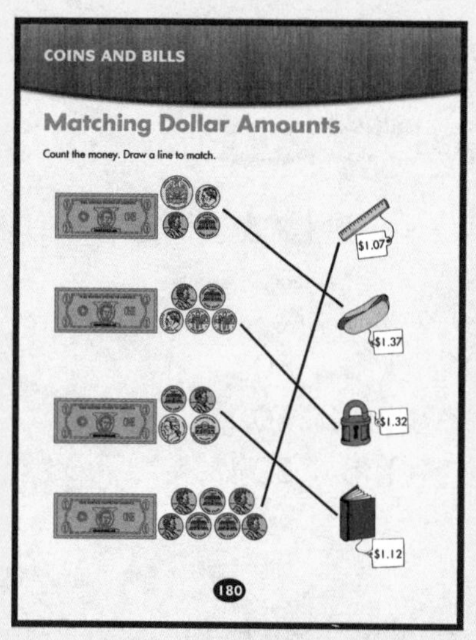

COINS AND BILLS

Matching Dollar Amounts

Count the money. Draw a line to match.

$1.07

$1.37

$1.32

$1.12

180

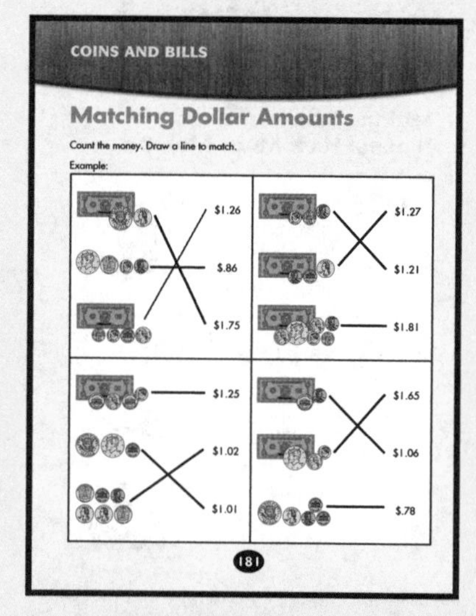

COINS AND BILLS

Matching Dollar Amounts

Count the money. Draw a line to match.

Example:

$1.26

$.86

$1.75

$1.27

$1.21

$1.81

$1.25

$1.02

$1.01

$1.65

$1.06

$.78

181

COINS AND BILLS

Counting Dollar Bills and Coins: How Much More?

Count the coins and bills. Find out how much more money you need to pay the exact amount.

How much money do you have? 1.27 ¢

How much more money do you need? 40 ¢

How much money do you have? 1.45 ¢

How much more money do you need? 30 ¢

Solve this puzzle.

How much more money does Anteater need?

25 ¢

182

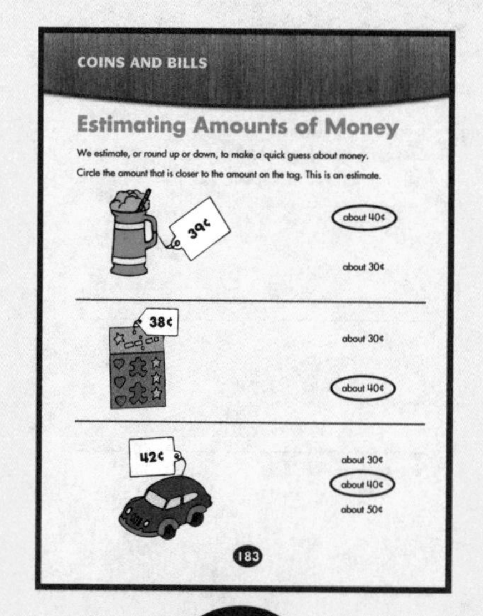

COINS AND BILLS

Estimating Amounts of Money

We estimate, or round up or down, to make a quick guess about money.

Circle the amount that is closer to the amount on the tag. This is an estimate.

39¢ — (about 40¢) / about 30¢

38¢ — about 30¢ / (about 40¢)

42¢ — about 30¢ / (about 40¢) / about 50¢

183

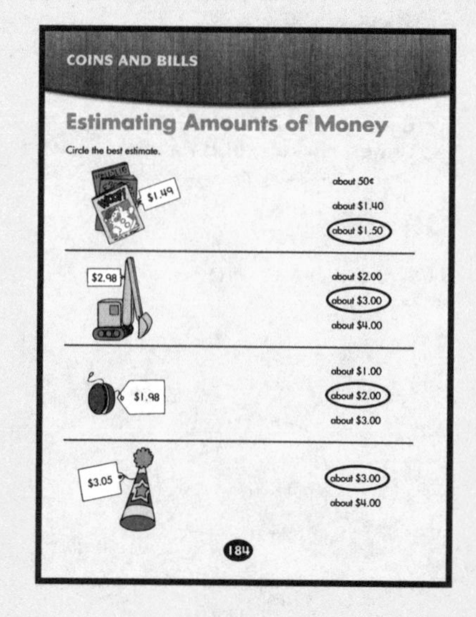

COINS AND BILLS

Estimating Amounts of Money

Circle the best estimate.

$1.49 — about 50¢ / about $1.40 / (about $1.50)

$2.98 — about $2.00 / (about $3.00) / about $4.00

$1.98 — about $1.00 / (about $2.00) / about $3.00

$3.05 — (about $3.00) / about $4.00

184

ANSWER KEY

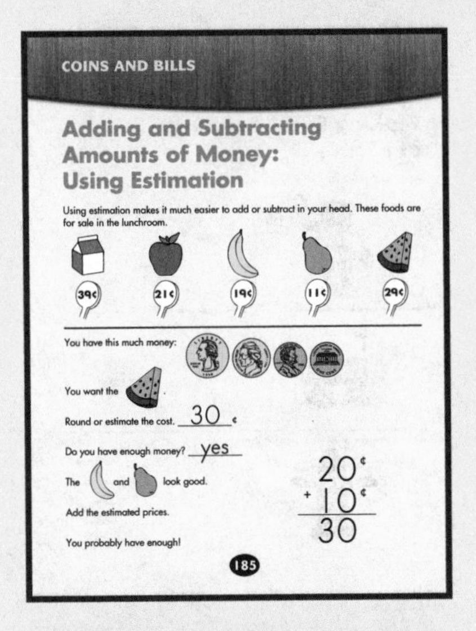

COINS AND BILLS

Adding and Subtracting Amounts of Money: Using Estimation

Using estimation makes it much easier to add or subtract in your head. These foods are for sale in the lunchroom.

39¢ 21¢ 19¢ 11¢ 29¢

You have this much money:

You want the

Round or estimate the cost. 30 ¢

Do you have enough money? yes

The and look good.

Add the estimated prices.

You probably have enough!

20¢
+ 10¢
30

185

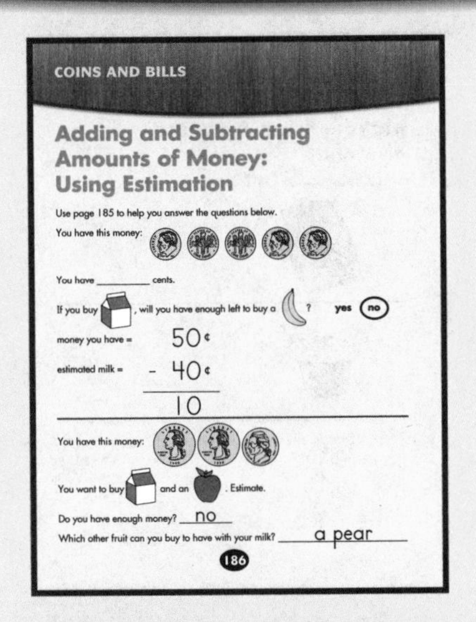

COINS AND BILLS

Adding and Subtracting Amounts of Money: Using Estimation

Use page 185 to help you answer the questions below.

You have this money:

You have ______ cents.

If you buy , will you have enough left to buy a ? yes (no)

money you have = 50¢

estimated milk = - 40¢

10

You have this money:

You want to buy and an . Estimate.

Do you have enough money? no

Which other fruit can you buy to have with your milk? a pear

186

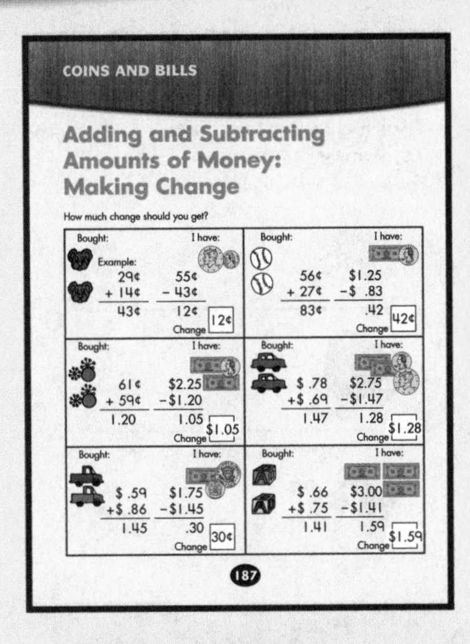

COINS AND BILLS

Adding and Subtracting Amounts of Money: Making Change

How much change should you get?

Bought:	I have:	Bought:	I have:
Example: 29¢ + 14¢ = 43¢	55¢ − 43¢ = 12¢ Change 12¢	56¢ + 27¢ = 83¢	$1.25 − $ .83 = .42 Change 42¢
61¢ + 59¢ = 1.20	$2.25 − $1.20 = 1.05 Change $1.05	$ .78 + $ .69 = 1.47	$2.75 − $1.47 = 1.28 Change $1.28
$ .59 + $ .86 = 1.45	$1.75 − $1.45 = .30 Change 30¢	$ .66 + $ .75 = 1.41	$3.00 − $1.41 = 1.59 Change $1.59

187

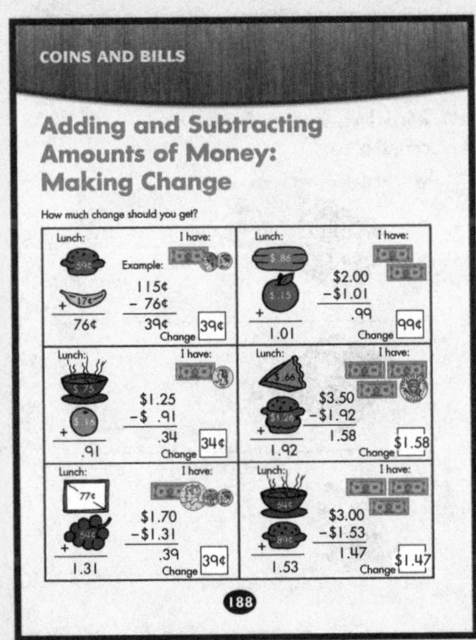

COINS AND BILLS

Adding and Subtracting Amounts of Money: Making Change

How much change should you get?

Lunch:	I have:	Lunch:	I have:
Example: 76¢	115¢ − 76¢ = 39¢ Change 39¢	1.01	$2.00 − $1.01 = .99 Change 99¢
.91	$1.25 − $ .91 = .34 Change 34¢	1.92	$3.50 − $1.92 = 1.58 Change $1.58
1.31	$1.70 − $1.31 = .39 Change 39¢	1.53	$3.00 − $1.53 = 1.47 Change $1.47

188

COINS AND BILLS

Making Change: Money Puzzles

Solve the puzzles. Show how much change you get.

1. Use 2 quarters. Pay 45¢. What change will you get? 5¢
2. Use 1 quarter, 2 dimes, and 2 nickels. Pay 53¢. What change will you get? 2¢
3. Use 3 quarters and 1 dime. Pay 76¢. What change will you get? 9¢
4. Use 3 quarters and 2 nickels. Pay 82¢. What change will you get? 3¢

189

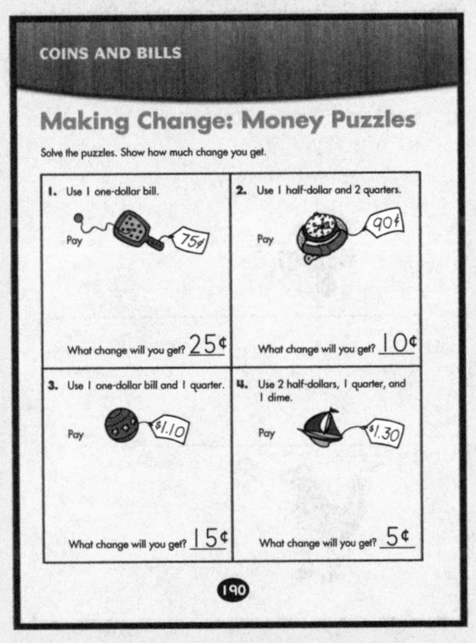

COINS AND BILLS

Making Change: Money Puzzles

Solve the puzzles. Show how much change you get.

1. Use 1 one-dollar bill. Pay 75¢. What change will you get? 25¢
2. Use 1 half-dollar and 2 quarters. Pay 90¢. What change will you get? 10¢
3. Use 1 one-dollar bill and 1 quarter. Pay $1.10. What change will you get? 15¢
4. Use 2 half-dollars, 1 quarter, and 1 dime. Pay $1.30. What change will you get? 5¢

190

COINS AND BILLS

Making Change: Money Puzzles

Solve the puzzles. Show how much change you get.

1. Use 3 half-dollars. Pay $1.12. What change will you get? 38¢
2. Use 1 one-dollar bill, 2 quarters, and 1 dime. Pay $1.54. What change will you get? 6¢
3. Use 1 one-dollar bill, 1 half-dollar, and 1 quarter. Pay $1.68. What change will you get? 7¢
4. Use 1 one-dollar bill and 2 half-dollars. Pay $1.51. What change will you get? 49¢

191

COINS AND BILLS

Making Change: Money Puzzles

Solve the puzzles. Show how much change you get.

1. Use 2 one-dollar bills. Pay $1.59. What change will you get? 41¢
2. Use 2 one-dollar bills. Pay $1.85. What change will you get? 15¢
3. Use 3 one-dollar bills. Pay $2.65. What change will you get? 35¢
4. Use 3 one-dollar bills. Pay $2.06. What change will you get? 94¢

192

COINS AND BILLS

Making Change: Money Puzzles

Solve the puzzles. Show how much change you get.

1. Use 4 one-dollar bills. Pay $3.55. What change will you get? 45¢
2. Use 5 one-dollar bills. Pay $4.15. What change will you get? 85¢
3. Use 3 one-dollar bills. Pay $2.80. What change will you get? 20¢
4. Use 2 one-dollar bills. Pay $1.95. What change will you get? 5¢

193

ANSWER KEY

COINS AND BILLS

Making Exact Amounts of Money

Pay for each toy. Show what coins you use.

60¢: 2 quarters, 1 dimes, ___ nickels, ___ pennies

55¢: 2 quarters, ___ dimes, 1 nickels, ___ pennies

Choose the price. Write it on the tag. Answers will vary.

¢: ___ quarters, ___ dimes, ___ nickels, ___ pennies

194

COINS AND BILLS

Making Exact Amounts of Money

Pay for each snack. Show what coins you use.

65¢: ___ quarters, 6 dimes, 1 nickels, ___ pennies

49¢: ___ quarters, 4 dimes, ___ nickels, 4 pennies

Choose the price. Write it on the tag. Answers will vary.

¢: ___ quarters, ___ dimes, ___ nickels, ___ pennies

195

COINS AND BILLS

Making Exact Amounts of Money

Pay for each robot. Show what coins you use.

85¢: 1 half-dollars, ___ quarters, 3 dimes, 1 nickels, ___ pennies

$1.00: 2 half-dollars, ___ quarters, ___ dimes, ___ nickels, ___ pennies

Choose the price. Write it on the tag. Answers will vary.

___ half-dollars, ___ quarters, ___ dimes, ___ nickels, ___ pennies

196

COINS AND BILLS

Making Exact Amounts of Money

Pay for each animal. Show what coins you use.

$1.50: 3 half-dollars, ___ quarters, ___ dimes, ___ nickels, ___ pennies

$1.35: 2 half-dollars, ___ quarters, 3 dimes, 1 nickels, ___ pennies

Choose the price. Write it on the tag. Answers will vary.

___ half-dollars, ___ quarters, ___ dimes, ___ nickels, ___ pennies

197

COINS AND BILLS

Making Exact Amounts of Money

Pay for each toy. Show what money you use.

$1.30: 1 dollars, ___ half-dollars, ___ quarters, 3 dimes, ___ nickels, ___ pennies

$1.55: 1 dollars, 1 half-dollars, ___ quarters, ___ dimes, 1 nickels, ___ pennies

Choose the price. Write it on the tag. Answers will vary.

___ dollars, ___ half-dollars, ___ quarters, ___ dimes, ___ nickels, ___ pennies

198

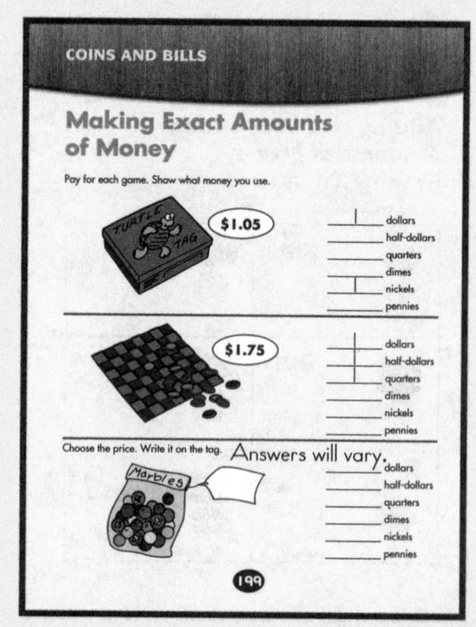
COINS AND BILLS

Making Exact Amounts of Money

Pay for each game. Show what money you use.

$1.05: 1 dollars, ___ half-dollars, ___ quarters, ___ dimes, 1 nickels, ___ pennies

$1.75: 1 dollars, 1 half-dollars, 1 quarters, ___ dimes, ___ nickels, ___ pennies

Choose the price. Write it on the tag. Answers will vary.

___ dollars, ___ half-dollars, ___ quarters, ___ dimes, ___ nickels, ___ pennies

199

MONEY REVIEW

Using Combinations of Coins to Pay

Pay for each cookie. Use as few coins as you can.

					Number of Coins Used
28¢	1			3	4
39¢	1	1		4	6
49¢	1	2		4	7
Choose the price. ¢	Answers will vary.				

200

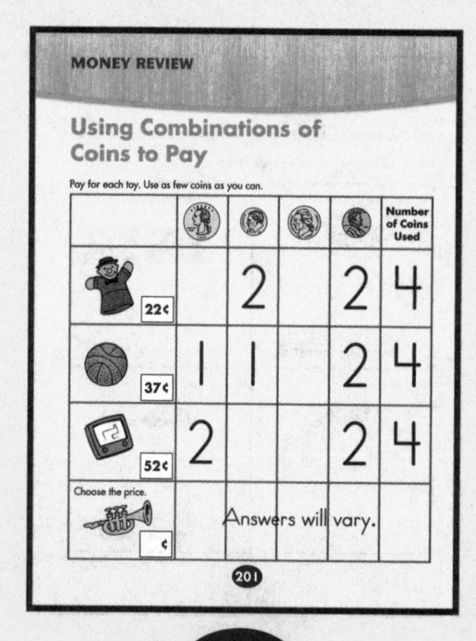
MONEY REVIEW

Using Combinations of Coins to Pay

Pay for each toy. Use as few coins as you can.

					Number of Coins Used
22¢		2		2	4
37¢	1	1		2	4
52¢	2			2	4
Choose the price. ¢	Answers will vary.				

201

MONEY REVIEW

Using Combinations of Coins to Pay

Pay for each book. Use as few coins as you can.

					Number of Coins Used
75¢	3				3
80¢	3		1		4
97¢	3	2		2	7
Choose the price. ¢	Answers will vary.				

202

ANSWER KEY

MONEY REVIEW

Using Combinations of Coins to Pay

Pay for each snack. Use as few coins as you can.

	(half-dollar)	(quarter)	(dime)	(nickel)	Number of Coins Used
$1.05	2			1	3
95¢	1	1	2		4
85¢	1	1	1		3
Choose the price.	Answers will vary.				

203

MONEY REVIEW

Using Combinations of Coins to Pay

Pay for each mask. Use as few coins and bills as you can.

	(dollar bill)	(quarter)	(dime)	(nickel)	Number of Coins Used
$1.75	1	3			4
$1.95	1	3	2		6
$2.50	2	2			4
Choose the price.	Answers will vary.				

204

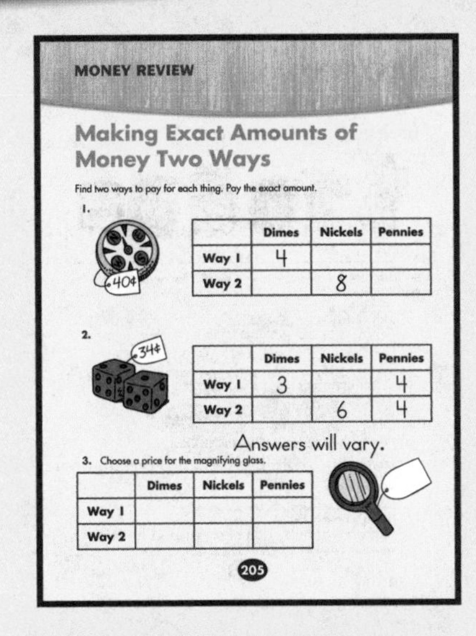
MONEY REVIEW

Making Exact Amounts of Money Two Ways

Find two ways to pay for each thing. Pay the exact amount.

1. 40¢

	Dimes	Nickels	Pennies
Way 1	4		
Way 2		8	

2. 34¢

	Dimes	Nickels	Pennies
Way 1	3		4
Way 2		6	4

Answers will vary.

3. Choose a price for the magnifying glass.

	Dimes	Nickels	Pennies
Way 1			
Way 2			

205

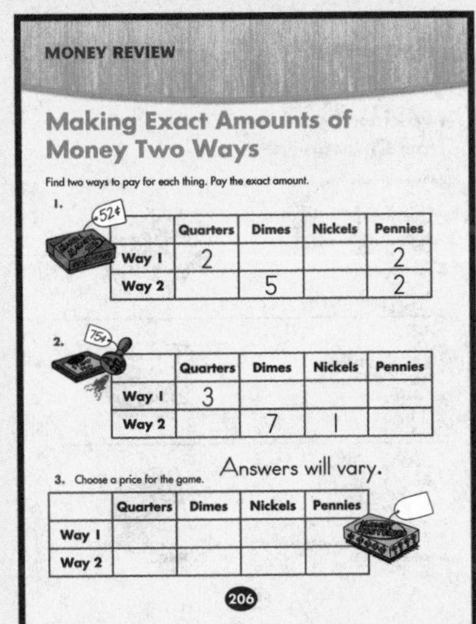
MONEY REVIEW

Making Exact Amounts of Money Two Ways

Find two ways to pay for each thing. Pay the exact amount.

1. 52¢

	Quarters	Dimes	Nickels	Pennies
Way 1	2			2
Way 2		5		2

2. 75¢

	Quarters	Dimes	Nickels	Pennies
Way 1	3			
Way 2		7	1	

Answers will vary.

3. Choose a price for the game.

	Quarters	Dimes	Nickels	Pennies
Way 1				
Way 2				

206

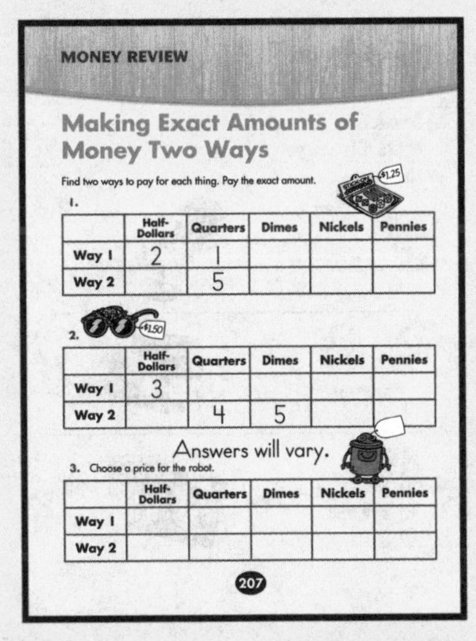
MONEY REVIEW

Making Exact Amounts of Money Two Ways

Find two ways to pay for each thing. Pay the exact amount.

1. $1.25

	Half-Dollars	Quarters	Dimes	Nickels	Pennies
Way 1	2	1			
Way 2		5			

2. $1.50

	Half-Dollars	Quarters	Dimes	Nickels	Pennies
Way 1	3				
Way 2		4	5		

Answers will vary.

3. Choose a price for the robot.

	Half-Dollars	Quarters	Dimes	Nickels	Pennies
Way 1					
Way 2					

207

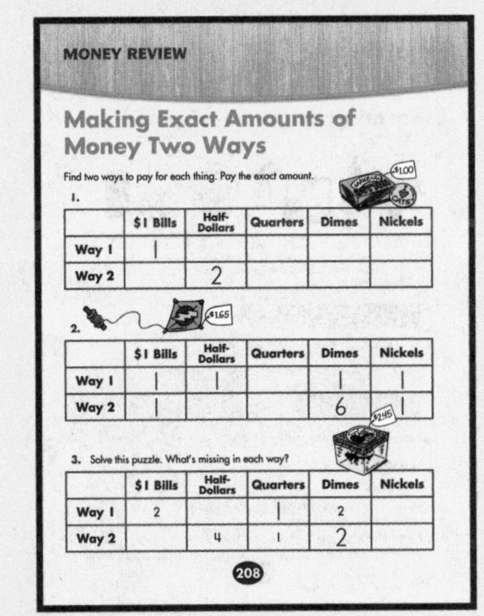
MONEY REVIEW

Making Exact Amounts of Money Two Ways

Find two ways to pay for each thing. Pay the exact amount.

1. $1.00

	$1 Bills	Half-Dollars	Quarters	Dimes	Nickels
Way 1	1				
Way 2		2			

2. $1.65

	$1 Bills	Half-Dollars	Quarters	Dimes	Nickels
Way 1	1	1		1	1
Way 2	1			6	1

3. Solve this puzzle. What's missing in each way? $2.45

	$1 Bills	Half-Dollars	Quarters	Dimes	Nickels
Way 1	2		1	2	
Way 2		4	1	2	

208

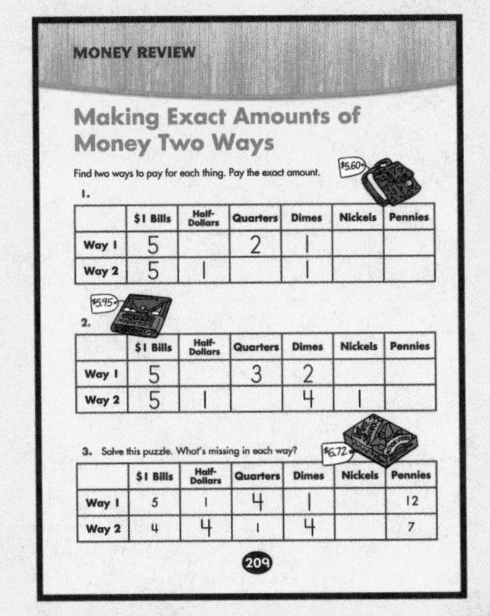
MONEY REVIEW

Making Exact Amounts of Money Two Ways

Find two ways to pay for each thing. Pay the exact amount.

1. $5.60

	$1 Bills	Half-Dollars	Quarters	Dimes	Nickels	Pennies
Way 1	5		2	1		
Way 2	5	1		1		

2. $5.95

	$1 Bills	Half-Dollars	Quarters	Dimes	Nickels	Pennies
Way 1	5		3	2		
Way 2	5	1		4	1	

3. Solve this puzzle. What's missing in each way? $6.72

	$1 Bills	Half-Dollars	Quarters	Dimes	Nickels	Pennies
Way 1	5	1	4	1		12
Way 2	4	4	1	4		7

209

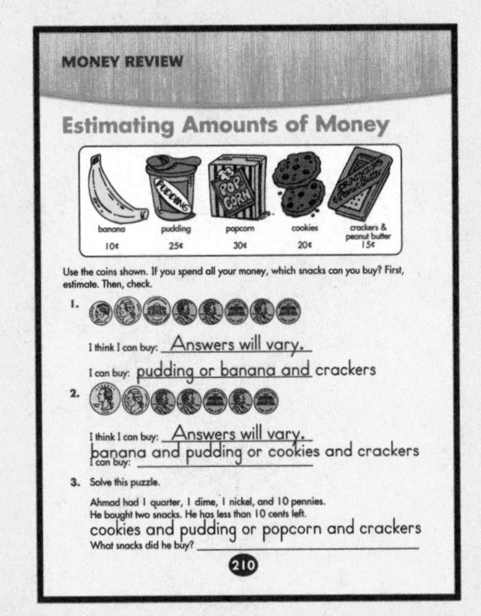
MONEY REVIEW

Estimating Amounts of Money

banana 10¢ | pudding 25¢ | popcorn 30¢ | cookies 20¢ | crackers & peanut butter 15¢

Use the coins shown. If you spend all your money, which snacks can you buy? First, estimate. Then, check.

1. I think I can buy: Answers will vary.

I can buy: pudding or banana and crackers

2. I think I can buy: Answers will vary.

I can buy: banana and pudding or cookies and crackers

3. Solve this puzzle.

Ahmad had 1 quarter, 1 dime, 1 nickel, and 10 pennies. He bought two snacks. He has less than 10 cents left.

What snacks did he buy? cookies and pudding or popcorn and crackers

210

ANSWER KEY

MONEY REVIEW

Estimating Amounts of Money

25¢ 65¢ 50¢ 55¢ 75¢ 35¢

Use the coins shown. If you spend all your money, which pet treats can you buy? First, estimate. Then, check.

1. I think I can buy: Answers will vary.
   I can buy: kitty treats and beef munchies or turtle delight and bird seed
2. I think I can buy: Answers will vary.
   I can buy: kitty treats, bird seed, and beef munchies
3. Solve this puzzle.
   Ismelda had 3 half-dollars. She bought 3 pet treats. She has less than 20 cents left.
   What treats did she buy? hamster donuts, dog cookies, and turtle delight

211

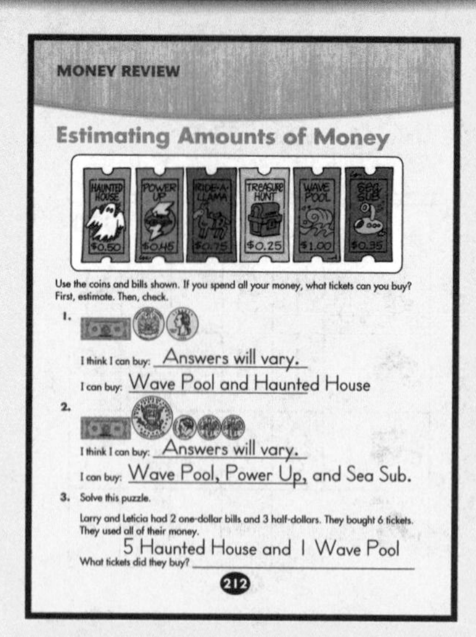
MONEY REVIEW

Estimating Amounts of Money

Use the coins and bills shown. If you spend all your money, what tickets can you buy? First, estimate. Then, check.

1. I think I can buy: Answers will vary.
   I can buy: Wave Pool and Haunted House
2. I think I can buy: Answers will vary.
   I can buy: Wave Pool, Power Up, and Sea Sub.
3. Solve this puzzle.
   Larry and Leticia had 2 one-dollar bills and 3 half-dollars. They bought 6 tickets. They used all of their money.
   What tickets did they buy? 5 Haunted House and 1 Wave Pool

212

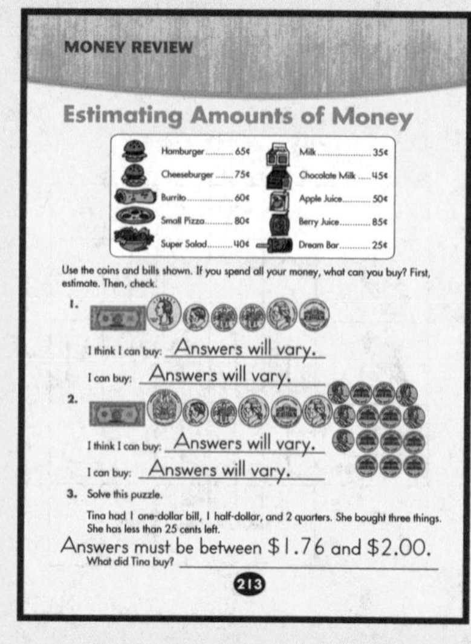
MONEY REVIEW

Estimating Amounts of Money

Hamburger	65¢	Milk	35¢
Cheeseburger	75¢	Chocolate Milk	45¢
Burrito	60¢	Apple Juice	50¢
Small Pizza	80¢	Berry Juice	85¢
Super Salad	40¢	Dream Bar	25¢

Use the coins and bills shown. If you spend all your money, what can you buy? First, estimate. Then, check.

1. I think I can buy: Answers will vary.
   I can buy: Answers will vary.
2. I think I can buy: Answers will vary.
   I can buy: Answers will vary.
3. Solve this puzzle.
   Tina had 1 one-dollar bill, 1 half-dollar, and 2 quarters. She bought three things. She has less than 25 cents left.
   What did Tina buy? Answers must be between $1.76 and $2.00.

213

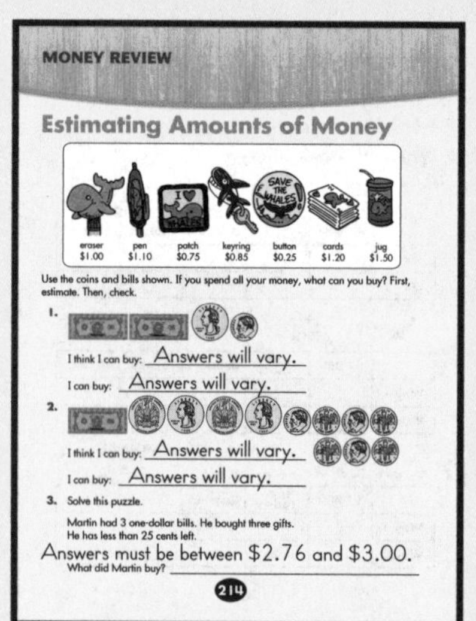
MONEY REVIEW

Estimating Amounts of Money

eraser $1.00 | pen $1.10 | patch $0.75 | keyring $0.85 | button $0.25 | cards $1.20 | jug $1.50

Use the coins and bills shown. If you spend all your money, what can you buy? First, estimate. Then, check.

1. I think I can buy: Answers will vary.
   I can buy: Answers will vary.
2. I think I can buy: Answers will vary.
   I can buy: Answers will vary.
3. Solve this puzzle.
   Martin had 3 one-dollar bills. He bought three gifts. He has less than 25 cents left.
   What did Martin buy? Answers must be between $2.76 and $3.00.

214

MONEY REVIEW

Making Exact Amounts and Change

Pay the exact amount. What change do you get back?

Amount you get back: 9 ¢

Amount you get back: 17 ¢

Amount you get back: 30 ¢

215

MONEY REVIEW

Making Exact Amounts and Change

Pay the exact amount. What change do you get back?

Amount you get back: 15 ¢

Amount you get back: 25 ¢

Choose a price between 75¢ and 90¢.
Write the price. Answers will vary.
Amount you get back: ____ ¢

216

ANSWER KEY

MONEY REVIEW

Making Exact Amounts and Change

Pay the exact amount. What change do you get back?

$0.81

Amount you get back: 19¢

$1.05

Amount you get back: 20¢

Choose a price between $1.15 and $1.28.
Write the price. Answers will vary.
Amount you get back: ______¢

217

MONEY REVIEW

Making Exact Amounts and Change

Pay the exact amount. What change do you get back?

$1.26

Amount you get back: 74¢

$2.67

Amount you get back: 33¢

Solve this puzzle.
What did Abby pay?
Write the amount on the tag.

$1.64

I had 2 one-dollar bills. I paid for the kite. I got back 1 quarter, 1 dime, and 1 penny.

218

MONEY REVIEW

Making Exact Amounts and Change

Pay the exact amount. What change do you get back?

$2.34

Amount you get back: $.66

$2.75

Amount you get back: $2.25

Solve this puzzle.
What did Dominic pay?
Write the amount on the tag.

$2.72

I had five one-dollar bills. I paid for the compass. I got back 2 one-dollar bills, 1 quarter, and 3 pennies.

219

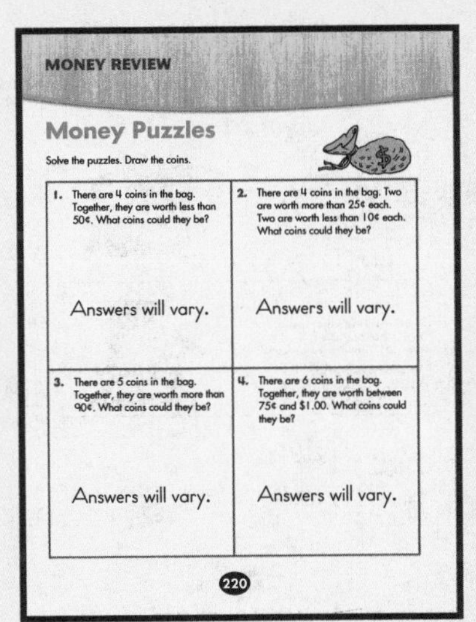

MONEY REVIEW

Money Puzzles

Solve the puzzles. Draw the coins.

1. There are 4 coins in the bag. Together, they are worth less than 50¢. What coins could they be? Answers will vary.	2. There are 4 coins in the bag. Two are worth more than 25¢ each. Two are worth less than 10¢ each. What coins could they be? Answers will vary.
3. There are 5 coins in the bag. Together, they are worth more than 90¢. What coins could they be? Answers will vary.	4. There are 6 coins in the bag. Together, they are worth between 75¢ and $1.00. What coins could they be? Answers will vary.

220

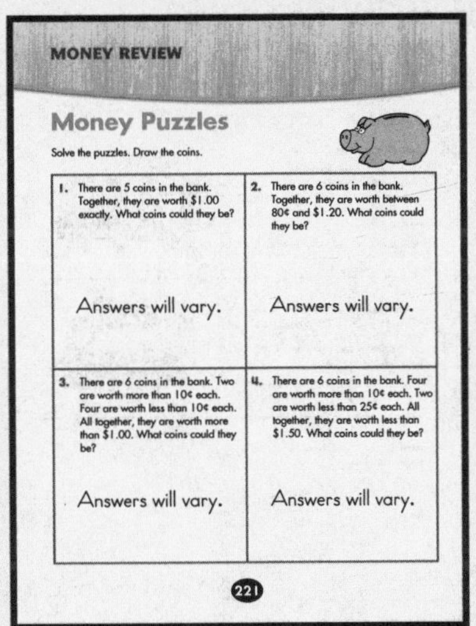

MONEY REVIEW

Money Puzzles

Solve the puzzles. Draw the coins.

1. There are 5 coins in the bank. Together, they are worth $1.00 exactly. What coins could they be? Answers will vary.	2. There are 6 coins in the bank. Together, they are worth between 80¢ and $1.20. What coins could they be? Answers will vary.
3. There are 6 coins in the bank. Two are worth more than 10¢ each. Four are worth less than 10¢ each. All together, they are worth more than $1.00. What coins could they be? Answers will vary.	4. There are 6 coins in the bank. Four are worth more than 10¢ each. Two are worth less than 25¢ each. All together, they are worth less than $1.50. What coins could they be? Answers will vary.

221

MONEY REVIEW

Using Combinations of Coins to Pay

Use the coins shown to make each amount.

Use 3 of the coins to make 25¢. What coins did you use?			2	1	
Use 4 of the coins to make 50¢. What coins did you use?		1	2	1	
Use 4 of the coins to make 66¢. What coins did you use?	1		1	1	1
Use 5 of the coins to make 96¢. What coins did you use?	1	1	2		1

222

ANSWER KEY

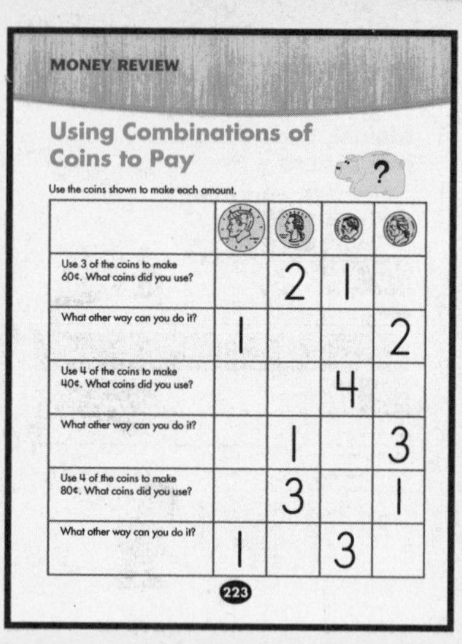

MONEY REVIEW

Using Combinations of Coins to Pay

Use the coins shown to make each amount.

	Half-dollar	Quarter	Dime	Nickel
Use 3 of the coins to make 60¢. What coins did you use?		2	1	
What other way can you do it?	1			2
Use 4 of the coins to make 40¢. What coins did you use?			4	
What other way can you do it?		1		3
Use 4 of the coins to make 80¢. What coins did you use?		3		1
What other way can you do it?	1		3	

223

MONEY REVIEW

Money Story Puzzles

Solve the money story puzzles.

Sean sees a box of magnets on sale for 50 cents. He takes 10 coins out of his pocket and buys the magnets.

What coins could they be?

nickels

Tonia sees a small bag of jacks for 58 cents. She takes 9 coins out of her pocket to pay.

What coins could they be?

5 dimes, 1 nickel, and 3 pennies

Dustin sees a toy hammer. He wants to buy it for his little brother. He pulls six coins out of his pocket and pays 75 cents.

What coins could they be?

1 quarter and 5 dimes

224

MONEY REVIEW

Money Story Puzzles

Solve the money story puzzles.

Matt buys a box of things for doing magic tricks. He takes an even number of coins out of his pocket and pays 65 cents.

What coins could they be?

Answers will vary.

Stacey buys a poster for 70 cents. She uses an odd number of coins to buy it.

What coins could they be?

Answers will vary.

Write a money story puzzle about buying the stuffed whale.

Answers will vary.

225

MONEY REVIEW

Money Story Puzzles

Solve the money story puzzles.

Amber put coins into her bank for a long time. She saved $6.25 in all. Amber saved $3.55 more than her sister Holly.

How much did Holly save?

$2.70

Collin and Jason each bought a watch. Jason paid $4.99 for his Flip-up Crocodile Watch. That was $1.20 more than Collin paid for his Dinosaur Watch.

How much did Collin pay?

$3.79

Write a money story puzzle about yourself and a friend.

Answers will vary.

226

MONEY REVIEW

Money Story Puzzles

Solve the money story puzzles.

Darci and Kara fed the horses at the fair. Kara's mother gave the girls 3 one-dollar bills, 3 quarters, 5 dimes, and 3 nickels. Darci and Kara divided the money equally.

How much money did each of them get?

$2.20

Josh and Ben washed cars one Saturday. When they finished, they had 3 one-dollar bills, 11 half-dollars, 3 quarters, 2 dimes, and 1 nickel in their money box. The boys divided the money fairly.

How much money did each of them get?

$4.75

Write a money story puzzle about earning money and dividing it equally.

Answers will vary.

227

MONEY REVIEW

Money Story Puzzles

Solve the money story puzzles.

Eric and Alicia took all the coins out of their pockets. They put the coins together and paid 65 cents for a bag of corn chips. Alicia paid 15 cents more than Eric.

How much did each of them pay?

Eric paid 25¢. Alicia paid 40¢.

Two friends put their money together and bought a package of stickers for $1.60. Rachel paid 20 cents more than Amanda.

How much did each girl pay?

Amanda paid 70¢.
Rachel paid 90¢.

Write a money story puzzle about buying something with a friend.

Answers will vary.

228